NELSON'S ANNUAL

Children's Ministry Sourcebook

2004 EDITION

NELSON'S ANNUAL

Children's Ministry Sourcebook

2004 EDITION

Vicki Wiley, Editor

THOMAS NELSON PUBLISHERS

Nashville

Nelson's Annual Children's Ministry Sourcebook, 2004 Edition

Copyright © 2003 by Thomas Nelson, Inc.

Published in Nashville, Tennessee, by Thomas Nelson, Inc.

Book design and composition by Mark McGarry,
Texas Type & Book Works, Dallas, Texas

Wiley, Vicki (ed.)
Nelson's annual children's ministry sourcebook, 2004 edition

ISBN 0-7852-5004-2

Printed in Canada

1 2 3 4 5 6 7—07 06 05 04 03

Contents

CONTENTS   vii

CONTENTS

Preface

"Mom, Adam and Eve sinned in the Garden of Eden and that's why there's sin in the world today!" my 5-year-old daughter announced as I picked her up from Vacation Bible School. Wow, I thought, what a brilliant young theologian! I continued the conversation by saying "You're right, Leigh. Do you know what they did?" She promptly answered, "Yep, they ate the Fruits of the Spirit!"

Many years have gone by since that time, but it still makes me smile. Knowing that young children "connect their own dots" between Bible stories, memory verses, activities, and crafts makes our tasks as teachers a little daunting. How can we introduce Bible stories, hold their interest, engage all their senses and intelligences, while maintaining biblical truth and focusing on one main point?

The *Children's Ministry Sourcebook* was written with this goal in mind. With a single biblical point as the focus, the foundation of the lesson is the children's Bible lesson. Activities, crafts, snacks, memory verses, and enrichment ideas help the lesson take root in the child's heart and mind. Each lesson contains an easy-to-understand story from the Bible, practical applications, activities that engage the senses, crafts that lock in the main point of the lesson, helpful memory verse activities, and stimulating enrichment information.

Faith develops when knowledge and experience combine. Facilitating this for our children at age-appropriate levels is the foundation for this book. With deliberate teaching and single-minded focus we teachers guide children to not only hear the story, but also to experience it for themselves.

How to Use This Book:
This book has been designed to provide flexibility for the teacher and to adapt naturally to your church's weekly schedule. The 52 dated weekly segments may be used one of two main ways:

A. Each session includes a midweek "teaser" to introduce the following Sunday's session. If your church provides a children's session during the week, use this first portion then.

B. OR, if you do not have a midweek program, use some of the introductory material to start your planning for Sunday and incorporate some of the ideas as supplementary activities for Sunday.

Weekly Features:

Each week's material contains several components, all of which work together to gently push the point of the lesson into the heart of children. These typically include:

Scripture: The Bible text from which the lesson is drawn.

Lesson Aim: The "target" of the lesson, the one thing to repeat from all elements so children can understand it clearly and apply it appropriately.

Bible Skill: A specific skill or concept from the Bible for children to practice.

Bible Lesson: An age-appropriate sermon, frequently using everyday objects as illustrations.

Song Suggestions: Current and traditional songs that enhance the lesson.

Bible Learning Activity for Younger Children: An activity to help younger children remember the point of the lesson.

Bible Learning Activity for Older Children: An activity designed for children in grades 3–6, to engage them with the Bible passage.

Enrichment for Younger Children: Information, conversation, or activity that will help the younger child more accurately grasp the lesson.

Enrichment for Older Children: Further background information about the passage such as the culture, archaeology, or life and times of the people and places.

Craft for Younger Children: A simple craft for younger children to create on their own that they can take home to remind them of the lesson.

Craft for Older Children: A take-home project for children in grades 3–6 to remind them of the lesson. These crafts are made from easy-to-find materials and supplies listed at the beginning of each craft.

Craft Simplification for Younger Children: When the same crafts and activities can also be used for younger children, suggestions for simplification are provided.

Snack: A lesson-related food item to make in class.

Memory Verse ICB: The memory verse from the International Children's Bible.

Memory Verse NKJV: The memory verse from the New King James Version.

Memory Verse Activity: An activity to help the children learn the memory verse.

Prayer Focus: A prayer "starter" that guides children to talk with God about the lesson. Consider adding your church's needs, children's prayer requests, and children's praises.

Special Holiday Activities: Activities, crafts, and information that coordinate with holidays, when appropriate.

Feature Articles: Special articles written by children's ministers to help and encourage you on your journey. You will find these collected near the back of the book.

It is my prayer that the *Children's Ministry Sourcebook* will equip you with the tools you need to provide a complete year of dynamic children's worship for your congregation. May God bless you in your efforts!

Vicki Wiley
Director of Children's Ministries
First Presbyterian Church, Honolulu

Contributors

Karl Bastian is Children's Pastor at the Village Church of Barrington, Illinois, and is the founder of Kidology, Inc., a non-profit organization committed to equipping and encouraging children's workers through quality training and affordable resources. He entertains and ministers to children around the world through puppets, magic, balloons, and other creative means. He started when he himself was a child. Karl holds a bachelor's degree in Bible theology from Moody Bible Institute, and will soon complete a master's in children's ministry at Trinity Evangelical Divinity School. You can find Karl at www.kidology.org. (Bible Lessons: June 27, July 11, September 5, December 12; Articles)

Ivy Beckwith is Minister to Children and Families at Colonial Church of Edina, Minnesota. Ivy has served churches in Boston, Chicago, and Minnesota and holds a Ph.D. in education from Trinity International University. Ivy also has worked for two curriculum publishers as a consultant and editor. (Bible Lessons: January 4, February 8, March 21, May 16, June 13, July 18, September 12, September 26, October 17, December 5)

Dr. Dan Chun is Senior Pastor of First Presbyterian Church, Honolulu. Dan and his wife, Pam, are the co-founders of Hawaiian Islands Ministries in Hawaii. Dan received his M.Div. and Doctor of Ministries degrees from Fuller Seminary. (Bible Lesson: November 7)

Judy Comstock is an educator and ministry consultant. Drawing on formal education training and rich experiences, Judy has equipped educators in conference settings for the past 20 years. She has partnered with churches as a mentoring education consultant and currently serves as Director of Children's Ministries at Church of the Resurrection in Leawood, Kansas. Previously, Judy worked with 19 schools in a gifted program in a large city in Michigan and served as Director of Christian Education in an inner-city church. She has a B.A. in elementary education from the University of Missouri and a master of arts in elementary leadership (administration) from Wayne State University. She is on the board of For Kids Only, Inc. and a corporate officer with the International Network of Children's Ministry. (Bible Lessons: February 22, April 11, June 6, August 1, October 31)

Dean-o is a Christian performer and president of BibleBeat Music. His awesome musical style and depth of spirituality draws him instantly to kids. Dean-o has a B.A. in Christian education from Biola University. Read more about Dean-o at www.biblebeatmusic.com. (Bible Lessons: January 18, March 28, October 10)

Roger Fields is president and creator of KidzBlitz, a ministry known around the world for its high-energy family events. He has been an ordained minister for over 20 years. His writings include children's ministry curriculum, Vacation Bible School programs, and articles. He is the editor of the Cold Water Café, an Internet site for children's pastors. You can find Roger at www.kidzblitz.com. (Contributor of Articles)

Amanda Garrett is the Director of Children's Ministry at New Life Community Church in Artesia, California. She is a graduate of Pacific Christian College (now Hope International University) with a bachelor's degree in Bible and cross-cultural communication and a master's degree in church growth. She has worked with children in Africa, England, and California, and with children from a wide variety of nationalities. Amanda loves reaching children for Jesus, seeing both a hunger for and a deeper understanding of Him develop in their lives. (Bible Lesson: February 15)

Mary Rice Hopkins is a singer and entertainer with a wonderful way of communicating the gospel truth through songs. She is a pioneer in the field of children's Christian music and has planted seeds that will last a lifetime with her upbeat style of music. You can learn more about Mary at www.maryricehopkins.com. (Bible Lessons: January 25, May 23, July 25, August 8, August 29)

Becky Howell is Director of Children's Ministries at Sierra Bible Church in Sonora, California. She has a background in Bible school and nursing. She had always planned to return to nursing but children's ministry is in her heart and soul. She's a preacher's kid and has been involved with children's ministries all her life. (Bible Lesson: May 30)

Rev. Barney Kinard is a full-time children's evangelist. He is also the President and Executive Director of Creative Children's Ministries (formerly Share-Time Int'l), located in Buena Park, California. Creative Children's

Ministries is a non-profit evangelistic organization whose ministry goal is to help churches and leaders evangelize children creatively. You can find Barney at www.kidhelper.com. (Bible Lessons: March 7, April 25)

Barbara Platt is a consultant with Gospel Light Publications and has taught in Sunday school conventions and churches for 20 years. She has a B.A. from Trinity College of the Bible. (Bible Lessons: October 3, November 14)

Terry Platt is the Midwest regional manager for Christian Education Services with Gospel Light Publications. Prior to that he was a minister of Christian education for 25 years. He lives in Oak Park, Illinois, with his wife, Barb. (Bible Lessons: February 1, October 24)

Johanna Townsend is president of For Kids Only. She has ministered to children for over 30 years as a public school teacher and Director of Children's Ministry. She has helped design curriculum used by Royal Family Kids Camps, and traveled nationally and internationally teaching training seminars for different Christian organizations. In 1990 Johanna got her master's degree at Vanguard University and received the Award for Excellence in Children's Ministry at Children's Pastors' Conference. (Bible Lessons: March 14, July 4, November 21, December 19)

Pat Verbal is the founder of Ministry to Today's Child and an inspirational guest speaker in churches, conferences, and the media. Pat holds a master's degree in pastoral studies and is a best-selling author who served 20 years as Pastor of Children and Christian Education. (Bible Lessons: January 11, February 29, May 2, August 15, August 22, November 28, September 19)

Vicki Wiley is the Director of Children's Ministries at First Presbyterian Church in Honolulu, Hawaii. She was the Creative Developer of www.KidsBible.com published by Thomas Nelson Publishers. Vicki has a master's degree in theology from Fuller Theological Seminary and has been in children's ministries for over 20 years. She loves to speak, study, and write about the faith and spiritual development of children and is on the faculty of the Bible Institute of Hawaii. (Bible Lessons: April 4, May 9, June 20, December 26; all crafts, Bible learning activities, enrichment, and Bible verse activities)

2004 Calendar

January 1	New Year's Day
January 4	
January 5	Epiphany
January 11	
January 18	**Sanctity of Human Life Sunday**
January 19	Martin Luther King, Jr. Day
January 25	**Superbowl Sunday**
January 26	Australia Day
February 1–29	Black History Month
February 1	**National Freedom Day**
February 2	Groundhog Day
February 8	
February 12	Lincoln's Birthday
February 14	Valentine's Day
February 15	
February 16	Presidents' Day
February 22	**Washington's Birthday**
February 25	Ash Wednesday
February 29	**First Sunday of Lent**
March 7	**Second Sunday of Lent**
March 14	**Third Sunday of Lent**
March 17	St. Patrick's Day
March 20	Spring Begins
March 21	**Fourth Sunday of Lent; Mothering Sunday**
March 28	**Fifth Sunday of Lent**

April 4	Passion / Palm Sunday; Daylight Savings Time begins
April 6	Passover
April 8	Holy Thursday
April 9	Good Friday
April 11	**Easter**
April 13	Jefferson's Birthday
April 18	**Holocaust Remembrance Day**
April 21	Administrative Professionals Day
April 22	Earth Day
April 25	
May 1	Labor Day
May 2	
May 6	National Day of Prayer
May 9	**Mother's Day**
May 15	Armed Forces Day
May 16	
May 20	Ascension Day
May 23	
May 30	**Pentecost**
May 31	Memorial Day
June 6	**Trinity Sunday**
June 13	
June 14	Flag Day
June 20	**Father's Day**
June 21	Summer Begins
June 27	
July 1	Canada Day
July 4	**Independence Day**

July 11	
July 18	
July 25	**Parents' Day**
August 1	**Friendship Day**
August 6	Transfiguration Day
August 8	
August 15	
August 22	
August 29	
September 5	
September 6	Labor Day
September 12	**Grandparents' Day**
September 15	Rosh Hashanah begins
September 19	
September 22	Autumn begins
September 24	Yom Kippur begins; Native American Day
September 26	
October 1–31	Pastor Appreciation Month
October 3	
October 10	**Clergy Appreciation Day; Children's Day**
October 11	Columbus Day; Thanksgiving Day (Canada)
October 16	National Boss Day
October 17	
October 24	**United Nations Day; Mother-in-Law Day**
October 27	Reformation Day
October 31	**Daylight Savings Time ends; Halloween**
November 1	All Saints' Day
November 2	Election Day

November 7

November 11   Veterans Day

November 14   International Day of Prayer for the Persecuted Church

November 21

November 25   Thanksgiving Day

November 28   First Sunday of Advent

December 5   Second Sunday of Advent

December 7   Pearl Harbor Remembrance Day

December 8   Hanukkah

December 12   Third Sunday of Advent

December 19   Fourth Sunday of Advent

December 21   Winter Begins

December 24   Christmas Eve

December 25   Christmas Day

December 26   Kwanzaa begins

December 31   New Year's Eve

WEEKLY SUGGESTIONS FOR 52 WEEKS

January 4

How Are We Going to Get to the Other Side?
By Ivy Beckwith

(NOTE to Teacher: All sessions except this one begin with a midweek pre-session that introduces the Sunday session. This one is a stand-alone session).

Scripture:
Exodus 14:21, 22

Lesson Aim:
God has the power to do what is impossible for us.

Bible Skill:
Children will realize they have God's power with them.

Bible Lesson: How Are We Going to Get to the Other Side?
Gather children together and ask, "Have you ever been to the ocean or to a very large lake?" Then, "Who can tell me what it was like?" Give many or most children time to tell about it. Prompt with questions like: "Could you see the other side? Do you think you could walk across it?" "So, if we can't walk across the ocean or the lake, how do we get to the other side?"

Explain that usually when people want to get to the other side of a big ocean or lake they need to take a boat or get into an airplane. But God gave us a story in the Bible about how some people got to the other side of a big body of water without a boat or an airplane.

God helped the Israelites escape from the cruel people who were making them slaves in the country of Egypt. God's people were very happy to be free, but they were also very scared. The armies from Egypt came after them to recapture them. So far they managed to stay ahead of the army.

But, when they came upon a sea, they had to stop. "How are we ever going to get across this water? We don't have boats. What are we going to do?" they might have asked. "We're going to be trapped here and the Egyptian army is going to catch up with us and make us go back to Egypt."

But the Bible tells us that God's people had a leader named Moses and he believed God would find a way for the Israelite people to get across this sea and stay ahead of the Egyptians. So Moses stood right on the edge of the water and stretched out his hand. And then the most amazing thing happened. The Bible tells us that God caused a very strong wind to blow. This caused the water to move and created a dry path for the people to walk on with a wall of water on both sides. The people could get across the sea to the other side. The dry path lasted just long enough for all the Israelites to get across the water.

The Egyptian army was close behind the Israelites! They could move faster because they had horses and chariots and the Israelites were on foot. As the Egyptians moved into the sea to follow the Israelites, God caused the wheels of their chariots to be clogged with mud so they didn't turn. The Bible tells us this great army started to panic and that while they were in a panic, the Israelites made it safely to the other side of the sea! The entire Egyptian army drowned in the sea, but God's people got safely to dry land.

The Bible tells us God saved the Israelites that day, and when they saw the impossible thing God did they believed in God and trusted their leader Moses.

This story reminds us that God has a lot more power than you or me or even armies. God doesn't need boats or airplanes to get to the other side of the sea. And this story helps us to remember that when we are faced with a problem that seems impossible to solve God has the power to do what we think is impossible. Remember the Israelites didn't think there was any way they could get across the sea—but God had a plan. God has the power to do the impossible!

 Song Suggestions:

Believin' On by Jana Alayra from "Believin' On" (Montjoy Music 2002)

Little Is Much by Mary Rice Hopkins from "15 Singable Songs" (Big Steps 4 U 1988)

Faith Will Do by Dean-o from "You Got It All" (FKO Music, Inc. 1997)

God's Power Songsheets published by CEF Press, P.O. Box 348, Warrenton, Mo. 63383

Craft for Younger Children: Fishy Necklace
Needed: one cord for each child, fruit loops, fish shapes cut from construction paper or sheets of thin craft foam

Say: Where do the fish live? Yes, in the ocean, the sea and lakes. When the Hebrew children were crossing the Red Sea, they saw lots of fish. Let's make a Fishy Necklace to remind us of what they saw.

Show children how to string one fish onto the cord followed by one fruit loop followed by one fish and so on to make necklaces.

 Craft for Older Children: Crossing the Red Sea Diorama
Needed: One shoebox for each child, blue cellophane or blue paper, clay or construction paper, glue

Say: We are going to make panoramas to illustrate the crossing of the Red Sea. What do you think it would have looked like if you were one of the people crossing it?

Help children think of what to create. Give ideas from the story such as crossing the Red Sea, what the water looked like when they were crossing, what the chariots looked like when they were being chased, etc. Show children how to make panoramas of the crossing by using blue cellophane or blue paper along the sides for the water. Suggest the children make people from clay or paper. Suggest they add wagons with supplies and animals.

Say: It is absolutely impossible to be able to cross a sea on dry land—unless God chooses to make it happen! God wanted to save his people, the Israelites, and God also knew just how to do it. God saved his people with his mighty power! Aren't you glad that we have a God who can do things that we think are impossible?

Ask: What other "impossible" things did God do in other Bible stories? (Burning bush, crossing of the Jordan River, feeding of 5,000 people, Jesus walking on water, etc.) God loves his people and wants to help us.

Red Sea Snack

Snack

Needed: Mix blue and green gelatin to make turquoise or aqua gelatin, gummy fish

Make gelatin as per instructions. Put fish into gelatin before it hardens. Serve to the children.

Say: This gelatin represents the Red Sea. The Red Sea wasn't really red; it was blue just like any other sea. It was named the Red Sea for another reason. The Red Sea is actually a bright turquoise color, but sometimes algae grow in the water. When the algae die, the sea becomes reddish-brown, and makes it look red. That is why it is called the Red Sea.

Memory Verse Activity: Hopscotch Through the Red Sea

Needed: 8 Pieces of blue paper

Preparation: Write the following phrases onto the 8 papers and arrange them "hopscotch" style on the floor. Tape down with masking tape.

Don't

Be afraid

Stand still

and you

Will see

the Lord

Save you today

Exodus 14:13

Say: Today we are going to learn a very important verse from the Bible. While you play "hopscotch" on the words you must say them. Let children take turns hopping and saying the verse. Say verse all together.

Ask: What do you think this verse means? When the Lord is going to save us, what do we do? How do we show we trust him? God loves us and God wants us to trust him. God wants us to keep walking in the direction he tells us to walk, to hear his instructions through the Bible, and then follow those instructions.

Memory Verse: Exodus 14:13 ICB

Moses answered, "Don't be afraid! Stand still and see the Lord save you today."

Alternate version (New King James)
And Moses said to the people, "Do not be afraid. Stand still, and see the salvation of the LORD, which He will accomplish for you today. For the Egyptians whom you see today, you shall see again no more forever.

Prayer Focus:
Dear God, thank you for protecting the Israelite people back in Bible times. Thank you for protecting us today, too! You are awesome and powerful. We know that you had a plan for your people, the Israelites, and we know that you have a plan for each of us today. We love you and we praise you. Amen.

January 7

The Worry Box, Midweek
By Pat Verbal

Scripture:
Exodus 25:10–22, 26:34
Joshua 3:1–7
2 Chronicles 35:3
Hebrews 9:4

Lesson Aim:
To help children understand that the way to overcome worry is to talk to God.

Bible Skill:
Children can talk with God about their worries and turn them into prayer. This helps them trust God in every situation.

Bible Learning Activity for Younger Children:
Ask: Do you ever worry about anything? Sometimes children worry about being in the dark. Have you ever been worried about being in the dark? What do you do if you are worried in the dark? (*ask mom to come in, have a nightlight, sing a song*). Did you know that you can also ask God to help you not be afraid? If you trust and obey God, you will find things to do during your fears, things that will stop your fears. He might suggest you count your blessings, or think a happy thought. You will see that God is with you and watching out for you.

Bible Learning Activity for Older Children
Ask: Do you worry? Jesus tells us not to worry about things we cannot change, like how tall we are or how long we will live. Did he mean not to

worry about darkness? Did he mean not to worry about school or tests? Did he mean not to worry about your friends liking you? No! Because those are things you can actually change when you let God show you what to do. So turn your worries into prayers.

He said, "Do not worry about anything. But pray and ask God for everything you need. And when you pray, always give thanks. And God's peace will keep your hearts and minds in Christ Jesus. The peace that God gives is so great that we cannot understand it."

Read this poem:

> *Lord, Make me a kite flying high and free in a heavenly blue sky.*
> *Teach me I cannot fly without wind.*
> *As the pressure of a forceful wind drives a delicate kite upward,*
> *Let the pressure of my life push me closer towards You.*
> *Help me remember when the stress of living blows in,*
> *I can soar in growth.*
> *I can float on faith.*
> *And I will!*

Pat Verbal, *Talking with God* (Chariot Books)

Enrichment for Younger Children: Worry Pictures

Ask: What makes you worried or afraid? Sometimes we get scared and frightened in the dark. We might even think there is a monster under the bed! You might want to sleep with the lights on because you are afraid or you might ask your mom or dad to look under the bed. What do you do when you are afraid?

Draw a picture of something you worry about. Talk about it with the class. Then write a prayer to God about that worry, and ask him what you should do about it. When you talk to God and then obey what he tells you, you show trust in God. For example, before bed you could:

1) Have family prayer time in the closet with a flashlight.

2) Hang a glow-in-the-dark Scripture verse above your bed.

3) Sing your favorite praise chorus over and over until you fall asleep.

Enrichment for Older Children:

Discuss current events with the children that they can understand but that aren't overly frightening. Ask: What worries you? War, bullies, getting stung by a bee? Did you know that no matter how worried we get we still can find out what to do, because of God? This a choice you make. You decide to talk with Jesus about your worries rather than just fret. You can hope in Jesus Christ no matter what happens in your life or in the world. You can decide to trust God to show you what to do. Hope comes from knowing that Jesus loves us and that God is preparing a home for us in heaven. ☺

Alternate:

Needed: current newspapers or magazines

Take the front-page section of the local newspaper to class. Divide children into small groups. Give each group a piece of the paper and several bold markers. Challenge them to locate and discuss articles that are scary.

Secondly, using a junior concordance, help students add next to each scary story a Bible verse that brings hope and comfort to the problem with the markers. Post newspaper on walls around your classroom. Suggest they look up words like "care" and "comfort" and "Jesus."

Thirdly, use the newspaper postings as a prayer guide. Show children how to move around the room praying for God's help to know what to do for each situation.

Say: The ark of the covenant was a box that contained three things: (1) the stone tablets with the Ten Commandments carved into them, (2) a gold pot filled with manna, a special food from God that represented God's provision, and (3) Aaron's rod that budded (Num. 17:1–10). These things remind us that God wants to take care of us, and will do that, especially when we ask him. ☺

Memory Verse: Philippians 4:6 ICB

Do not worry about anything. But pray and ask God for everything you need. And when you pray, always give thanks.

Alternate and expanded version (New King James)

Be anxious for nothing, but in everything by prayer and supplication, with thanksgiving, let your requests be made known to God; and the peace of God, which surpasses all understanding, will guard your hearts and minds through Christ Jesus.

January 11

The Worry Box
By Pat Verbal

Scripture:
Exodus 25:10–22, 26:34
Joshua 3:1–7
2 Chronicles 35:3
Hebrews 9:4

Lesson Aim:
To help children understand that the way to overcome worry is to talk to God.

Bible Skill:
Children will talk with God about their worries and turn them into prayer. This helps them trust God in every situation.

Bible Lesson: Some Worries Never Come True
Tell this story: There was once a poor, old lady who lived in the most broken down house in town. The tattered shingles on the roof matched perfectly with the faded siding. The front window was cracked, but it didn't matter since the little old lady hadn't washed the glass in years.

Neighbors offered to fix up the house for her, but the poor woman refused to let anyone near her property.

She worried that someone might steal something.

She worried restaurants had dirty kitchens, so she never went out to eat.

She worried that dry cleaners used chemicals, so she wore only cotton.

She worried cars went too fast, planes flew too high, and buses were too crowded, so she walked everywhere.

She worried that banks and churches only wanted her money, so she avoided them.

But all her worries left her very lonely.

The whole town felt sorry for the poor, old lady . . . until she died. Then they learned the real truth. When the city tore down her shabby house to build a new convenience store, they discovered a roughhewn wooden box stuffed with money . . . lots of money, hundreds of thousands of dollars. In fact, the town's poorest person turned out to be the town's richest. The headline in the local newspaper read, "Worry Robs Wealthy Citizen."

To keep worry from stealing your happiness, turn your worries into prayer. Talk to God so He can show you what to do.

Ask, and allow each child to answer: *What do you worry about?*

Then let each child practice a sentence prayer asking God for help in this worry. Ask: *What is a prayer you might say about a worry?*

Continue your story with: We've talked about a modern day woman. Here is a story about Bible times: The ark of the covenant was a beautiful box which caused a lot of worry. The Gentiles worried about its powers. The Romans worried about its contents. The Jews worried about its safety. It was said to be so holy that if a man touched it with his bare hands, he would die. Sounds dangerous, doesn't it? So, why was this box so important?

When God's people suffered as slaves in Egypt, they had no specific place to worship. Some thought God had forgotten them. Then God sent Moses to lead the people to the Promised Land. Moses led the people to a place called Mount Sinai where he went up the mountain to pray. When he took a long time to come back, the people built a golden calf and worshiped it.

Song Suggestions:

No Need to Worry by Jana Alayra from "Jump Into the Light" (Montjoy Music 1995)

Pray, Pray, Pray by Mary Rice Hopkins from "Good Buddies" (Big Steps 4 U 1994)

Let the Lord Have His Way Songsheets published by CEF Press, P.O. Box 348, Warrenton, Mo. 63383

I Will Obey You by Cindy Rethmeier from "I Want To Be Like Jesus" (Mercy Vineyard 1995)

This was not the worship object God wanted. Because of this sin, God refused to let them enter the Promised Land.

As they wandered in the wilderness for forty years, God patiently taught them about worship and gave them an object that represented His presence. It was called the ark of the covenant or the Box of Agreements. It eventually rested in the holiest place of worship. But for awhile they carried it with long poles.

God gave instructions to build a sacred box made of acacia wood covered in gold. It was about 45 inches long, 27 inches wide and 27 inches high. Gold covered the wood and two cherubim (a type of angel) sat on top. They didn't worry when they walked behind the ark. It became their most sacred representation of God's presence.

Today God is present everywhere we go. We remember this by talking to him inside our heads. This is called prayer. As we talk to him he shows us what to do about our worries, and gives us his power to do that something.

 Craft for Younger Children and Craft for Older Children: Create a "Me Box"

Needed: One box per child and magazines with pictures. These boxes can be baby wipes containers, fast food take out containers or shoeboxes.

Give each child a box. Direct them to cut and paste magazine or newspaper pictures to the outside of the box that represent their lives: favorite foods, activities, interests, pets, sports, family, vacations, favorite subject in school, etc. Take time to let each child tell about his or her "Me Box."

Then direct the children to cut and paste pictures that represent their worries or fears on the inside of the box. Encourage them to add words with markers. Give children permission to put the lid on the box without showing their worries to the group and to talk to God about the worries privately. Invite each child to say one worry aloud so the group can suggest a prayer to pray about that worry. For example: I worry about my sick grandmother. "God show me how to make her a card or to visit her in a way that helps her feel better."

Special Holiday Activity: Pipe Cleaner Flag

Needed: several packages of red, white, and blue beads and white pipe cleaners.

Make sample patterns with the beads on the pipe cleaners. Set the remaining beads and pipe cleaners on a table and allow the children to copy any of the patterns on their own pipe cleaners. Assist younger children in making the flag they want to make. ☺

Worry Chocolate?

Present a box of assorted chocolates and watch the children pick one. Some will be very cautious. Other children will dive right in, but take a bite out of several until they find a chocolate they like. A few kids will eat anything through politeness or kindness.

Say: Did you know that the way you tried the chocolate shows how people react to worry? Some of you bit quickly. Some of you investigated to find out what was inside first before you tried it. Some of you wondered what it would taste like. Worrying is similar. Some worries are easy to get over, and some take more time. Unlike a box of chocolates, God knows what's inside each worry and how to help you keep from a bad taste. He can help us know what to do about each thing that we worry about. That's exciting, isn't it?

Memory Verse: Philippians 4:6 ICB

Do not worry about anything. But pray and ask God for everything you need. And when you pray, always give thanks.

Alternate and expanded version (New King James)

Be anxious for nothing, but in everything by prayer and supplication, with thanksgiving, let your requests be made known to God; and the peace of God, which surpasses all understanding, will guard your hearts and minds through Christ Jesus.

Memory Verse Activity
Needed: Strips of paper 2 inches by 11 inches, markers
Have children write the entire verse on a strip of paper. Wind the paper around their wrist like a bracelet and let them wear it.

Say: When you are worried today, read this verse and think of what God wants you to do about each worry. Remember that God will always take care of us.

Prayer Focus:
Dear God, forgive me for the time I spend worrying about things rather than obeying you in your plans to fix those things. I'm glad that you see the inside of my heart. I give you my fears and concerns. Please show me what to do about them. I trust you to be my peace. Amen.

January 14

Whose Words Are They Anyway?, Midweek
By Dean-o

Scripture:
I Thessalonians 2:13

Lesson Aim:
The words of the Bible actually come from God, its author, not from people.

Bible Skill:
Kids will understand that reading God's word on a daily basis changes our lives.

Bible Learning Activity For Younger Children: God's Words
Needed: One Bible (hidden in the room), cleaning supplies such as rags for dusting, and a broom for sweeping.

Say: Today we are going to clean our room! Show children how to sweep and dust. Tell them that there is a very special book hidden in the room and that they might find it while they are cleaning.

When they have found the Bible say: Oh yes! You have cleaned our room and now you found a very special book. Let's hear a story about a little boy that did the same thing!

(Go on to enrichment activity)

Bible Learning Activity for Older Children: Instructions! Instructions!
Guide children to do the following by first listening to the directions and then trying to remember and follow the directions: Sit down, stand up, hop on your right foot, sit down, clap three times, cross your legs, shake someone's hand, stand up.

Enrichment for Younger Children: Josiah Cleans the Temple

Tell this Bible story: One of the kings of Judah was named Josiah. Josiah became king when he was only 8 years old. The whole time Josiah was the king, he chose to do good and right things. So his reign was remembered as a good one. King Josiah realized that the people no longer loved God. He wanted them to love God. While repairing the worship center, his workers found the scrolls that had God's words on them. These scrolls were part of what we now know as the Old Testament. Have you ever helped your family clean? What things have you found—maybe something you weren't even looking for? Josiah found the most special thing of all—God's word! ☺

Enrichment for Older Children: Josiah, the Boy King

Tell this Bible event: The country of Judah had become very evil. The people did not worship God. One day, a very young boy became king and chose to act kindly instead. He was only 8 years old! His name was Josiah. Josiah was a good king and he was very wise even though he was so young. While Josiah was the king, his reign was good. These years were among the happiest years experienced by the people in Judah. This is what happened:

Josiah decided to clean the temple, a special place of worship, and fix it up. While his workers were cleaning they found a great surprise! They found scrolls with God's word written on them! These scrolls likely contained all or a part of the Bible book of Deuteronomy.

King Josiah was happy and asked that the word of God be read to the people. The Hebrew people had forgotten to show love to God for many years and now Josiah wanted them to know God again! Josiah began to devote himself to pleasing God and having God's word read to the people. The people loved what they heard and they began to follow God and do what God said to do.

Because of that, even though he was young, Josiah led an entire nation back to God and God blessed him while he was king. The workers took good care of the scrolls that they found and later these scrolls became part of the Bible! ☺

Ask: Was that hard to remember? Why?

Write the same instructions on a white board or poster board. After you write them, say: Now try it this way. Read and follow the instructions as you read them. Cheer as the children follow the directions.

Ask: What is the difference? Why is it easier to follow written directions than spoken directions?

Use children's comments to explain that this is why God instructed people to write the Bible for him. God told them what to write. We can remember God's instructions better because they are written down.

Memory Verse: 1 Thessalonians 2:13 ICB

Also, we always thank God because of the way you accepted his message. You heard his message from us, and you accepted it as the word of God, not the words of men. And it really is God's message. And that message works in you who believe.

Alternate version (New King James)

For this reason we also thank God without ceasing, because when you received the word of God which you heard from us, you welcomed it not as the word of men, but as it is in truth, the word of God, which also effectively works in you who believe.

January 18

Whose Words Are They Anyway?
By Dean-o

Scripture:
1 Thessalonians 2:13

Lesson Aim:
The words of the Bible actually come from God, its author, not from people.

Bible Skill:
Kids will understand that reading God's word on a daily basis changes our lives.

Bible Lesson: "You've Got G-Mail!"
Gather children together and ask: Have you ever wondered who really wrote the words of the Bible? (Genesis, Exodus, Leviticus, Numbers, Deuteronomy, and Matthew, Mark, Luke, etc.) How many different people wrote the words of the Bible? (*40 different authors, from 5 different continents, in 3 different languages*) Where did they get the words? (*from God*)

Stress that the words of the Bible actually came from God, and there is something special that the Bible can do for us that no other book can do. Continue the story: God gave us a verse in the Bible that describes his words. Invite a child to read 1 Thessalonians 2:13.

Then explain: A man named Paul wrote a letter to his believing brothers and sisters in the city of Thessalonica. He thanked God that they understood that the Scriptures were the word of God. For us today, this means that the words Bible recorders like Paul, Matthew, Luke, John and others wrote were actually words that God gave them to write. There have been many creative and poetic writers throughout our history who have given us words to entertain us and make us think. But the only book that can forever change our lives and give us eternal life is the Bible. Why? These words do not come from brilliant men, but from the eternal God.

Isn't that amazing? God is the author of the Bible, which means that the words are perfectly placed for our benefit. God is aware of our daily needs, so he has given us the words of the Bible to help us grow strong as we live each day for Jesus! The Bible also teaches that it is at work in those who believe in Jesus. That's right, at work! That means that we can actually depend on the word of God to help us make the right decisions.

The Bible is not just a book full of history or stories of old, but is actually useful for us! It's like an instruction book from God, who always knows what is best for us. The Bible is full of heroes, who gave us examples of how we can really trust God with everything we do. Those heroes are real people just like you and me who made mistakes and made good choices.

The Bible also gives us great words of praise and wisdom, so that we can remember each day how awesome and loving God is.

To help remind you what the Bible can do for us, I call the Bible "G-Mail," which stands for "God-mail." The Bible is actually a great, big message from God! And you know what? There are so many messages in that great, big book that we can have a new one each day to help us live the way Jesus wants us to live! So boys and girls, here's my challenge: Read the Bible every day. Even if you just read one verse, and think about what it means, you'll be on your way to dedicating your day to God. Pretty soon you'll be reading a couple of verses a day, and then a whole chapter! The bottom line: You've got G-Mail, so depend on it every day!

♪ **Song Suggestions:**

G-Mail! By Dean-o from "Soul Surfin'" (1999 FKO Music / ASCAP)

God's Holy Book from "God's Big Picture" (Gospel Light)

The B.I.B.L.E. (Traditional)

God Wrote Us a Letter by Mary Rice Hopkins from "Come Meet Jesus" (Big Steps 4 U)

I Believe the Bible (CEF Press, P.O. Box 348, Warrenton, Mo. 63383)

Craft For Younger Children: Letter From God

Needed: Envelope for each child addressed to them, and the memory verse written on paper.

Say: God's word is the Bible. The Bible is like a letter that God wrote just to us! Have you ever gotten a letter? What did it say? Today we are going to decorate our envelopes and send a letter to ourselves. When you get the letter in the mail, you can read God's word!

Help the children put the memory verse in the envelope and stamp it. Encourage them to watch for the letter in their home mailboxes in about three days. Mail the letters to the children.

 Craft for Older Children: Phylactery

Needed: a small gift box, jewelry box, or raisin box for each child, string or cord, brown paper bags torn into pieces about 4 inches by 6 inches

Say: Back in Bible times, people had a way to remember the words of God. It was a container called a phylactery. A phylactery was a little box in which they put pieces of paper or leather with Scripture words written on them. They could open it up any time they wanted to read the word of God. Today we are going to make a phylactery.

Show children how to attach the cord to the box by punching holes in the box to string the cord through.

Next take the paper bag paper and write this part of the memory verse on it: "And it really is God's message. And that message works in you who believe" (1 Thess. 2:13). Say: This paper looks like the parchment paper that they used in Bible times. Put the verse into the box and tie it around your head. Yep, your head! If you tie it around your head you won't lose it. That's what many Bible people did.

Bible Cookies

Needed: Square black wafer cookies, alphabet cereal, and icing.

Explain: God tells us many things in his word. What are some of the words God tells us? Let's make a cookie with a Bible word in it. Find alphabet cereal letters to spell one of God's words and then put it on your cookie. Show children how to spread a thin layer of icing on their cookie and then put letters on top to spell one of the words from the memory verse (or any other words from the Bible).

Snack

Memory Verse Activity: Who's Message Is It?

This verse tells us that God's word is from God and not people. Let's play a game to decide which words are from God and which are from men. Write the following phrases on the board:

Be kind

Do whatever you want

Love one another

I am the Way, the Truth and the Life

Get every toy that you can

Cheating is okay as long as you are nice

Don't steal

Don't kill

Obey your parents

Honor your mother and father

God loves you

Jesus died for you

Guide children to separate the phrases into two piles: words from God and words from people.

Ask: Which words should you trust and follow? Encourage the children to suggest more words from God and from people.

Stress: You can always trust what God says, God always tells the truth.

Memory Verse: 1 Thessalonians 2:13 ICB

Also, we always thank God because of the way you accepted his message. You heard his message from us, and you accepted it as the word of God not the words of men. And it really is God's message. And that message works in you who believe."

Alternate version (New King James)

For this reason we also thank God without ceasing, because when you received the word of God which you heard from us, you welcomed it not as the word of men, but as it is in truth, the word of God, which also effectively works in you who believe.

Prayer Focus:

Dear God, thank you for your word, the Bible. Thank you for all that you tell us, all the words that help us which are in it. We praise you for all you do for us. Amen.

January 21

Tuned Up and Ready, Midweek
By Mary Rice Hopkins

Scripture:
1 Corinthians 9:24

Lesson Aim:
To teach children to always be prepared.

Bible Skill:
Kids will discover how important Bible study is.

Bible Learning Activity for Younger Children: Running for the Prize!
Needed: Clouds cut from white paper posted on a wall.

Say: Today we are going to run a race. The prize for the race will be heaven! Start all children at the same place. Let them all race toward the clouds, all together at the same time. Have them stop when they touch the clouds.

Say: You all win! You all win the prize of heaven. But you don't get that prize by running. You get it by loving God and believing in Jesus.

Bible Learning Activity for Older Children: Race to Win!
Needed: Paper and pens.

Guide children to trace around their feet onto the paper. Cut the footprints out. Write on each footprint "Run to Win!"

Say: Have you ever been in a race? Did you win the race? What strategies did you use to win, or try to win, the race?

After several children share, explain that when Paul was writing the letter to the Corinthian people, Paul said, "Run to Win." Do you think he was talking about running a race?

Explain that Paul was talking about running the "race of life" and that more than one person can be first place winners in this race. Ask: What strategies that you use for physical running can apply to running the race of life? (*Samples: Pace yourself; always play fair; cheer on your teammates; give 110%.*)

Say: If you win the "race of life" you will get a prize which is eternal life with God. What a great prize! You also have fun while running.

Enrichment for Older Children: Olympics

Ask: What would it be like to go to the Olympics? Do you think you could win? How is being in the Olympics like and not like games that you play? What event would you want to be in? What would you have to do to be in that event?

Explain: It takes lots of practice to be in the Olympics!

Share these fun facts: Did you know that the Olympics and running races have been run for many, many years? Long ago, the first Olympic Games were held as part of religious festivals honoring Zeus who was someone the Greeks called a god. The athletes were all male citizens from every corner of the Greek world, coming from as far away as Iberia (Spain) in the west and the Black Sea (Turkey) in the east.

The Olympics were named after Mt. Olympus, the highest mountain in mainland Greece. In Greek mythology, Mt. Olympus was the home of the greatest of the Greek gods and goddesses that they believed in.

Invite a child to read 1 Corinthians 9:24 while the others follow along in their Bibles. When the apostle Paul talked about "running for the prize" he was talking to these Greek people who knew all about running! He wanted them to know that the "prize" was not a physical something they actually won, but eternal life in Jesus Christ! Paul wanted them to stop believing in the Greek gods and learn to believe in the true God! ☺

Further Enrichment for Older and Younger Children: Silly Olympics

Say: *Today we are going to have our own Olympics. Each child will partici-pate in every event. Are you ready?*

Guide the children to participate in the following events:

Backward race across classroom

Javelin throw with drinking straws

High jump over stretched out rope

Swimming race with children running and making "swimming" motions with their hands

Long jump with children jumping backwards

Summersault relay race

Say: *Were those events hard or easy? What made them so hard? (Samples: I'm only good at one of them; they were hard to do that way.) What made them easy? (They were skills we don't have to practice.) Why were they fun?*

Communicate that as Christians we can all be winners, and that there is a lot of happy fun in running our life for God. We don't have to beat another believer to be the person God wants us to be. Encourage the children to tell you what this means with questions like: *How is running for God like winning a trophy? What strategies do you use in games that you can also use in living as a Christian? Where do you keep your trophies? What physical reminders show you the prizes you win as Christians?*

Ask: What are some ways your parents say to you "Do your best!" That's what the apostle Paul was telling the people. He told them to keep trying hard to reach the goal. The goal he was talking about was not the finishing line in a game, or an Olympic medal. It was life forever with God. That excellence shows in the kind way you treat your brothers and sisters, the dedicated way you work at school, the fair way you play games, and in the good books you read. ☺

Memory Verse: 1 Corinthians 9:24 ICB

You know that in a race all the runners run. But only one gets the prize. So run like that. Run to win!

Alternate version (New King James)

Do you not know that those who run in a race all run, but one receives the prize? Run in such a way that you may obtain it.

January 25

Tuned Up and Ready
By Mary Rice Hopkins

Scripture:
1 Corinthians 9:24

Lesson Aim:
To teach children to always be prepared.

Bible Skill:
Kids will discover how important Bible study is.

Bible Lesson:
Tell a story about preparation. For example: Before I get ready for a concert, I always make sure my guitar is tuned. I also have to "warm up" my voice and practice singing. It's important to be prepared and ready to go. Sometimes I have to change my strings. I have to change my strings so that they sound their best. These are important parts of doing the best possible job. If you do not play the guitar, change the example to fit your interest such as "When I get ready to paint a picture I get my very best paints out," or "When I get ready to work on a business deal I make sure I have all the information that I will need."

Continue: Athletes who want to perform their best have to stretch to get ready for a race or a game. If they don't they could be unprepared or even injure a part of their bodies. Good athletes remember to stretch before they run and probably stretch afterwards as well.

Did you know that the Bible says we need to be prepared by knowing the Bible and knowing what we believe? It's like we are in a spiritual race. Before we start our day we can get ready by spending just a little time with God. It's

Song Suggestions:

Running for the Prize by Mary Rice Hopkins from "15 Singable Songs" (Big Steps 4 U, 1988)

Every Move I Make by David Ruis from "Ablaze With Praise" (Revelation Generation Music 2001)

Speed of Sound by Dean-o from "Soul Surfin" (FKO Music, Inc. 1999)

Yes I Can! Songsheets published by CEF Press, P.O. Box 348, Warrenton, Mo. 63383

sort of like getting ready for a concert or getting ready for a race. We tune up before we go out on the stage, OR we stretch before going out onto the track of life. In the same way, we should start our morning by reading his Bible so he can tell us how to be ready for our day. We also ask throughout the day for God's ideas, strength, and protection.

Invite a child to read 1 Corinthians 9:24.

 Craft for Younger Children: Trophy Time

Needed: Bring for each child a toilet paper roll and a 3-inch circle cut from stiff paper or cardboard. Write: "I Did My Best!" on each circle.

Provide crayons for the children to color the tubes. Attach a circle to the top of each toilet paper roll by cutting a slit in the top of the tube for the circle to slide into. This creates a trophy.

Say: What do trophies look like? Tell about a time you won a trophy or saw someone else win a trophy. What is a trophy for? When you win trophies, it means that you were the best in that contest! Our trophies say that you did your best this morning. God wants us to always do our best!

Craft for Older Children: I Did My Best!
Needed: Bring for each child a blue ribbon 1 inch wide by 7 inches long and 3-inch round circles cut from white poster board or thin craft foam.

Make "Blue Ribbons" by attaching circle to the top of the ribbon. Write "I Did My Best!" on the circle.

Discuss, using the final paragraph of the Craft for Younger Children.

Prayer Focus:

Dear God, thank you for all the wonderful things you do for us. We know that you have given us your very best. Help me to do my best for you always. Amen.

First Place Ribbons

Bring for each child six inches of fruit roll up and a round cookie such as a vanilla wafer, plus a dab of icing for "glue."

Make First Place Ribbons by attaching vanilla wafer to top of piece of fruit roll up, forming a prize ribbon.

Snack

As children eat the ribbons, ask: Have you ever won a ribbon like this or a trophy? Tell us about it. What did you do to win it?

Explain: It's fun to win a trophy, ribbon, or prize because it shows you were one of the best in that contest! The apostle Paul tells us in the Bible that if we want to win we have to be prepared. How did you prepare to win those awards? Did you practice your swimming? Did you practice your spelling or your art?

Ask: Tell me some times and places you could read your Bible to prepare to be a Christian? What are some tips you would find in the Bible? What are some prayers you pray and where do you pray them?

Explain: It is very important to be prepared in our lives. Reading the Bible shows us what to do in day-to-day events such as friendship, getting along with family, learning at school, and more. Each caring action is a way to show we love Jesus. When we are prepared, we are closer to God and to people. We can be ready for whatever happens in our lives.

Memory Verse: 1 Corinthians 9:24 ICB

You know that in a race all the runners run. But only one gets the prize. So run like that. Run to win!

Alternate version (New King James)
Do you not know that those who run in a race all run, but one receives the prize? Run in such a way that you may obtain it.

Memory Verse Activity: Running for the Prize!

Needed: Prepare for each team several pieces of paper with one or two words of the verse written on each one. Mark a starting and finishing line on the floor with masking tape. Have kids line up into two teams behind the starting line.

Say: We are going to have a relay race. You must run to the line and then choose the word that goes next in the verse. You must then carry it back and put it on the floor. You must get the words in the correct order. When you put the word in order on the floor, the next person can go and get their word. Ready?

Conduct the race, guiding the kids to put verse together.

Say: Let's read the verse together.

Lead children in reading the verse from the cards together several times until it becomes a chant. Invite volunteers to recite the verse.

Explain: The apostle Paul knew that life was hard. He knew that we will run up against sad and bad things and we must be able to jump them, run around them, or fight until we win over them. Sometimes our own bad choices cause these problems. Other times another's bad choice causes these problems. Learning how to stop bad and start good is one way to be prepared. This fights sin—doing wrong or failing to do right. God wanted us to know that life is like a great race. In the "Race of Life" we should keep going, we should not get discouraged, but instead we should keep training and keep running.

Ask: What is our prize if we follow God in our "Race of Life"? *(happiness here on earth and eternal life with God!)*

January 28

Bought Again, Midweek
By Terry Platt

Scripture:
1 Peter 1:18

Lesson Aim:
To help children embrace God's deep commitment to them.

Bible Skill:
Children will explore the meaning of redemption through Christ.

Bible Learning Activity For Older Children and Younger Children: The Salvation Message

Needed: 1 small baby food jar for each child, colored sand or sand-type candy in these colors: yellow, black, red, white, green, OR use beads of the same colors and make a necklace or bracelet.

Say: Today we are going to learn the very best part of the Bible, the salvation message. When your jar is filled, it will help you remember the salvation message.

Pass around the YELLOW (or gold) sand.

Guide children to place into their jar 1/2 inch of yellow sand.

Ask: What does this gold remind you of? (*money, jewelry, more*)

Explain: Those things are very valuable and special. But today the gold is going to represent something even more valuable and special. That something is heaven. The Bible gives an image of heaven having streets of gold. God tells us many other things about heaven. No one is ever sick there. No one ever dies. There is no night there. Heaven is a very special place.

Pass around the BLACK sand.

Guide the children to add about 1/2 inch black sand on top of the gold sand.

Ask: There is one thing that can never be in heaven. Does anyone know what that is? *(sin)*

Explain: The black sand stands for sin. Sin is anything we think, do, or say that is wrong and does not please God. It hurts us and it hurts other people. Sin can also be failing to do something good, like not invite someone to sit at our lunch table. Because God wants us to live in heaven and because we sin, God thought of a plan to bring us there.

Pass around the RED sand.

Guide the children to add about 1/2 inch red sand on top of the black sand.

Say: God loved us so much and wanted us to be in heaven with him. So he came to earth in the person of Jesus Christ. Jesus lived on earth just like we do, but Jesus never sinned. He showed us how to live. We can imitate him to find the happiness we seek. The Bible tells us that Jesus died on the cross even though he did nothing wrong. Instead of dying for his sin, he died for our sin. The red stands for the blood of Jesus.

Pass around the WHITE sand.

Guide the children to add about 1/2 inch white sand on top of the red sand.

Say: God wants to forgive your sins, the times you do wrong and the times you refuse to do right, and make it so that they never happened at all. No matter how good you are, you still choose some sins. Only one very special person can take away your sin—Jesus. You can receive Jesus. How do you do that? You tell Jesus that you know you are a sinner. You tell Jesus that you believe in him and that you want him to be your Savior and your Lord. As Savior he takes care of sin; as Lord he shows you how to avoid sinful choices in the future.

Then when God looks at you he doesn't see the sin, he only sees the "clean" part of you, that has no sin at all. The white sand will stand for a pure heart.

Pass around the GREEN sand.

Guide the children to fill the rest of the jar with the green sand and put on the lid.

Explain: The color green reminds me of things that are growing, like trees, plants, and grass. When you are a Christian and have received Christ, you begin to grow too. You learn more and more about Jesus and that means you are growing in Christ!

Ask: Would anyone like to receive Jesus and become a Christian right now? We are going to pray and when we pray let's all bow our heads. I will tell you what you can say, and if you want to receive Christ, you can pray along with me, okay?

Prayer Focus:

Dear Jesus, I know that I am a sinner because I do wrong and I fail to do right. So I would like to receive you right now so that you can be the Lord of my life. I love you and I want to follow you. Please forgive me for my sins and come into my life. Thank you, God. Amen.

Say: Let's review what the colors mean so you can tell others about Jesus Christ! Invite children to take turns naming a color and what it means. Let every child have a turn. Affirm each child fervently. ☺

Memory Verse: 1 Peter 1:18b, 19 ICB

You were bought, but not with something that ruins like gold or silver. You were bought with the precious blood of the death of Christ, who was like a pure and perfect lamb.

Alternate version (New King James)
Knowing that you were not redeemed with corruptible things, like silver or gold, from your aimless conduct received by tradition from your fathers, but with the precious blood of Christ, as of a lamb without blemish and without spot.

February 1

Bought Again
By Terry Platt

Scripture:
1 Peter 1:18

Lesson Aim:
To help children embrace God's deep commitment to them.

Bible Skill:
Children will explore the meaning of redemption through Christ.

Bible Lesson: Bought Twice

Tell this story: Not too long ago a man named Terry decided to sell some of his things to make space *for* some new things. Many people showed up at the sale and Terry got excited about selling so many things! When a dealer of old books offered him a price that seemed very tempting, Terry was really happy! He didn't really want those old books so he took the money.

The man picked up the box and loaded it in the trunk of his car. But when Terry looked at him, he got worried. He had the biggest smile on his face! Terry wondered why? Did he make a mistake by selling those books?

Soon after that event, Terry went to an antique shop and began looking at the old children's books. They looked familiar and he even commented that he once had those same titles. His eyes were drawn to a favorite book. When he opened it to see the price he nearly dropped it—it was his book; it was a special book that his grandfather gave him when he was in second grade.

The price of the book was many times what the dealer paid for the whole box! He took the book to the dealer and told him it was his book and he would like it back. The dealer just smiled and said, "Sure, you can have it back—just pay the price for it!"

Terry told him "You don't understand, it was my book. I shouldn't have sold it to you. I can't pay that price."

He said, "Pay the price, or leave it."

The dealer wanted cash only and would not accept a credit card or check. Terry told the dealer he did not have that much cash. The dealer did not care. He repeated that the book would stay if the price was not paid.

Can you imagine how frustrated and disappointed Terry was?

"I'll buy it," a stranger's voice said. Terry was wide eyed as the man paid the price and watched the special book go into a bag. With that the man handed Terry the bag and simply said, "I understand."

He paid the high price for Terry's mistake.

Did you know that Jesus is like that? Everyday we sin and cannot pay the price for what we do. But everyday Jesus says, "I'll pay the price for their sin." Just as the man paid the price for my book so that I could have it back without deserving it, Jesus paid the price for our sins so that we could have eternal life—a happy life that starts now and lasts long after we die—without deserving it. Jesus died so that we could live!

 Song Suggestions:

He Paid a Debt (Traditional)

Nothing But the Blood Songsheets published by CEF Press, P.O. Box 348, Warrenton, Mo. 63383

Love with the Love by Mary Rice Hopkins from "Miracle Mud" (Big Steps 4 U 1998)

Before We Say Goodbye by Jana Alayra from "Believin' On" (Montjoy Music 2002)

Craft for Older Children: Sugar Cube Cross
Needed for each child: 15 sugar cubes, 1 strip of green construction paper 6 inches long and 2 inches wide, and water to make the cubes stick together.

Guide children to cut the green construction paper so that one long side looks like grass, to glue 9 cubes into a 3x3 square. This will be the base of the cross.

Then guide them to glue 4 cubes in a row, then one cube on each side of the third cube to form a cross. Glue the resulting cross standing up to the middle cube of the base.

Say: The Christians back in Bible times were so sad when Jesus died on the cross. But he didn't stay dead! No! He came back to life just like he said he would do. Today, we use the symbol of the cross to remember Jesus.

 Craft for Younger Children: Torn Paper Cross
Needed for each child: 5 inch cardboard square, small pieces of torn tissue paper

Show children how to draw a cross on the cardboard with the glue. Let the children create a cross by attaching the torn tissue paper to the glue. Say: The Christians back in Bible times were so sad when Jesus died on the cross. But he didn't stay dead! No! He came back to life just like he said he would do. Today, we use the symbol of the cross to remember Jesus.

Rocky Roads

Needed: Graham crackers, chocolate chips, peanut butter (check for allergies), small sandwich bags

 Show children how to put one graham cracker, a few chocolate chips and a spoonful of peanut butter into a sandwich bag. Crush and mix ingredients inside the bag, form into a ball and eat!

Say: Sometimes our lives have some "rocky roads" and things do not go smoothly for us. When we go through hard times, we remember that Jesus went through hard times too. He will walk right beside us. He died for us and then came back to life. He is still alive and can help us through our rocky roads.

Prayer Focus:

Dear God, thank you for coming to earth to show us how to live. Thank you for coming in Jesus and paying the price for our mistakes. Thank you for eternal life. We praise you. Amen.

Memory Verse: 1 Peter 1:18b, 19 ICB

You were bought, but not with something that ruins like gold or silver. You were bought with the precious blood of the death of Christ, who was like a pure and perfect lamb

Alternate version (New King James)
Knowing that you were not redeemed with corruptible things, like silver or gold, from your aimless conduct received by tradition from your fathers, but with the precious blood of Christ, as of a lamb without blemish and without spot.

Memory Verse Activity: You Were Bought

Needed: Construction paper, small play coins (about 5 for each child), glue.

Write the verse on a white board or poster. Let the children copy the verse onto the construction paper to make their own memory verse posters. Glue on the coins for effect.

February 4

The Most Important Command, Midweek
By Ivy Beckwith

Scripture:
Matthew 22:34–39

Lesson Aim:
God wants us to love him and our neighbor.

Bible Skill:
Children will discover that treating people kindly and refusing to lie about them is a way to show love for God. It shows the kind of "neighboring" that God wants us to show.

Bible Learning Activity for All Ages:
Option #1
Involve kids in a service project to help them experience some ways they can love their neighbor. For example, suggest that they take the snack (below) to someone in their neighborhood or to a friend at school whom they don't know yet. Insist that they take a parent along when going to a house other than their own.

Option #2
Show pictures of people with a variety of appearances (different ethnic and racial groups, old and young, male, female). As you show each picture ask: "Is this person your neighbor?" Show as many pictures as possible so that the children will understand that ALL people are neighbors. Stress: Neighbors are more than the people who live next door or on your block. Every person matters to God and to you. This does not mean you go up to every person, but together with your parents, you speak kindly to every person, and treat every person at your school like you want to be treated.

Enrichment for Younger Children: Knock, Knock, Neighbor!
Preparation: Have children sit in a circle.

Play Duck, Duck Goose substituting KNOCK KNOCK NEIGHBOR! For duck, duck, goose. Make certain children do not knock hard on each other's heads.

Let children play until all children have had a turn to be "it".

Ask: Who is your neighbor?

Clarify that everyone here is your neighbor, and that God wants us to love everyone and be a neighbor to everyone! You did that first by not knocking each other's heads.

Ask: What are some other ways to be a neighbor? ☺

Enrichment for Older Children:
In the Old Testament, believers thought a neighbor was a friend, close associate, or a person who lived nearby. When God made his covenant with Abraham, God gave guidelines to the Israelites about how to act toward these neighbors. God commanded believers to show concern for their neighbors. Two ways to do this, according to the ninth and tenth commandments (Ex. 20:16–17; Deut. 5:20–21), are to not say untrue things about a neighbor, and not to be jealous of a neighbor's wife, servant, livestock, or other possessions.

God also insisted that believers not cheat or rob from neighbors. This command is in Leviticus 19:13. Rather than getting a neighbor back worse than he got you, God said to be fair. He described it like this: "eye for eye, tooth for tooth" in Leviticus 24:19–20. Despising one's neighbor is wrong, as is leading him morally astray or deceiving him, then saying, "I was only joking" (Prov. 14:21; 16:29–30; 26:19). God does not want us to even think evil about a neighbor (Zech. 8:17).

Jesus expanded the concept of neighbor to include strangers, as in the parable of the Good Samaritan (Luke 10:25–37). In that story religious people passed by a man who was hurt simply because he didn't meet their definition of neighbor. The apostle Paul declared that to "love your neighbor as yourself" is very important (Rom. 13:9–10). ☺

Memory Verse: Matthew 22:37 ICB

Love the Lord your God with all your heart, soul and mind.

Alternate and extended version (New King James)

Jesus said to him, " 'You shall love the LORD your God with all your heart, with all your soul, and with all your mind.' This is the first and great commandment. And the second is like it: 'You shall love your neighbor as yourself.' On these two commandments hang all the Law and the Prophets."

February 8

The Most Important Command
By Ivy Beckwith

Scripture:
Matthew 22:34–39

Lesson Aim:
God wants us to love him and our neighbor.

Bible Skill:
Children will discover that treating people kindly and refusing to lie about them is a way to show love for God. It shows the kind of "neighboring" that God wants us to show.

Bible Lesson: Tell the Truth
Gather children together. Ask, "*Who can name some of the things God commands us to do?*" Respond to each child's answer with comments like: That's right. God asks us to be honest. God asks us to worship only God. God asks us not to take what isn't ours. God asks us to treat other people well. God asks us to respect our parents. Whew! God asks us to do a lot of stuff. How are we ever going to remember all the things God wants us to do? How are we ever going to do all the things God wants us to do?

Well, did you know that when Jesus was here on earth some people were asking that very same question: How can I ever get it right? These people thought maybe it would help if God would tell them which commandments were more important than the rest. Then they could make sure they at least kept the ones that were most important. One man walked up to Jesus and said, "Teacher, which commandment is the most important?" The man was hoping Jesus would give him two or three commandments he could be sure to obey and then tell him that the rest were only important to obey when he remembered what they were.

Well, Jesus surprised the man by saying there are really only two commandments. Jesus said the first commandment is, "You shall love the Lord your God with all your heart and with all your soul, and with all your mind." What do you think this means? It means that we are to love God with everything that is inside of us. We are to think about why we love and trust God and then to obey him with our actions and soul even if we don't feel like doing the right thing.

Then, Jesus said there was a second command: "You shall love your neighbor as yourself." What do you think that means? It means that you should treat other people in the same way you like to be treated. You put yourself into that person's situation and do what you would want them to do for you. For example if you are trying to find a seat in the lunchroom, you hope someone will notice and invite you over. So you notice and invite people over.

Now why do you think Jesus thought he could take all the commandments God gave us and make them into only two commandments? Because if we do these two things, if we love God and if we love our neighbor as we want to be loved then we end up keeping all of God's commandments. The other commandments simply spell out how to love God and how to love people. If we only love God, God is the only one we will want to worship. If we truly love other people we won't want to steal from them or tell lies about them because we wouldn't want to be treated this way. So instead of remembering all the commands God gave us in the Bible Jesus made it really easy for us to do the things God wants us to do: Love God and love your neighbor.

 Song Suggestions:

Lovin' God Is Livin' Great! by Dean-o from "You Got It All" (FKO Music, Inc. 1997)

Who Is Your Neighbor? by Mary Rice Hopkins from "Come on Home" (Big Steps 4 U 2002)

Love the Lord Your God, Love Your Neighbor from "Kids on the Rock" (Gospel Light Publishers 1995)

I'm a Winner Songsheets published by CEF Press, P.O. Box 348, Warrenton, Mo. 63383

Craft for Older Children: Love Your Neighbor Plate
Needed for each child: a paper plate, house shape cut from thin colored foam sheets or construction paper. Letter "Love Your Neighbor as Yourself" on each paper plate.

Let children glue the house onto the plate. Ask: *What kind things can you do for someone in your own house or apartment? In a house that you go to?* Let children add plants and details with markers.

Ask: Who is your neighbor? Did you know that Jesus thought that everyone was your neighbor, not just those who live close to you? Jesus wanted you to show great love for everyone!

Friendly Neighbor Snack

Needed: Pretzels, small chocolate candies, peanuts, corn cereal, snack size plastic bags. Place the snack foods in bowls and set on a table.

Say: Today we are going to make a snack for ourselves and one for our neighbor. Each of you will make two bags, one to eat and one to give away.

Show children how to walk around the table and take small amounts of snack foods from each bowl and place them into the plastic bags.

Ask: Did you make both bags the same? When you are giving something to your neighbor, it should be something you would like too. When you go home, give one of these bags to someone you and your parents pick. This might be a friend at school or someone you and your parents go to visit. Say to this person: "Thank you for being my neighbor!" or "I made this for you because I am glad you are my friend."

Prayer Focus:

Dear God, thank you for loving us so much. Please help us to love everyone like Jesus did. Thank you for all you do for us. Thank you for our friends and neighbors and all the strangers that we don't know. We love you. Amen.

Memory Verse: Matthew 22:37 ICB
Love the Lord your God with all your heart, soul and mind.

Alternate and extended version (New King James)
Jesus said to him, " 'You shall love the LORD your God with all your heart, with all your soul, and with all your mind.' This is the first and great commandment. And the second is like it: 'You shall love your neighbor as yourself.' On these two commandments hang all the Law and the Prophets."

Memory Verse Activities All Ages:
(can be used for Valentine's Day activity too)
Needed: Red construction paper, markers
    Activity #1   Cut large hearts out of construction paper. Write the verse on each heart.
    Cut heart into an age-appropriate number of puzzle shapes and let children reassemble the puzzle.
    Activity #2   Write one word of the verse on each heart. Hide the hearts around the room and let children find the hearts and then put the verse together by laying the hearts in order. Encourage them to reference their Bibles.

Special Holiday Activity: Valentine's Day Craft
    Needed for each child: Three small hearts (about 3 inches across) cut from thin colored foam sheets or construction paper, red and pink beads, ribbon.
    Preparation: Punch hole through top of each heart and string it on a ribbon. Let the children add beads. Put three hearts on each necklace to stand for "heart, soul and mind."
    Say: These hearts will remind us to love our neighbors and friends! The hearts stand for all the ways that we are supposed to love God, with our hearts, our souls and our minds. Who can name a way to show love toward a friend your age? Toward someone who is older? Toward someone who is younger?

February 11

Misfits, Midweek
By Amanda Garrett

Scripture:
Mark 10:46–52

Lesson Aim:
Jesus loves each of us regardless of how different or awkward we may feel.

Bible Skill:
Kids will realize Jesus accepts all of us and we can accept each other.

Enrichment for Younger Children: Miracles
Ask: What is a miracle? (Something really extraordinary that happens) Can you do a miracle? Explain that a miracle is something that happens only through God's help. It is not the same as a magic trick. A magic trick is something anyone can do if they just learn how. A miracle is something only God can do.

God has special power and that special power can bring miracles. Have you ever prayed for someone who got well? Getting well can be a miracle. God worked many miracles in the Bible times and God works miracles in our lives today too!

Enrichment for Older Children: Miracles
Say: When Jesus healed a blind man, it was called a miracle. But what is a miracle? A miracle is something that happens "supernaturally" or with super power. This kind of special power comes only from God.

Are miracles the same as "magic"? No. What is the difference between magic and miracle?

If we look in the dictionary, we will find these definitions:

✂ **Bible Learning Activity All Ages: Concentration!**
   Needed: Index cards. Make two sets of cards, writing on each
   card the elements of the Bible story; Jericho, Jesus, Bartimaeus,
a cloak, a crowd, eyes closed, eyes open, etc. Or if you have older children,
plan to let the children write the elements with your guidance.

   Play the game by guiding children to take turns turning over two cards
at a time to find a match. If the cards match, that child may turn two
more. If they do not match, the next child takes a turn.

   Say: Sometimes we find a match and sometimes we don't. Sometimes
it may feel like no one understands us, like we have no match. But there is
often another person—parent, teacher, friend—that has experienced the
same thing. When you talk about your problems to someone, they can
usually help you. God provides his help through people. He
also provides his help through himself. He always understands.

Magic—A comprehensive name for all of the *pretended* arts, which claim
to change events using secret forces in nature or enchantment or witchcraft.

   That means that magic is the name for when you are *pretending* to do
something supernatural.

   Now, let's look at what the dictionary says about miracles.

   Miracle—A wonder or wonderful thing. An event or effect different
from the normal way things are, different from what usually happens in
nature; a supernatural event, or one that goes beyond the ordinary laws by
which the universe is governed.

   That's a lot of hard words! But these words mean that miracles are real
and wonderful! They are different from magic because they are not pretend.
They are real.

   Ask: Can you think of any miracles in the Bible? Here are examples:

   Loaves and fishes   Blind man healed
   Lazarus raised from the dead   The men saved from the fiery furnace
   Daniel saved from the lions   Jesus' birth
   Woman healed from sickness   There are many, many more!

Jesus did many miracles, not to prove he was the Son of God, but to
show us that he was the Son of God. Do miracles help you believe in God?
Can you believe in God without miracles? As children discuss, clarify that
God gave us miracles to help some people believe. But none of us has to
have a miracle to believe.

Memory Verse: Ephesians 5:2a ICB

Live a life of love. Love other people just as Christ loved us.

Alternate and extended version (New King James)
And walk in love, as Christ also has loved us and given Himself for us, an offering and a sacrifice to God for a sweet-smelling aroma.

February 15

Misfits
By Amanda Garrett

Scripture:
Mark 10: 46–52

Lesson Aim:
Jesus loves each of us regardless of how different or awkward we may feel.

Bible Skill:
Kids will realize Jesus accepts all of us and we can accept each other.

Bible Lesson:
Have you ever played "*One of these things is not like the other*"? The goal of this game is to look for the one that doesn't match the others. Let's see how well you do.

Call up a group of girls and one boy—line them up. Which one is different? That's right, he's a boy.

Call up kids wearing blue and one not—line them up. Which one is different? That's right, she's not wearing blue.

Say: We cited two ways to divide person from person: boy/girl, and color of clothes. Differences like these can make us feel like misfits. But there are many more things that are alike about us than are different; so actually we do fit together. For example, boys and girls both feel happy sometimes and both feel sad sometimes.

Ask: What are other things we use (or have seen others use) to make people feel they are different or that they just don't fit? (*Brand of clothes, skin color, wealth, skill, intelligence, etc.*) Wow! Many of those could feel pretty hurtful if they were used to exclude us or make us feel like a misfit. All of us could be in a group where we're different, where we feel like we're misfits.

We aren't actually misfits but we feel like one. God wants us to prevent this problem.

In the Bible in the Gospel of Mark, Jesus was walking through Jericho. There was a man living there who everyone considered a misfit. He was blind. Because he was blind he was not able to work enough to feed himself and he became a beggar. This made him feel like a misfit for two reasons: He was a beggar and he was blind. As Jesus walked nearby, this misfit whose name was Bartimaeus, called out to Jesus "Jesus, Son of David, have mercy on me!"

Everyone told him to be quiet—that Jesus had no time for someone like him. We do that to people sometimes too. We ignore them or wish they would just go away or even make fun of them. But, Jesus heard Bartimaeus and he stopped and told Bartimaeus to come to him. We can be just like Jesus.

After Jesus was nice to the man, the crowd acted much nicer to Bartimaeus. Have you ever noticed how that happens—when you're nice to someone, other people act nicely too? They told him to cheer up and get up because Jesus wanted to see him. Bartimaeus was so excited that Jesus listened to him that he left all his stuff behind and went to Jesus.

Jesus asked Bartimaeus, "What do you want me to do for you?" Bartimeus was very honest and said "Rabbi, I want to see." Jesus said, "Go, your faith has healed you." And it was true! Bartimaeus could see, but he didn't go anywhere. He joined the crowd and followed Jesus.

Jesus has time and attention for everyone. He wants us to act the same way as he acts. He wants us to give our time and attention to other people. It doesn't matter how many differences we see or feel. We can listen like Jesus listens and give attention like Jesus did. He will sometimes help other people

---

 Song Suggestions:

For God So Loved by Dean-o from "You Got It All" (FKO Music, Inc. 1997)

You're In My Heart To Stay by Jana Alayra from "Dig Down Deep" (Montjoy Music 1997)

Miracle Mud by Mary Rice Hopkins from "Miracle Mud" (Big Steps 4 U 2000)

Four-Letter-Words from L-O-V-E Songsheets published by CEF Press, P.O. Box 348, Warrenton, Mo. 63383

through us, and help us through other people. That means we don't have to worry about being a misfit because we'll always fit with Jesus and Jesus will always give us people to fit with. In fact, any two people are more alike than they are different.

Remember to learn from Jesus and Bartimaeus how to treat each other. If Jesus has time and attention for everyone then we can have time and attention for everyone too. We can be friends with all kinds of people, including those that some people might call misfits.

Craft for Older Children: Treasure Boxes

Needed for each child: One margarine tub or similar container, gold spray paint, jewels or beads, glue. Spray paint the containers prior to class.

Ask: Do any of you have a treasure box? A treasure box is something that we keep our treasures, or our special things, in. We are going to make treasure boxes. Show children how to put glue onto container lids and then place jewels or beads into the glue.

Explain: This treasure box will be fun to put special things into. It will remind us that God treasures us and wants us to treasure each other.

Craft for Younger Children: Treasure Hearts

Needed: Construction paper, wax paper, colored tissue paper

Show children how to fold construction paper in half and then cut out a heart. Glue piece of wax paper (a little larger than the cut out) onto the "heart window".

Guide children to tear different colors of tissue paper into small pieces. Show children how to glue small bits of tissue paper to wax paper. When it dries, show children how to hold up the tissue paper mosaic to the light to see it through the heart window.

Say: We can see this beautiful heart through this heart window. Isn't it pretty? It's like a treasure! We are treasures to God. God loves us and we look beautiful to God! He then shows us how to see and treasure the beauty in each person we go to school with, each person we see anywhere.

Make It Your Own!

Needed: graham crackers, saltines or round crackers, frosting, peanut butter or jelly, and a variety of small toppings such as raisins, coconut, mini chocolate chips or M&M Minis, etc.

Snack

Say: Today we are going to create our own snack. Everyone can make their cracker the way they want to. Guide the children to create three separate, individual, edible masterpieces.

After they finish, ask: Did they all turn out the same? No, of course they didn't! They are all different. And they are all delicious. God made us all different and we all make things differently! Each of us is yummy to know.

Prayer Focus:

Dear God, thank you for understanding all our thoughts and feelings, even when we feel like misfits. Thank you for helping us show acceptance to others so no one will feel like a misfit. Thank you for giving us others who treat us kindly, like you did with Bartimaeus. In Jesus' name, Amen.

Memory Verse: Ephesians 5:2a ICB

Live a life of love. Love other people just as Christ loved us.

Alternate and extended version (New King James)
And walk in love, as Christ also has loved us and given Himself for us, an offering and a sacrifice to God for a sweet-smelling aroma.

Memory Verse Activity:

Needed: Balloons and small pieces of paper

Preparation: Write one word of the verse on each slip of paper. Put each slip of paper into its own balloon and blow up balloons.

Say: Today we are going to learn a new verse. Each child (or group of children) has a balloon. We will pop the balloons and find the paper inside. After all the balloons are popped, we will put the verse together.

Let children pop the balloons and assemble verse. Help them if needed. Then say verse together as a group several times.

February 18

Smarter Than a Little Pig, Midweek

By Judy Comstock

Scripture:
Matthew 7:24–27

Lesson Aim:
To help children understand that they can feel secure with Jesus.

Bible Skill:
Children will discover why and how to build their lives on Jesus Christ.

Enrichment for Younger Children:

Needed: blocks, small pan of sand

Let children build houses out of blocks in the pan of sand. Put one house on sand and show children how shaking the sand slightly makes the house collapse!

Say: Jesus knew we needed a strong foundation and that sand was not strong! We use sand for many things, but not for building houses on! What can we do with sand? (Build sandcastles, play, dig) Those are fun things, aren't they? But when we build a house we need something that will not shift or move. We need something strong and steady. ☺

Enrichment for Older Children: Houses in Palestine

Optional: cedar for children to smell

Houses were very different in Palestine. If you were wealthy, you might make your house out of stone and brick and really nice wood. Wealthy home-builders used hewn stone and highly polished marble. They used cedar for their wall paneling and ceilings. Ask: Who has smelled cedar? What does it smell like? Today some people line closets and chests with cedar. A cedar-lined chest is often called a cedar chest.

Houses also could include moldings of gold, silver, and ivory.

Some wealthy landowners built "winter houses" and "summer houses" for their comfort in those seasons. They built the summer houses partly underground and paved them with marble. These houses generally had fountains in the central court, and were constructed to bring in currents of fresh air. This made them very refreshing in the torrid heat of summer. We don't know very much about winter houses.

The houses most people lived in had only one room made with mud walls. The builders reinforced these walls with reeds and rushes, or with stakes plastered with clay. Sometimes, the family lived in the same house with their animals! If they did this, they usually slept on a platform above the animals. The windows were small holes high in the wall, perhaps barred.

Whether a fancy house or a simple house, the owners dedicated their new homes to God before they moved into them. They asked God's blessing upon the house and the people who would live in it. Both fancy houses and simple houses needed a good solid foundation. No house, no matter how strong the materials, would stand very long on a shifting foundation. ☺

Bible Learning Activity All Ages:
Needed: Craft sticks, blocks, words of verse written on index cards, two words on each card.

Let children build a "house" with the blocks. Tape the words to the blocks and say the verse. Let children take turns knocking down the block house.

Guide children to build the house again while chanting the verse. Build and knock down the house several times until each child can recite the verse.

Then explore the meaning of the verse by asking: What "house" is this verse talking about? Is it really talking about a house?

Use children's words to explain that this house is our lives, and that the foundation is Jesus himself. To build our house on him we do what is good and right and pure. Invite children to each name one action that shows we are building our lives on the solid rock of Jesus Christ.

Memory Verse: Matthew 7:24 ICB

Everyone who hears these things I say and obeys them is like a wise man. The wise man built his house on rock.

Alternate version (New King James)
Therefore whoever hears these sayings of Mine, and does them, I will liken him to a wise man who built his house on the rock.

February 22

Smarter Than a Little Pig
By Judy Comstock

Scripture:
Matthew 7:24–27

Lesson Aim:
To help children understand that they can feel secure with Jesus.

Bible Skill:
Children will discover why and how to build their lives on Jesus Christ.

Bible Lesson: Smart Pigs and Smart People

Needed: Big Book of Three Little Pigs, large rock (preferably 4–5"), sand in sealed bag

Show the pages that match each part of the story as you tell it. Begin by showing the four main characters in the story as the details unfold.

Do you know the story about the three little pigs? Each pig constructed a house from three different kinds of building material. Allow time for children to respond by each giving you one detail of the story.

Then continue: After the houses were finished, the pigs were each visited by a wolf. The wolf said, "Little Pig, Little Pig, let me in, or I'll do what?" If they don't remember this line, guide them to say in unison and in a wolfish voice: "I'll huff and I'll puff and I'll blow your house in."

Recall that the wolf was able to blow in the first and the second houses. Ask: From what material did the first pig build his house? After students say "Straw", affirm, "Yes! He built his house from straw. There are places in the world where you can see real straw houses, but straw houses are not strong." Continue by explaining: The first little pig would not let the wolf into his house. The wolf decided to go in without permission. He tried to blow the house down and he did.

Ask: What happened to the second pig's house? Of what was it built? As students give the answer, affirm with: "That's right! The house of sticks fell down when the wolf huffed and puffed at the door.

Continue with a mixture of questions and telling the story to discuss the third pig's house. Include: In the nursery rhyme, the third little pig was smart. What material did he use to build his house? (bricks.) The third little pig used bricks, which are very strong. Did his house collapse when the wolf huffed and puffed and tried to blow down the brick house? (Wait for "No" answer.) The house did not fall.

There is a story in the Bible that Jesus told to a crowd of people. The lesson we can learn from that story is even more important than the lesson told in the Three Little Pigs story. Jesus wanted the people to understand that the way we build our lives matters. It's smart to practice what Jesus teaches. Knowing is good. Doing is smart. Jesus said doing what he teaches is like a wise man who built his house on the rock. (Show the large rock.) Rock is a great thing to use as the foundation of a house. The foundation is the place on which the house is built. Rock is solid and not shaky. If the bottom of a house is not sitting on rock, the house will not be strong even if it is built out of strong materials. The house could fall when the wind and rain blow hard and beat against it.

Jesus warned the people about the dangers of building a house upon sand. When something heavy (like a house) is on sand, it moves. When wind comes sand moves. When water comes sand moves. It looks steady, but it's not. (Show the bag of sand and move it to illustrate shifting characteristics.) Sand moves very easily. When the wind blows and the rain comes down, the house built on sand will fall.

 Song Suggestions:

You Are the Rock by Mary Rice Hopkins from "Come on Home" (Big Steps 4 U 2002)

Generation Filled with Righteousness by Cindy Rethmeier from "I Want 2 Be Like Jesus" (Mercy Vineyard Publishing 1995)

Go! Songsheets published by CEF Press, P.O. Box 348, Warrenton, Mo. 63383

The Wise Man Built His House Upon the Rock Traditional

In this story from the Bible, Jesus was not really talking about building a house. He was talking about building life habits, and life friendships and life relationships. If you build your life on shaky ideas, ideas that are not from the Bible, you will eventually have a mess. Things in your life will fall apart. For example, you might think it's OK to lie every now and then, especially if it gets you something you want. But then the foundation of trust washes away just like sand. And your friends and family won't trust you. Then you feel like collapsing. And it's hard to rebuild. Jesus wants to help you know good ideas, true ideas you should believe in and practice. He said doing the things he was teaching and living by his ideas is like building your life on solid rock. For example: When you choose to tell the truth, you build solid friendships, solid family closeness, and a safe place to stand.

Jesus wants us to be very, very smart. He wants us to be wise, very wise. We are wise if we build our lives on the important things we read and hear from the Bible. What are some of these? (Give each child a chance to give one example. Prod them gently so they will have confidence to speak.) Stress that building our lives on Jesus makes us smarter than the three little pigs.

Craft for Older Children: Wise Man's House

Needed: Strong paper plate, a large rock, craft sticks and bits of construction paper or sheets of colored craft foam.

Guide the children to make a picture of the story putting a house from sticks on the rock. Encourage bushes and other fun details.

Write across the top of the paper plate—"A Wise Man's House Is Built on the Rocks."

Say: Our story was about building a house on top of rocks and how a house built that way will stand up, even when there is bad weather. I wonder:

If Jesus is the rock, what would the house be? (*Our lives*)

What would the bad weather represent? (*Bad things that happen in our lives*)

Who would the foolish man be? (*Someone who doesn't obey Jesus*)

 **Craft for Younger Children:**
Needed: House shapes cut from thin colored sheets of craft foam or construction paper, paper plates, and stones/pebbles.
Letter "A Wise Man's House" across the top of the paper plate.
Guide the children to glue pebbles onto the plate. Let children glue the house on top of the pebbles. Say: "This is the wise man's house like in our story. Why do we call him a wise man? (Because he was smart enough to build his house on top of rocks) The wise man did a wise thing, didn't he?

Build Your House!
Needed: Graham crackers; precut into halves for walls and triangles for ceiling front and back. Each child will need 6 halves and 2 triangles, icing for "glue", small candies for decorations.

Say: In Bible times, home owners built their own houses. Today we are going to make a house by ourselves too! Show children how to form a house with the crackers.

Simplification idea: Make houses FLAT instead of 3D. Give each child a square and a triangle. Let them make a house and decorate it with windows, door, etc.

Prayer Focus:
Dear God, thank you for being a solid foundation in our lives. Help us to always trust in Jesus and to build our lives on you. We pray that we will always live our lives for you. We love you and we praise you. Amen.

Memory Verse: Matthew 7:24 ICB
Everyone who hears these things I say and obeys them is like a wise man. The wise man built his house on rock.

Alternate version (New King James)
Therefore whoever hears these sayings of Mine, and does them, I will liken him to a wise man who built his house on the rock.

Memory Verse Activity:

Letter the following words onto the craft sticks: (make one set per group of three children) Write only two or three words on each stick, divided as indicated:

> Everyone
> who hears
> these things I say
> and obeys them
> is like a
> wise man
> who built
> his house
> on rock.

Give each group a set of sticks. Let them try to put it together correctly and say the verse.

Say: What words is Jesus talking about? What is a wise man? How can you be wise? Jesus wants us to be wise, listen to what he says, and have a strong foundation in our lives.

February 25

The Power of a Song, Midweek

By Pat Verbal

Scripture:
2 Chronicles 20: 1–12, 21–22

Lesson Aim:
To help children discover the power of praise.

Bible Skill:
Singing helps me focus on God. Focus on God is praise.

Enrichment for Younger Children: A Game of Praise

Needed: Music player and music; your church's hymnals.

Play a game of musical chairs, but don't eliminate a child who is left without a chair. Instead, let him or her sing one line of their favorite song and keep playing.

Say: Singing as the penalty for getting "out" makes us almost want to miss. What do you like about singing? What are your favorite songs?

Make a list on the board of the favorite songs.

Say: There's a lot to like about singing and about songs! God loves songs too, and God loves for us to praise him with songs. ☺

Enrichment for Older Children: Hymns of the Church

Tell this story: The music we enjoy is a gift from God. Psalms are poems that can be sung. The Bible book of Psalms was a hymnbook for believers. Jesus himself may have sung from it. Later he used the book of Psalms when he preached and taught. Different psalms express joy, sorrow, and thanksgiving. Each one sings to God, as a type of prayer. David was inspired by God to write many of the psalms. In a similar way, Christian songwriters throughout history have inspired faith with their music.

Here are examples: The "Battle Hymn of the Republic" written in 1861 by Julia Ward Howe played an important role the Civil War. It was said to bring tears to the eyes of President Abraham Lincoln every time he heard it and became the theme of his war-torn presidency.

The hymn "Onward Christian Soldiers" was written for a children's program in 1864 in Yorkshire, England. The song didn't become popular until 1941 when Franklin Roosevelt and Winston Churchill requested it. They requested it when their two countries united to oppose Hitler in World War II.

George Bennard preached as a traveling evangelist. After an especially difficult campaign in 1913, he spent time thinking about the cross as a symbol of Christianity. Deciding the cross was the very heart of our faith, Mr. Bennard wrote the most frequently requested hymn in history, "The Old Rugged Cross."

Pass out hymnals and guide children to: Find a song in your church hymnal and do a search to find its history. Show children where to find this information in the hymnals.

Guide children to write their own praise song, perhaps setting words to the tune of a commercial jingle. Begin by guiding children to list what they want to praise God for. Then put these phrases into the song.

Guide another group of children to write a poem based on a Bible passage. Encourage others to think of a tune they could use. Merge the two groups to create a theme song for your class, being careful to quote from every piece. ☺

Bible Learning Activity for Older Children: Instruments in the Bible
Explain that there were many different musical instruments in the Bible. Some of them are still used today! Provide paper and urge children to draw the instruments as you tell about each one:

Bells were common in Palestine but they weren't used for singing! Instead, tiny bells of pure gold were fastened to the hem of the priest's robe.

Cymbals were another instrument that was used by priests. These instruments made a loud, distinctive sound when banged together. They were used to accompany trumpets (Ezra 3:10).

The lyre, a small harp-like instrument, was also used for worship.

Gong is the word used by some English translations for a type of cymbal sounded at weddings or other happy occasions. The phrase "noisy gong" is used in 1 Corinthians 13 to describe going through the motions of Christianity without the heart.

The flute or fife is mentioned in the book of Psalm. Some flutes were made of silver, while others were made of reeds, wood, or bone. Ask: Do any of you play the flute, bells, or cymbals?

The musical instrument mentioned more often than any other in the Bible is the harp. The harp is the instrument that David used to soothe the "distressing spirit" that troubled King Saul. The harp, considered by many to be the most noble of all musical instruments, was used both for worship and everyday use. Although David apparently plucked the strings with his fingers, the harp was usually played by stroking the strings with a pick, much as a guitar is played. The harp had from three to twelve strings. The harp was often made of silver or ivory.

The trumpet is mentioned several times in the Bible. This instrument was used by the priests during services of sacrifice, especially to signal the Day of Atonement (Lev. 25:9). The trumpet was also used to rally troops on the battlefield (Josh. 6:4).

The shophar was a very special type of trumpet. This trumpet was made from a ram's horn. It signaled war and peace, the new moon, the beginning of the Sabbath, approaching danger, and the death of a dignitary. Some even believed the shophar had power to drive out evil spirits and to heal by magic. The sound of the shophar could be heard from a great distance (Ex. 19:16, 19). It can produce only the first two tones of the musical scale and those not very accurately. The ram's horn is rarely mentioned with other musical instruments. Its main function apparently was to make noise.

What instrument do you play? Is it one of the ones from the Bible? ☺

Bible Learning Activity for Younger Children: Priest's Walk

Needed: Bells

Distribute bells. Explain: In the Bible, the priests sewed bells onto their clothes. When they walked, everyone knew that they were coming. Let's pretend that we are priests—hold your bell and shake it while we walk.

Ask: Why do you think priests used these bells? They make a nice sound, don't they? There are lots of musical instruments in the Bible; bells are just one of them. ☺

Enrichment Activity for All Children: Make Cymbals

Needed: Two aluminum pie plates for each child, two 6" x 2" pieces of felt per cymbal

Explain: You can make your own Bible time's cymbal as follows: Glue the ends of the felt onto the back of two pie plates, creating handles for the cymbals. Then bring the pie plates together to make noise. Encourage the children to clang away!

While children make their cymbals and then play them, talk further about instruments in the Bible. ☺

Memory Verse: Psalm 96:1 ICB

Sing to the Lord a new song. Sing to the Lord, all the earth. Sing to the Lord and praise his name. Every day tell how he saves us.

Alternate version (New King James)
Oh, sing to the LORD a new song!
Sing to the LORD, all the earth.
Sing to the LORD, bless His name;
Proclaim the good news of His salvation from day to day.

February 29

The Power of a Song
By Pat Verbal

Scripture:
2 Chronicles 20: 1–12, 21–22

Lesson Aim:
To help children discover the power of praise.

Bible Skill:
Singing helps me focus on God. Focus on God is praise.

Bible Lesson: A Song Wins a Battle

Ask: Do you play a musical instrument? How well do you like to practice? Practice can seem like it takes the fun out of music, but it puts the power in performance. Here are two stories about performances with musical instruments:

Once there was a girl named Susan. Susan stood back stage rubbing her sweaty palms. For weeks she had prepared for her fourth-grade piano recital, but now all she wanted to do was run home and hide under her bed.

At Susan's right elbow, her mom kept fidgeting.

On Susan's right, Mr. Harper, her piano teacher, paced back and forth like a caged rat wrinkling his nose. "Oh, no!" Mr. Harper said frowning at the first row. "The judges really loved Leslie Ann's original piece. She'll probably get first place."

Susan shook all the harder. She tried to picture in her mind the first few bars of music, but drew a blank. A little voice inside began to laugh as if it knew she would soon embarrass herself, her mom, and Mr. Harper.

Susan was looking for the EXIT sign when she heard her name called from the podium. With a hug from her mom and a little shove, Susan walked across the stage and sat down at the most beautiful grand piano she'd ever seen.

Even my mom is nervous. The judges don't like me. I don't have a chance. I can't remember a note. "Help me, Lord," she heard herself whisper as she put her right hand on the keyboard. She struck one note . . . then another and then a third. Her left hand effortlessly responded. To her surprise the melody seemed to take charge. The notes tumbled out like crystal water bubbling from an underground spring. It filled the room, commanding her to relax and go with it.

That night Susan's Grandma called. "How was the recital, Princess? We prayed for you."

"Oh, Nana, I was so nervous, but no one ever told me about the power of a song. Once I began to play, God sort of took over and I did great! All the practice was worth it. The recital was wonderful!"

King Jehoshaphat might have understood Susan's feelings. He faced three mighty armies at the same time. What was his brilliant military strategy? How did his well-trained army seek victory over their fierce enemies?

The king barely opened court that morning when a servant came running in. "A vast army is coming against you from Edom." the servant shouted. "The Moabites and the Ammonites joined the Meunites and they are already on the other side of the sea."

The news spread like wild fires. People from every town in Judah rushed to the palace. Everyone had an idea of what should be done, but before King Jehoshaphat was ready to give marching orders, he led his people in prayer.

In this great prayer, the king honored God for who he was: "O our God, did you not drive out the inhabitants of this land before your people Israel?"

 Song Suggestions:

You Are a Wonderful God Songsheets published by CEF Press, P.O. Box 348, Warrenton, Mo. 63383

You Reign by Kurt Johnson from "Kid Possible" (Kurt Johnson 1995)

Create in Me by Mary Rice Hopkins from "15 Singable Songs" (Big Steps 4 U 1988)

Outta Sight by Dean-o from "Soul Surfin'" (FKO Music, Inc. 1999)

Jehoshaphat simply told God about the problem. "But now there are men coming to drive us out of this land you gave us." Finally, Jehoshaphat declared his faith, "We have no power to face this vast army. We don't know what to do, but our eyes are on you. Amen."

After Jehoshaphat prayed, the Spirit of the Lord came to him and laid out the battle plan (2 Chr. 20:15–17). Jehoshaphat's prayer is a good model for us:

1. Don't be afraid.
2. Take a stand and stand firm.
3. Do not be discouraged.
4. Have faith in the Lord your God.
5. Sing to the Lord.

Jehoshaphat appointed men to sing to the Lord and praise him for the splendor of his holiness as they went out at the head of the army. He said: "Thank the Lord. His love continues forever" (2 Chr. 20:21 ICB).

As the soldiers began to sing at the top of their lungs, the Lord set an ambush for their enemies. Hearing the noise all around them, the enemies got confused and fought one another. By the time the men of Judah reached the scene, the battle was over. Not one of King Jehoshaphat's soldiers was hurt.

What a party they had when they got home! Can you imagine how their families sang praises to the Lord? The Bible tells us, "They entered Jerusalem with lyres, harps and trumpets and went to the Temple of the Lord" (2 Chr. 20:28). There's even an expression called, "jumping Jehosaphat." It means great excitement!

Craft for Younger Children:
Needed: For each child bring one film container, rice, and stickers

Let each child decorate a film container with stickers. Put a small amount of rice into the container and put the lid on. Let them shake the "musical shaker."

Craft for Older Children: Musical Shaker

Needed: For each child bring one film container, a pony bead, twelve inches of curling ribbon, and plenty of glue, and rice (or other options from below).

To make a musical instrument with which to praise God, poke a hole in each film container lid with an ice pick. Cut a 12" piece of curling ribbon, thread it through the hole in the film container, and tie the curling ribbon to a pony bead. The bead will not be seen once you close the lid; but it will hold the ribbon.

Add more pieces of contrasting/complimentary ribbon until the film container looks festive and fun. Curl the ends of the ribbon with the side of a pair of scissors.

Fill the container half full with rice, beans, pennies, or whatever you want to use to make noise. Place the lid onto the container and shake away!

Musical Munchies

Needed: cups, snack crackers shaped like a bugle, round oat cereal

Mix the two ingredients together and pass out small amount to each child in a cup.

Say: These bugle-shaped crackers will remind us of instruments that we can use to praise God and the round cereal will remind us of the notes on the music!

Prayer Focus: Sing a Prayer!

Sing The Johnny Appleseed Song:

The Lord is good to me, and so I thank the Lord
For giving me the things I need
The sun and the rain and the appleseed
The Lord is good to me!

Memory Verse: Psalm 96:1 ICB

Sing to the Lord a new song. Sing to the Lord, all the earth. Sing to the Lord and praise his name. Every day tell how he saves us.

Alternate version (New King James)
Oh, sing to the LORD a new song!
Sing to the LORD, all the earth.
Sing to the LORD, bless His name;
Proclaim the good news of His salvation from day to day.

Memory Verse Activity: Praise the Lord!
Needed: 10 glass drinking glasses, spoons to tap the glasses with.

Guide the children to fill the glasses with different amounts of water and arrange the glasses so they can play tunes.

Say: People who wrote the songs (or Psalms) in the Bible used to sing them. They were written as songs. Let's try to make up a tune and sing this Psalm to it.

Let children experiment with tapping the glasses lightly with a spoon until they make a melody. Make up a tune to which to sing the verse.

March 3

Christians Are Like Tea!, Midweek
By Barney Kinard

Scripture:
James 1:2–4

Lesson Aim:
To show that having problems doesn't give an excuse to do the wrong thing. Instead, as we choose to do right during problems we show that we have faith in God.

Bible Skill:
Children will do the right thing even when they have problems.

Enrichment for Younger Children: And the Flavor Is . . .

Bring several items that can be recognized by their smell, such as cookies, an onion, an orange, a banana, vanilla, an apple, and bread. Let the children guess what each is by smelling it. Do this by putting each in a paper sack open only enough for children's noses.

Ask: How did you guess what you smelled? Was it hard or easy to guess? Which ones did you want to eat after you smelled them?

What do you think the "flavor" or "smell" of a Christian would be? Would it be good? Would it be sweet? Would you want to be around it all the time?

Explain: When we are Christians we should "smell good"! Everyone should want to be around us because we are like Jesus Christ! ☺

Enrichment for Older Children: Hot and Cold

Needed: Large piece of paper or white board on which you have written *Hot* on one side and *Cold* on the other. Marker for each child

Say: We are going to list things that happen in our lives and compare them to "hot" and "cold." Some things feel hot and some things feel cold.

As children think of things, direct them to write or draw these hot and cold items on the paper or white board. Ideas:

Under HOT: Actions with good effects, such as: Building friendships, a habit of helpfulness, doing homework every day, playing fair, taking turns, sharing the last cookie.

Under COLD: Actions with bad effects such as: Getting picked last for a team, being left out by a friend, feeling sick, being sick, getting into trouble, not doing homework, a parent being cruel, you being cruel whether by accident or on purpose.

Explain: The things we do that we listed under "cold" make us sad or make someone else sad. If we do these cold actions, we "smell bad" to God and other people. But if we choose the hot things, we create happiness for God and other people. We "smell good." Sometimes this isn't easy: You don't want to do homework because you want to watch TV instead. But God will help you find a way, such as recording the show you want to watch in the afternoon and watching it after your homework is done.

Invite the children to give more examples, letting each child take a turn.

Explain: The Bible tells us that whether we go through bad things or good things, he will always be there to help us do the right thing. As you choose to do the right thing no matter how tough it gets, your life will smell wonderful. You will smell wonderful to both God and people. ☺

Memory Verse: James 1:4 ICB

Let your patience show itself perfectly in what you do. Then you will be perfect and complete. You will have everything you need.

Alternate version (New King James)
But let patience have its perfect work, that you may be perfect and complete, lacking nothing.

Bible Learning Activity for Younger Children: Getting Warmer!
Needed: Cut out construction paper in the following shapes:
Cross, heart and dove. Write a good action on each such as: tell the truth, share equally, take turns, listen rather than do all the talking, not hit or kick, and more.

Show the shapes. Say: We are going to play a game. Two of you will leave the room while I hide these shapes. Let two volunteers leave. Let the other children see where you hide the shapes, and let them be partially visible.

Call the two volunteers back into the room. Say: Look for the shapes that I have hidden. The class will help you by telling you that you are "warmer" when you get close and by saying that you are "colder" when you get far away from them.

Play game and let children find shapes. Talk about what is written on each shape and why we need those actions. Explain: When Christians choose to live these actions in their lives, they stay out of trouble and create happiness for people. This is a great way to grow in their faith!
Just as you have done here, help the people around you choose
to find good actions.

 Bible Learning Activity for Older Children: Hot Potato Problems!
Needed: One "potato" either a real one or a small ball to represent a potato, music.

Say: Sometimes our problems can seem "hot" or difficult to handle. But with friends to pass it back and forth, we can do the right thing no matter how tough it gets. We are going to play a game to talk about the kind of problems that you might have.

Have children pass the potato while music plays. When the music stops, the person holding the potato must tell something that causes a big problem for kids their age, such as: lying, cheating, not doing homework, being selfish, keeping a messy room, etc.

After you have played for awhile, say:
What would you do during each of these problems to do the right thing anyway? What friend could help you do the right thing?

How will you put the hot problem in God's hands and talk
with him about it? Say the actual prayer you would say.

March 7

Christians Are Like Tea!
By Barney Kinard

Scripture:
James 1:2–4

Lesson Aim:
To show that having problems doesn't give an excuse to do the wrong thing. Instead, as we choose to do right during problems we show that we have faith in God.

Bible Skill:
Children will do the right thing even when they have problems.

Bible Lesson: In Hot Water
Make a pot of tea with a commercial tea bag (one gallon) on which you've written CHRISTIAN on the label attached at the end of the string. Or just bring a teabag of any size with CHRISTIAN on the label. By actually making a pot of tea and pouring a cup while you give your talk, you visualize the message. This makes the lesson more interesting and understandable. It also holds children's attention.

Tell this story while you make a pot of tea. What I have here, today, is a giant teabag. Maybe you have never seen one this big before, but this larger sized bag is used in restaurants to make a lot of tea at one time. You will notice that on the label, here, I put the word "Christian." That's because I like to think of Christians as like tea.

Let me explain: In order to make tea, you have to put the teabag, which has ground up tea leaves, into some hot water. Or the water can be warm or cold. It just takes longer. The hot water slowly dissolves the tea. Then you let it "steep." That means you let it soak in the hot water long enough for it to

Song Suggestions:

He's Got Plans by Dean-o from "Soul Surfin'" (FKO Music, Inc. 1999)

I Do Believe by Jana Alayra from "Dig Down Deep" (Montjoy Music 1997)

Grow Me Up Like You by Mary Rice Hopkins from "Come on Home" (Big Steps 4 U 2002)

More Precious than Silver Songsheets published by CEF Press, P.O. Box 348, Warrenton, Mo. 63383

dissolve the tea flavor into the water. The tea both flavors and colors the water. The water turns brown rather than clear. You can observe the presence of the tea. When it is as dark as you like it, it is ready to use as a refreshing hot drink. Or you can add ice to have iced tea instead.

How are Christians like tea? Well, a true Christian's real strength comes out when he or she gets in hot water! It is easy to do the right thing when everything is going happily. But doing the right thing when you are sad, or mad, or sick isn't so easy. You can tell what Christians are really made of when they respond to trials. Jesus helps them choose the right thing and the color of their Christian character seeps out into the world around them. You see, the tea is in the bag, but it's not too useful until it gets affected by the water.

So Christ can be in you, but he may not be visible to anyone else until you experience some trials or problems. Then if you respond by doing the right thing during trials, Jesus spreads into the world. Others will observe that he is actively working in your life. They can tell that you have the "flavor of Christ," in your response to problems. They want a taste of that Jesus who can help them do the right thing no matter how bad things get.

Craft for Older Children: Tea Bag Verse Reminder
Needed: Rectangles of construction paper 4" x 3", tea bags, coffee cups

Let children make "labels" for their tea bags by writing these words to the verse on the rectangles: "Let your patience show itself perfectly in what you do." Attach to the tea bags. If desired, fill a small basket with the tea bags.

Say: It is very important to remember how to deal with bad things in our lives. Just remember to do the right thing no matter how tough it is. This tea bag will help you remember our story today, that Christians are like tea!

Let children drop the tea bag into a plastic coffee cup and let the verse/tag hang over the side. Take home as a reminder of the lesson.

Craft Simplification for Younger Children:
Make the labels for the children. Let them decorate them and attach to the tea bag.

Don't Give Up Ice Cream
Needed: for each 4–6 children bring one 1 lb coffee can, one 3 lb coffee can, 1 cup of cream, 3/4 cup milk, 1 t vanilla, 1/2 cup sugar, crushed ice and rock

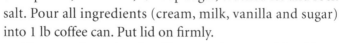 salt. Pour all ingredients (cream, milk, vanilla and sugar) into 1 lb coffee can. Put lid on firmly.

Place one lb can inside 3 lb can and surround it with ice and rock salt. Put lid on firmly.

Have children stand several feet from each other and roll the ice cream makers back and forth between the children. Remind them to have patience as they do this! The ice cream should be made in 10–15 minutes but it seems like a long time. The reward for choosing to patiently keep going is great tasting ice cream!

Prayer Focus:

Dear God, please give us patience to do the right thing no matter how long it takes or how hard it is. We know that you love us. When we have problems, please help us to find joy and give it to others. Help us to be helpful to others so that we can give and receive joy too! Amen.

Memory Verse: James 1:4 ICB

Let your patience show itself perfectly in what you do. Then you will be perfect and complete. You will have everything you need.

Alternate version (New King James)
But let patience have its perfect work, that you may be perfect and complete, lacking nothing.

Memory Verse Activity: Stick to It!

Needed: Pieces of paper

Verse: *Let your patience show itself perfectly in what you do.*
Then you will be perfect and complete. You will have everything you need.

Print three or four words from the verse on each paper. Give one set of verse cards to each team of 4–6 children. Scramble up the verse and have children straighten it out in front of them on the table or floor. When they finish and it is correct, the team should sit down.

Say: That was a long verse! Did it take "patience" to put the whole verse together?

When are other times that you need patience in your life? Does your patience help you in your life?

March 10

Frog in the Kettle, Midweek
By Vicki Wiley

Scripture:
Proverbs 7:1, 15:21

Lesson Aim:
Children will do the right thing even when they have problems.

Bible Skill:
To teach children what the Bible says about wisdom.

 Bible Learning Activity for Younger Children: Frogs on the Lily Pads

Needed: Six lily pad shapes cut from construction paper with these words written on the shapes, one word on each shape: "Do What God Says to Do." Arrange lily pads in correct word order.

Say: Let's pretend that we are frogs in a small lake. Frogs like to sit on lily pads. Can you jump from one lily pad to another? When you jump, say the word on the pad. (Tell children what the words are as you demonstrate what they are supposed to do.)

Guide children to go from pad to pad saying the words in the correct order.

Bible Learning Activity for Older Children: Pressure, Pressure!

Needed: One soda unopened in a can

Say: Do you know what WISDOM is? The Bible talks about wisdom and says that all we have to do to get wisdom is to ask God for it. How do we do that? Yes, we pray! Praying is both talking to God and listening to God.

Ask: What happens if we don't have wisdom and we have a big problem? (begin to shake the soda, slowly at first) Yes, pressure within us begins to get bigger and bigger. We begin to worry and get stressed, (shake can harder) then we really BLOW up! Pretend to open can (or if you are outside open it so it points away from the children).

Yep, just like this can of soda—we explode! Which is better when you have a problem; to explode or ask for wisdom? Of course, ask for wisdom!

Enrichment for Younger Children: St. Patrick

Needed: Shamrock (real or paper)

This week we will celebrate St. Patrick's Day. On that day you may choose to wear some green because if you don't someone might pinch you! That's kind of a silly thing to do, but it is a tradition we have chosen. St. Patrick was a very special person.

St. Patrick loved God very much. He told many, many people about God. He also loved to use "shamrocks" to tell people about God. Have you ever seen a "shamrock"? This is what it looks like. (Show shamrock) Since Patrick didn't have books to give the people to teach them about Jesus he gave them shamrocks. It has three leaves and Patrick used the three leaves to explain that God had three important parts: God the Father, God the Son, and God the Holy Spirit.

Now on St. Patrick's Day you will know who St. Patrick was and how much he loved God! ☺

Enrichment for Older Children: St. Patrick's Day

St. Patrick was born in Wales a long time ago, about A.D. 385.

When Patrick was 16 years old, people who raided his village sold him as a slave. During his captivity, he became closer to God. (Does this remind you of what happened to Joseph? Joseph's brothers sold him as a slave and he also became closer to God!)

Patrick escaped from slavery after six years and he began to study about God. He learned all he could about God for about twelve years. During his training he knew that God wanted him to convert people who were "pagan" (didn't believe in God at all) to Christianity.

Patrick was very good at telling people about God. He traveled throughout Ireland, building schools and churches. These buildings gave him a place to teach people about Jesus. He died on March 17 and that day has been celebrated as St. Patrick's Day ever since.

Since Patrick didn't have books to give the people to teach them about Jesus, he used what he did have—lots of shamrocks. Have you ever seen a shamrock? It has three leaves and Patrick used the three leaves to explain the Trinity.

He told the people that each leaf stood for something very important; part of God; The Father, the Son, and the Holy Spirit. He used it in his sermons to represent how the Father, the Son, and the Holy Spirit could all be separate but at the same time they could all be one God. ☺

Memory Verse: Proverbs 7:1; 15:21 ICB

My son, remember what I say. Treasure my commands.
A man without wisdom enjoys being foolish. But a man with understanding does what is right.

Alternate version (New King James)
My son, keep my words,
And treasure my commands within you.
Folly is joy to him who is destitute of discernment,
But a man of understanding walks uprightly.

March 14

Frog in the Kettle
By Johanna Townsend

Scripture:
Proverbs 7:1; 15:21

Lesson Aim:
Children will do the right thing even when they have problems.

Bible Skill:
To teach children what the Bible says about wisdom.

Bible Lesson: Frog in the Kettle
Needed: Stuffed or plastic frog, a large kettle, and Bible with scripture identified ready to be read.

Tell this story: Have any of you ever tasted frog legs? (Wait for response) I understand they taste very much like chicken. Interesting fact, isn't it? I learned another interesting fact about frogs not long ago that really amazed me! (Hold up the frog and the kettle.) Now this isn't a live frog but if I did put a live frog in this kettle, filled the kettle with water, and put it over heat, the water would get hotter and hotter. Could the frog get out of the kettle? (Wait for response) Of course it could get out any time it wanted to. But typically a frog would choose to stay there. Because it is cold blooded it gets used to whatever temperature is around it. It would remain sitting unaware of any danger, yet slowly cook till dead! No joke—it would stay there until it croaked! Isn't that unbelievable? Ask: Did you know that we humans can be just as foolish? For example: Have you ever lied to someone or taken something that didn't belong to you without getting caught? Lying and stealing without getting caught is similar to the frog sitting in the heating water of the kettle. We talk ourselves into believing that a little bit of wrong here and there is OK. Like the frog, the person guilty of lying or stealing can chose to quit any time or continue on until tragedy comes. Not only you, but those you lie to and steal from, will get cooked.

What advice does God give about tolerating wrong behavior in yourself? Proverbs, a book in the Bible has this to say in chapter 7, verse l: *My son, remember what I say. Treasure my command*s. In that verse God advises us to learn and keep his rules. When God created us he knew the difficulty we would have keeping out of trouble so he gave us rules to live by. His top ten are called the Ten Commandments and two of them (numbers 8 and 9) tell us not to lie or steal. Another verse in Proverbs 15:21 says, *A man without wisdom enjoys being foolish. But a man with understanding does what is right.*

A wise boy or girl will obey God's rules, not foolishly disobey them. This will make three folks happy. Who are those? (you, other people, and God!) Disobeying God's rules is called sin and it hurts three folks. Who are those? (you, other people, and God!)

It is important to stay serious about obeying God's rules so you won't ever be caught like the foolish frog in the kettle, headed for trouble that can never be fixed.

 Song Suggestions:

God's Way Right by Dean-o from "You Got It All" (FKO Music, Inc. 1997)

Big Steps for Little Feet by Mary Rice Hopkins from "15 Singable Songs" (Big Steps 4 U 1988)

Make Your Home in My Heart by Cindy Rethmeier from "I Want 2 Be Like Jesus" (Mercy/Vineyard Publishing 1995)

Happiness Is the Lord Songsheets published by CEF Press, P.O. Box 348, Warrenton, Mo. 63383

Craft For Younger Children: Frog puppet

Needed: For each child bring 3-inch circles cut from green paper, much smaller black and yellow circles and small piece of red curling ribbon.

Guide children to make frog puppets according to these directions: Fold a circle in half to make a frog's head, with the open part forming the frog's mouth. Glue yellow and black circles for eyes onto the top of the head, and tape a piece of red curling ribbon inside the mouth for a tongue. Then glue green paper strips, folded accordion style, to the back of the frog's head for legs. To work the puppet, hold it by the fold and pinch the mouth open and closed.

Say: Have you ever seen a frog? What sound does a frog make? Frogs are fun to play with and watch. But frogs are foolish and not very smart. Invite children to repeat the story as they play with the frogs.

When we follow God we are wise, something a frog cannot be!

Wise Crackers

Needed: Can of cheese, or string cheese, large crackers

Say: We are going to make "wise crackers" today. Show children how to write the word "Wise" with the cheese on the crackers.

Wisdom is a great thing to have. How do we get wisdom? Are you wise now? God will give you wisdom; all you have to do is ask for it!

Prayer Focus:

Lord, help all of us here today keep the rules you have given us to live by. We trust you know what is best for us. You created us and understand the different kinds of troubles we can have. Keep us from doing wrong when we find ourselves in bad situations. Speak to us when we are in trouble by the gentle voice of your Holy Spirit and give us the courage to obey your advice. Amen.

Craft for Older Children: Frog

Needed: For each child bring one large green pompom, two wiggle eyes, and green construction paper

Guide children to make frogs by gluing the eyes onto the pompom and cutting legs from construction paper to add to frog.

Say: According to our lesson, frogs are not very smart, are they? Invite children to repeat the story as they play with the frogs. When we follow God we are wise, something a frog cannot be!

Let's look at FROGS a little differently now to remind us of that truth.

Instead of talking about little, slimy things that croak, let's say that FROG stands for Forever Relying On God! What would that mean?

If you RELY on God, what does that mean? We should rely (trust) on God all our lives! You let him show you how to do the right thing no matter how much heat comes. What are some of the things we can do that will show we are relying on God? What are some of the ways that WE DO NOT rely on God and trust ourselves instead?

This frog will remind you that we should Forever Rely On God!

Alternate Craft: FROG Bracelet

Purchase lettered beads (F.R.O.G. for each child) and lacing
Let children make bracelet or necklace with letters on it. Use dialog above.

Memory Verse: Proverbs 7:1; 15:21 ICB
My son, remember what I say. Treasure my commands. A man without wisdom enjoys being foolish. But a man with understanding does what is right.

Alternate version (New King James)
My son, keep my words,
And treasure my commands within you.
Folly is joy to him who is destitute of discernment,
But a man of understanding walks uprightly.

Memory Verse Activity:

Needed: Paper cut into strips

   Preparation: Write the words of the verse on the strips, one or two words on each strip. Hide the strips throughout the classroom.

   Let the children search for the scripture strips one at a time. Direct them to the strips by saying, "You're getting hotter/colder."

   Throughout the game remind the children that when we need to search for wisdom as hard as we would search for hidden treasure that God will come through for us. He will show us what good action to do and how to do it. Wisdom comes from God's word and wisdom is a treasure from God.

   When all verse strips have been collected, lead the children in putting the verses together in order.

March 17

God's Words, Midweek
By Ivy Beckwith

Scripture:
Psalm 19:7–10

Lesson Aim:
Kid's understand that God's words in the Bible are very special.

Bible Skill:
Kids will learn to love God's words.

 Bible Learning Activity for Younger Children:
Needed: Honeycomb and honey, craft sticks.

Say: *The verse today talks about honey and honeycomb. Do you know how we get honeycomb?* Explain the process of honeymaking, including that bees deposit the honey in the honeycomb and that this honeycomb is near where the bees live. *Have you tasted honey?* Put small amount of honey on craft stick for each child. Let them taste honey. Say: *What does the honey taste like? Is it sweet? I wonder why the Bible says that God's teachings are like honey.* Guide children to open in their Bibles to the verse that says this. Give a clean craft stick to use as a bookmark.

Bible Learning Activity for Older Children: Many Teachings from the Bible

What are some of the things people think are very valuable today? (Gold, silver, expensive houses, jewelry) Those things were also valuable in Bible times. But God wanted us to know that his teachings were even more valuable.

The passage today contains many wonderful teachings from the Bible. Let's read a few of them and talk about what they mean.

Take time to read each teaching and discuss its meaning with the children.

Enrichment for Older Children: Sayings from the Bible

Explain: There are many wise sayings in the Bible. But there are some wise sayings that people think are in the Bible, but really aren't! What is true? Let's choose which of these is in the Bible and which is not. Allow children to use a concordance so they can look up the words in the verses to find out if they come from the Bible. A computer concordance is easiest to use, but a complete concordance in book form is helpful too. Assure children that the concordance in the back of their Bible won't have every Bible word.

Spare the rod and spoil the child (true)

Give me liberty or give me death! (false)

An apple a day keeps the doctor away (false)

A friend loves at all times (true)

It is better to give than to receive (true)

A penny saved is a penny earned (false) ☺

Enrichment for Younger Children:

Needed: Honey and small spoons

Sit down with the children in a circle.

Say: Our verse today says that the Bible is sweeter than honey. Let's taste this honey. (Allow children to taste by putting the honey on each child's own spoon.) Can you imagine anything sweeter? This is so sweet! But God knows that his word, the Bible, is even sweeter! That means, if we like this honey, we'll like God's word even better! ☺

Memory Verse: Psalm 19:7–10 ICB

The Lord's teachings are perfect. They give new strength.
The Lord's rules can be trusted. They make plain people wise.
The Lord's orders are right. They make people happy.
The Lord's commands are pure. They light up the way.
It is good to respect the Lord. That respect will last forever.
The Lord's judgments are true. They are completely right.
They are worth more than gold, even the purest gold.
They are sweeter than honey, even the finest honey.

Alternate version (New King James)
The law of the LORD is perfect, converting the soul;
The testimony of the LORD is sure, making wise the simple;
The statutes of the LORD are right, rejoicing the heart;
The commandment of the LORD is pure, enlightening the eyes;
The fear of the LORD is clean, enduring forever;
The judgments of the LORD are true and righteous altogether.
More to be desired are they than gold,
Yea, than much fine gold;
Sweeter also than honey and the honeycomb.

March 21

God's Words

By Ivy Beckwith

Scripture:

Psalm 19:7–10

Lesson Aim:

Kid's understand that God's words in the Bible are very special.

Bible Skill:

Kids will learn to love God's words.

Bible Lesson: Words So Sweet You Can Eat Them

Gather children together. Show them a Bible. Ask: What is this?

Ask: What is the Bible?

After several children respond, explain that God gave us the Bible so we could know who God is. God gave us the Bible so we could know God loves us. God gave us the Bible so we could understand the best way for human beings to live.

Ask: What are some of your favorite parts of the Bible? Do you have a favorite Bible story? Why is that your favorite Bible story? Give EVERY child an opportunity to respond.

Follow their stories with: Did you know that the people who wrote the Bible didn't know they were writing the Bible? They were just writing stories about God that God encouraged them to write or writing songs to God to thank him for loving them. They had no idea that some day everything they wrote would be put in this book I'm holding. But, still, some of the writers were thankful God gave them an understanding about the best way to live and these writers wrote songs called the psalms to praise and thank God for this. Open the Bible and show the children the book of Psalms. Guide the children to find the Psalms in their own Bibles.

Our Bible verses for today come out of one of these songs, Psalm 19. Show the children Psalm 19 and help them find it in their own Bibles. In this song the writer thanks God for giving him God's special words. And the writer paints pictures with words to help us understand how wonderful God's words truly are. The psalmist says that God's words are perfect. What does the word perfect mean? It means that no one can find anything wrong with God's words. All of God's words are right. They also apply perfectly to every situation.

The psalmist says that God's words are true. What do you think that means? It means that God will never lie to us. God will always tell us the truth. The writer of Psalm 19 tells us that God's words are more valuable than gold. Does anyone know how valuable gold is? Gold is a precious metal and is usually worth many hundreds or thousands of dollars. So this means that having God's words with us is worth more than having a piece of gold worth hundreds or thousands of dollars. And the last thing the psalmist tells us about God's words is that these words are sweeter than honey. Who can tell me about the sweetest thing you've ever tasted? Did it taste really good? Did you want more of it because it was so sweet? Well, the person who wrote this psalm says that God's words are sweeter than any cake, or cookie, or ice cream we could ever eat.

So you see the stories and songs and poems God gave us in the Bible are very special. They tell us the truth about God and how much God loves us. They help us to know who God is and understand God's ways better. People who love God love the words God gave us. Why? Because we like hearing from people we love. The Bible is a way God talks back to us after we pray to him. Let's bow our heads and pray, thanking God for giving us these special words in the Bible.

 Song Suggestions:

Free Inside by Dean-o from "Soul Surfin'" (FKO Music, Inc. 1999)

Turn It Over by Dean-o from "God City" (BibleBeat Music 2001)

Walk Like Jesus by Mary Rice Hopkins from "15 Singable Songs" (Big Steps 4 U 1988)

I Believe the Bible Songsheets published by CEF Press, P.O. Box 348, Warrenton, Mo. 63383

Craft for Younger Children: Favorite Bible Stories

Needed: For each child fold several pieces of paper into a book by folding the paper lengthwise and stapling the center of the book.

Say: What are your favorite stories in the Bible? (as needed, suggest Noah, Daniel, David, birth of Jesus, and show where each is in that child's Bible) Let's draw and color pictures of our favorite stories and make a book of them.

Have children color the stories as you write the captions on the pictures so that others will know what the story is and can ask them to tell the details of the picture.

 Craft for Older Children: Bible Story Book: Favorite Bible Stories

Needed: For each child fold several pieces of paper into a book by folding the paper lengthwise and stapling the center of the book.

Say: Today we are going to make a book of Bible stories. The Bible is a very precious book and it has many great stories in it. What are your favorite stories? (as needed, suggest Noah, Daniel, David, birth of Jesus, and show where each is in that child's Bible)

Guide children to write the Bible story on one side of the paper and illustrate the story on the other. Allow enough time for this activity so that they can write and illustrate at least three stories. Decorate a special cover for the book.

Sugar Cookies

Provide kids with unfrosted sugar cookies. Provide tube frosting used in cake and cookie decorating. Help kids write "God's Word" on the cookie. As they enjoy the snack remind them that God's words are sweet, just like the cookie and frosting.

Memory Verse Activity:

The Lord's teachings are perfect. They give new strength.

(When I read the Bible I become stronger in my faith. Being strong in faith includes emotions, actions, attitudes, and more.)

The Lord's rules can be trusted. They make plain people wise.

(God only gave us good rules, the kind that make us wise. Wisdom is applied knowledge. If we are wise we know how to act and how to start that good action.)

The Lord's orders are right. They make people happy.

(When we follow what God told us to do, we will be happy. People near us will be happy too.)

The Lord's commands are pure. They light up the way.

(God's commands are so pure they show us what to do.)

It is good to respect the Lord. That respect will last forever.

(When you learn to have respect for the Lord, you will see how and why he does what he does, and how and why to make your life match his.)

The Lord's judgments are true. They are completely right.

(When God says something, it is always the truth.)

They are worth more than gold, even the purest gold.

(All these things that God says are worth more than gold or money or any physical wealth.)

They are sweeter than honey, even the finest honey.

(They taste better than your favorite food.)

Psalm 19:7–10 ICB

Ask: What would your life be like if you read this everyday? Let each child respond with good reasons to listen to God each day through reading the Bible. Isn't it great advice? God gives rules that can be trusted, pure commands, perfect teachings, and true judgments. They are worth more than GOLD! As an added activity, let children write this verse down to keep in their school notebooks or a place at home.

Memory Verse: Psalm 19:7–10 ICB

The Lord's teachings are perfect. They give new strength.
The Lord's rules can be trusted. They make plain people wise.
The Lord's orders are right. They make people happy.

The Lord's commands are pure. They light up the way.
It is good to respect the Lord. That respect will last forever.
The Lord's judgments are true. They are completely right.
They are worth more than gold, even the purest gold.
They are sweeter than honey, even the finest honey.

Alternate version (New King James)
The law of the LORD is perfect, converting the soul;
The testimony of the LORD is sure, making wise the simple;
The statutes of the LORD are right, rejoicing the heart;
The commandment of the LORD is pure, enlightening the eyes;
The fear of the LORD is clean, enduring forever;
The judgments of the LORD are true and righteous altogether.
More to be desired are they than gold,
Yea, than much fine gold;
Sweeter also than honey and the honeycomb.

Prayer Focus:
Dear God, your word is so wonderful. Your teachings are perfect and they give me strength. Your rules make me wise. Your orders make me happy. Your commands light up my way. Your word is sweeter than honey and worth more than gold. Thank you and praise you for your word. Give me courage to obey it because I love you. Amen.

March 24

Get Up for the Word of God!, Midweek
By Dean-o

Scripture:
John 20:31

Lesson Aim:
The Bible shows us the way to eternal life.

Bible Skill:
Kids will understand that eternal life comes from believing God.

 Bible Learning Activity for Older Children: The Bible
John wrote the Bible book of John because he wanted people to know how important it is to believe in Jesus. John's book is part of the whole Bible. If we didn't have this Bible it would be much harder to know who Jesus is, how he lived on earth, and how to believe in him. Let's make a list of the things that the Bible tells us about Jesus.

List on the board everything that the children say, urging them to look through the Bible book of John for ideas, especially the first chapter. You don't want children to just remember what they've learned in past sessions, but to learn something new today. Looking through their own Bibles is a great way to do this. Ideas include:

Jesus was in the beginning

Jesus is called the word

Jesus did miracles

People followed Jesus

Jesus was the Son of God and someone we can believe in and trust!

Bible Learning Activity for Younger Children: Fish Symbol
Needed: For each child 1 chenille wire and 32 glow-in-the-dark pony beads (or color of choice)

Explain: The Christians in the first century needed a secret symbol to show that they were believers. Today we are going to make one of these symbols. Show children how to put the beads on the pipe cleaner and then form into a fish symbol.

Say: Keep this fish to remind you that you are a Christian and you don't have to hide it! The glow-in-the-dark feature reminds children of this.

Enrichment for Younger Children: Gotta Go Fishing!
Needed: Fish shapes cut from construction paper, fishing pole with magnet on the end, paper clips. Put one paper clip on each fish shape.

Say: Many people who followed Jesus were fishermen before they became followers of Jesus. Let's go fishing today!

Show children how to "fish" by dropping the magnet end of the fishing pole down to a paper clip on the end of a fish. Guide the group to take turns.

Say: The fish reminds us of Jesus because Jesus' followers were fishermen and the secret symbol of the Christians was the fish! Show how to make the fish symbol with two people, one drawing each side of the fish with a half oval. Christians believed in Jesus and wanted to follow him. Many years later, some of them recorded the Bible. ☺

Memory Verse: John 20:31 ICB
But these are written so that you can believe that Jesus is the Christ, the Son of God. Then by believing you can have life through his name.

Alternate version (New King James)
but these are written that you may believe that Jesus is the Christ, the Son of God, and that believing you may have life in His name.

Enrichment for Older Children:

Tell this story: When Jesus died, many of his followers were persecuted. This forced them to worship in secret places. Often these believers would scratch the secret symbol of a fish in the ground or in the sand to show other Christians that they were also Christians. Show children how to draw a half oval on the chalkboard, and then let another child complete the fish. Say this was a way to let each other know they were Christians.

Then explain: The fish was an easy two-person sketch but it had other meanings. Not only was fish a common food of the day, but fish were often used by Jesus during His ministry. To make it even more special, the letters which make up the Greek word for "fish" also spell out a secret message about our Lord which was "Jesus Christ, son of God, Savior."

The name of Jesus means so much to Christians. The symbols of the cross and the fish remind us of our relationship with God and Jesus. ☺

March 28

Get Up for the Word of God!
By Dean-o

Scripture:
John 20:31

Lesson Aim:
The Bible shows us the way to eternal life.

Bible Skill:
Kids will understand that eternal life comes from believing God.

Bible Lesson: Why the Bible Was Written

Gather children together and ask: Have you ever wondered why the Bible was written? Was it to give us an important history lesson? Was the Bible written to give us important rules to live by? Or was the Bible written to show us the way to heaven? Or was it a combination of these?

God gave us a verse in the Bible that tells us the main purpose of the Bible. The word of God was written so that we would believe in Jesus, and as a result receive eternal life in his name. Once we have that, we can start living that eternal life by obeying the Ten Commandments and the other guidelines in the Bible. Cool! We're talking about everlasting life here! We can learn several things from this verse that can help us appreciate what the Bible, the word of God, can do for us every day.

The Bible teaches that the Bible book of John was written so that we may believe! And not just believe any old thing, but believe that Jesus is real. When you believe Jesus is real, you change how you live. This is a belief with all of our hearts that Jesus is the Christ, the Savior of the world, and that he is really the one and only Son of God. I can remember when I believed this for the first time. I realized that it was true, that God was real and that Jesus was really his Son. I knew that I was not alone in this world.

The Bible also teaches that there is a reward for believing that Jesus is God's son. That's right, a reward and it's a big one! When we believe that Jesus is the Son of God, we believe that he died on the cross so that our sins, the things we do wrong, will be forgiven. This means that our sins will not stand in the way of our getting into heaven. God will accept us lovingly, because we believe that he gave us his Son. By believing, we can have life in his name—that's eternal life in the name of Jesus!

To celebrate this, let's "GET UP FOR THE WORD!" To get up for the Word means to be excited about the promises God gives us in the Bible where his words are recorded. The Bible is holy, true, and never changing. And here's the best part—His word is heaven-assured! This means that the result of believing his word is a place in heaven, and I'm pretty sure we're all up for that!

So boys and girls, here's my challenge: Make the choice to get up for the Word every day. No matter the circumstances you're in, think about what the Bible says, believe it to be true, obey it, and you'll be on your way to celebrating your day. Remember that you belong to God, and that he loves you. The bottom line is this: Get up for the Word, and don't leave home without its promises!

 Song Suggestions:

Up for the Word by Dean-o from "Soul Surfin'" (FKO Music 1999)

The B.I.B.L.E. Traditional

Treasure of My Heart by Jana Alayra from "Jump Into the Light" (Montjoy Music 1995)

God's Love by Mary Rice Hopkins from "Good Buddies" (Big Steps 4 U 1994)

Craft for Younger Children: Promises! Promises!

Needed: For each child bring one piece of light blue construction paper. Bring also glue and colored paper torn into small pieces in these colors: red, yellow, green, blue.

Say: Have you ever promised to do something? Did you do it?

In the Bible, God makes many promises and he always does what he says he will do. One of the greatest promises in the Bible was when God made a promise with a rainbow. He did that so that every time we see a rainbow, we will remember that promise. Let's make a rainbow to remember the promise.

Put glue on the paper in the shape of a rainbow. Let children put the torn paper onto the glue to create a rainbow in this order: red, yellow, green, blue.

Say: "This rainbow will remind us of a great promise; that God will never destroy the earth with water." That is a promise in the Bible and God always does what God promises!

 Craft for Older Children: Promise Jar

Needed: For each child: one baby food jar or other small jar or can with lid. Bring also paper and markers or pencils.

Say: "Have you ever made a promise? Did you do what you promised to do? Has anyone ever promised you anything? Did they keep their promise?"

Very often people don't keep their promises to us, but God always keeps his promises! God's promises are in the Bible. Today we are going to make a "promise jar" so that we can remember promises.

Pass paper to children. Let them write the following on the papers:

God promises to be your friend. John 15:14, 15

God promises to be your comfort. 2 Corinthians 1:3, 4

God promises you are his child. Galatians 3:26

God promises to help you do good works. Ephesians 2:10

Say: Let's put these papers inside our jars so that we can always read them and remember the promises that God made to us. God never breaks his promises, so we can believe all of these!

Fishy Snack
Needed: Large fish-shaped crackers, cheese spread

 Show children how to spread cheese between two crackers to create sandwich.

Ask: When you eat this "fishy snack" what does it remind you of? Use children's answers to affirm that in Bible times, the fish reminded people of Jesus!

Prayer Focus:
Dear God, thank you so much for your son Jesus Christ and for the Bible. Thank you for talking to us through the Bible. Thank you that you gave us all the very special words in it. We believe in you and we praise you! Amen.

Memory Verse: John 20:31 ICB
But these are written so that you can believe that Jesus is the Christ, the Son of God. Then, by believing you can have life through his name.

Alternate version (New King James)
But these are written that you may believe that Jesus is the Christ, the Son of God, and that believing you may have life in His name.

Memory Verse Activity: Find That Verse!
Needed: Slips of paper
   Preparation: Write two or three words of the verse on each slip of paper and hide in the room.
   Let children hunt for the papers and then put verse together. Say the verse all together.
   Ask: Why was the Bible written?
   What will you have if you believe?
   Who should you believe in?

March 31

Who Is This Man?, Midweek

By Vicki Wiley

Scripture:
Matthew 21:1–3, 6–11

Lesson Aim:
That the children will learn that even though we can't see Jesus, we can know him.

Bible Skill:
Kids will learn that they can know all about Jesus from the Bible.

 Bible Learning Activity Younger Children: Who Is This?
Needed: a small mirror.

Say: Who are your favorite people? When you see one of them, how do you know it is them?

Say: "Let's look in the mirror and guess who you can see." One by one let children look into the mirror and say who it is.

Say: "How did you know who was in the mirror?" (We could see them; we knew what they look like.)

Now say: "It's easy to know who someone is when we know them and see them, but it is hard to know who someone is if we don't know them, isn't it?" That's what happened to Jesus in our story.

Bible Learning Activity for Older Children: Who Is This?
Needed: For each child a small amount of craft dough.

Say: "Who are your favorite people in the Bible? Let's sculpt some of our favorite Bible characters with our craft dough." Let children sculpt models of their favorite person. Help children with ideas, if needed.

Say: "Let's guess who these people are." Let children guess and try to figure out who they are. (Wrong answers are great here, so try to get kids to see this as a light-hearted activity.) "What should we do if we want to learn more about someone? What should we do if we want to learn more about Jesus?"

Say: "It's hard to know who these people are because we don't really know what they looked like, we only know *about* them. That's what happened to Jesus in our story; the people had heard about him, but some of them had never seen him so they didn't know who he was."

Enrichment for Younger Children:
Needed: Palm branches either real, or create from green construction paper and wrapping paper tube

Say: "Have you ever been to a parade? Well, Jesus was in a big parade!

"One day Jesus was going to come into the town of Jerusalem. The children were so excited to see him that they waved branches like these to praise him! They lined the streets and watched as Jesus came down the street on a special donkey.

"The children said, 'Hosanna, Hosanna!' Can you say that too?

"Can you pretend that you are the children praising Jesus?" Choose one child to be Jesus and let the children reenact the story. ☺

Enrichment for Older Children: Shadows of Faith

Needed: One darkened room, white wall, flashlight, paper

Create a darkened room and show the children how to make "shadow pictures" by putting your hand in front of the flashlight and projecting it onto the wall.

Let children experiment by projecting things (object or fingers) onto the wall by shining the light at them. Let children guess what the objects (or body parts) are.

Have children (one at a time) stand up with paper taped to the wall at their head height. Shine flashlight so that their shadow is created on the paper and have someone trace around their "head" on the paper.

Put all papers out and let children try to guess which "head" belongs to which child.

Say: "How can you tell which picture belongs to which child? If you didn't know any of these children, would you be able to tell which one belonged to each child? What if you didn't know them, but you had heard a lot about them?"

Even though we have never seen Jesus, we can know a lot about him by reading the Bible. That won't help us know what he looked like, but it will help us know what he is like. ☺

Memory Verse: Luke 19:38 ICB

[They said,]
"God bless the king who comes in the name of the Lord!
There is peace in heaven and glory to God!"

Alternate version (New King James)
"'Blessed is the King who comes in the name of the LORD*!'*
Peace in heaven and glory in the highest!"

April 4

Who Is This Man?
By Vicki Wiley

Scripture:
Matthew 21:1–3, 6–11

Lesson Aim:
That the children will learn how unique and special Jesus is.

Bible Skill:
Kids will learn that they can know all about Jesus from the Bible.

Bible Lesson: Who Is This Man?

Needed: Photographs or pictures of recognizable men from the present and the past (suggestions Abe Lincoln, George Bush, your pastor, and one picture of Jesus).

Hold up one of the pictures (any except Jesus) and say, "Who is this man?" (Let children answer. Do the same for each picture, except don't show picture of Jesus yet.)

Ask: "How did you know who this was? Have you ever seen this person?" Let children discuss how they knew who the person was.

One day, Jesus was coming to town and the people were so excited that they all came out to see him. In fact, all of a sudden there was sort of a parade for him. People stood on the sides of the road and waited for him!

Some of the people knew who he was because they had actually seen him before. Some of the people knew who he was because they had heard about him, and some people knew who he was because they believed others who told them who he was. All those people lined the streets and praised him by shouting, "Hosanna! Hosanna!" as he rode by on a donkey.

But there were some other people there too. These people didn't know who he was, but they sure knew he was important. How do you think they could tell he was important? They could tell he was important because of how everyone else was acting. They saw people waving palm branches; they saw people take off their coats and put them on the ground; they saw people worship him. They saw that everyone loved him!

"Who is this man?" they said to each other. (Show picture of Jesus) Boys and girls, who is this? (they will answer Jesus) That's right! This is a picture of Jesus, but it isn't a real picture. We really don't know what Jesus looked like—no one painted his picture, and there were no cameras in Bible times, so we really don't know. If we saw Jesus today how would we know it was him? (by the way that he was acting, by the things he said, how kind he is, etc.)

We can't know what Jesus looks like, but we can know who he is. We can learn more about him by reading our Bibles and listening to our teachers at church. Our parents can tell us more about Jesus too. This week, as we get ready for Easter, let's try to learn more about who Jesus is. Let's try to learn more about what he taught us and how much he loves us. That way if you are talking about Jesus and one of your friends says, "Who is this man, Jesus?" you will know things about him that you can share!

 Song Suggestions:

Believin' On by Jana Alayra from "Believin' On" (Montjoy Music 2002)

Hallelujah Ballad Songsheets published by CEF Press, P.O. Box 348, Warrenton, Mo. 63383

Oh, How Great a Love by Jana Alayra from "Believin' On" (Montjoy Music 2002)

We Will Shout for Joy by Cindy Rethmeier from "I Want To Be Like Jesus" (Mercy Vineyard 1995)

Craft for Younger Children: Praise Ribbon
Needed: Several pieces (about 10 inches long) of ribbon. Hide the pieces of ribbon about the room.

Let children search for the ribbon. When they find the ribbons, have them come and sit down. Encourage them to share ribbons so that each child has at least two.

Say, "One day Jesus came into the town. The people were so excited to see him that they waved things and shouted 'Hosanna!' Lets make a Praise Ribbon and we can shout Hosanna too!"

Show children how to tie their own ribbons together to form a longer ribbon. Lead them in waving the ribbons as you say "Hosanna!"

(Keep ribbons for use in the memory verse activity.)

Alternate activity: Praise Shakers
Needed: containers with a lid such as oatmeal containers or margarine tubs, dry beans or rice.

Show children how to put a small amount of beans or rice into their container and put the lid on. Let them decorate the container if you wish. Shake to make noise!

 Craft for Older Children: Palm Branches
Needed: Green construction paper, paper rolls (from paper towels)

Show children how to cut green paper into palm branch shapes and glue onto paper roll to form a palm branch.

Say: "When Jesus was coming into Jerusalem the people waved palm branches because they were easy to find. We will make a palm branch today that is similar to the ones they waved."

(You will use palm branches in the memory verse activity.)

Praise Person!

Needed: Cubes of cheese, grapes, stick pretzels

Say: "Today we are going to make a 'praise person.' The cube of cheese will be the body, the grape will be the head, and the pretzels will make arms and legs."

Show children how to form the "praise person."

Ask: "Does this look like a real person? Of course, it doesn't! Can real people praise Jesus? How do they praise Jesus?

"We can praise Jesus because he loves us. We praise him by saying, 'Praise you, Jesus, we praise you, we love you and praise you.' You can also praise Jesus by saying 'Hosanna,' just like they did."

Prayer Focus:

Dear Jesus, we praise you and we love you. We praise you because you are God and you do wonderful things. We love you. Amen.

Memory Verse: Luke 19:38 ICB

[They said,]
God bless the king who comes in the name of the Lord!
There is peace in heaven and glory to God!

Alternate version (New King James)
"'Blessed is the King who comes in the name of the LORD!'
Peace in heaven and glory in the highest!

Memory Verse Activity:

Using palm branches from craft activity, let children line both sides of the room. Wave palm branches and say, "God bless the king who comes in the name of the Lord! There is peace in heaven and glory to God!" Repeat several times.

The people actually said these words as Jesus came through their streets.

Special Holiday Activity: Palm Sunday
Act out the Bible lesson of Jesus entering into Jerusalem. Using palm branches made in earlier activities, have them act out the lesson. (You can also use celery for the palm branches.) Let one child be Jesus and one the donkey. As Jesus rides the donkey through the crowd, they wave their palm branches, saying, "Hosanna, Hosanna!" ☺

April 7 Easter Week

A Toy that Won't Quit, Midweek
By Judy Comstock

Scripture:
2 Kings 4:1–7

Lesson Aim:
Recognize that God's power can supply what you need and keep supplying even more than you need.

Bible Skill:
Children will know that they can rely on the power of God.

Bible Learning Activity for Older Children: An Easter Basket Full of Meaning: The Story of Jesus' Life

Needed: There are many items needed for this lesson, but you can use as many or as few as you like. Whatever number you choose, bring one of each

---

 Bible Learning Activity for Younger Children: An Easter Basket Full of Meaning

(Simplification for younger children)

Needed: For each child bring a small basket or box and one of each item below for each child (halo, Easter grass, cotton ball, star, fish crackers, cross, empty egg, and chicks). Bring also an Easter basket to show, and Easter grass.

Use the script from Bible Learning Activity for Older Children with only these items: halo, Easter grass, cotton ball, star, fish crackers, cross, empty egg, and chicks.

---

for each child and bring an inexpensive basket to put the items into. (A shoebox or strawberry basket can be used.)

Say: I'm going to give you several objects that tell the story of Jesus' life. During Easter we celebrate Jesus' life, but mostly his resurrection. Resurrection means he rose from death. Only Jesus can do that and he can do it because He is God.

So, here is a basket for each of you. When I give you an item, put it in your basket.

STONE (small)

The first thing we are putting into the basket is a small stone. Can anyone remember a Bible story that has a small stone in it? Yeah, you're right! David and Goliath! David killed a giant with God's help and a small stone. What does this have to do with Jesus?

Jesus was from the family of David. David was one of Jesus' relatives and God told David that his relatives would be kings. The stone will remind us that Jesus was from the same family that David was from.

HALO (out of chenille wire)

The second thing we will put in is a halo. The halo will remind us of the angel who told Mary that she was going to have a baby. That baby was Jesus.

EASTER GRASS

Now, we are finally putting some Easter grass into the basket. This will remind us of how Jesus was placed in a manger when he was born. There was hay in the manger because a manger is a bed of hay from which animals ate. The Easter grass is shaped kind of like hay.

COTTON BALL

Why do you think we would put a cotten ball in next? Well, this cotton ball looks sort of like a sheep. This cotton ball will remind you of the shepherds who saw the angels and then came to find the baby Jesus.

STAR (made of paper)

Now we are going to add a star. Why do you think we would do that? Yes, you're right. This will remind us that the wise men found Jesus by following a beautiful star that led them to him.

Baby Jesus grew up and he began his ministry. The next symbols happened when Jesus was an adult.

DOVE (feather)

This feather will remind us of a bird. What kind of bird was important in

Jesus' life? A dove! When Jesus was baptized, the Holy Spirit came down like a dove and said, "This is my dear son, and I am so pleased with him." That told Jesus that his father, God, liked what he was doing.

FISH (crackers)

Now we are going to put in some fish crackers. When Jesus started preaching to the people, he needed some helpers. He found some fisherman and asked them to be his disciples. These fish will remind us that Jesus chose some fishermen to be his disciples.

FLOWER (paper or silk)

Jesus taught about flowers. Often, he went into gardens to pray or teach. One time when Jesus taught in the garden he told everyone that God loves the flowers so much that he made them very beautiful. That also means that God will take care of you because God loves you more than the flowers.

SALT (small restaurant style packets)

Another thing that Jesus taught is that we should be like salt. How can we be like salt? That's kind of weird. Well, salt makes food taste better and Christians should make the world seem better. It also preserves what is good. This will remind us that Jesus told us to be like salt.

COINS (pennies)

Something else Jesus taught us was to give money. These coins will remind us that God tells us to give money, but to do it in secret and not show off while we are doing it.

BAND AID™

Why do you think we are going to put a Band Aid™ in now? This Band Aid™ will remind us that Jesus healed people. Jesus cared so much about people that if they were sick, he made them well.

MATZO

This is a cracker called matzo. Matzo was the kind of bread that the Hebrew people ate at Passover time. Passover was the last supper that he had with his disciples before he died. We will put some matzo in to remember the Passover supper.

LICORICE WHIP

After Jesus ate the Passover supper, some Roman soldiers came to arrest him. They whipped him with a whip, except it had pieces of glass and bone in it. It would hurt much more than this licorice whip. We will put this in to remember that.

CROSS (out of paper)

After he was beaten up, Jesus died on the cross. We use the cross to remember Jesus' death.

EMPTY EGG (empty plastic Easter egg)

But . . . he didn't stay dead! This egg is empty and will remind us of the empty tomb. Jesus was alive again!

CHICKS (Marshmallow)

These chicks will remind us of new life. When we believe in Jesus we have new life. It is like we are born all over again, just like little chicks and bunnies are in the spring.

CHOCOLATE EGGS

Foil-covered chocolate Easter eggs will remind us of the shiny streets of gold in heaven where Jesus is. We will be there with him one day too!

FISH (out of chenille wire)

This last fish reminds us that when Jesus went back to heaven, he told his disciples not to go back to fishing for fish but instead to fish for people! That meant that Jesus wanted them to tell people all about him, and to live so people would want to live for God. This "fish" became the secret sign of a Christian.

Go back through the symbols to ask children to tell you what each one stands for. Supplement their ideas.

Enrichment for Younger Children:

Needed: Small jar of cooking oil

Ask: Have you ever touched oil before? Would you like to see what it feels like? (Let children put their finger in the oil.) What does it feel like? What word would you use to describe it? (*Samples: slimy, slippery, etc.*)

Do you know what this kind of oil is used for? (Cooking, frying) Does it taste good all by itself? No, it probably doesn't, but if you want to taste the oil on your finger you may. It really doesn't have much of a taste, does it? But when you mix it with other things it becomes very helpful. We use oil all the time. God knew the widow needed oil too, so he gave her all that she needed. ☺

Enrichment for Older Children: Oil

Ask: Oil is very important today. What do we use oil for? (*Samples: cooking, for our cars, etc.*)

Then explain: In Bible times, olive oil was used so much that it is mentioned over 200 times in the Bible! There were different kinds of olive oil for different uses. Pure olive oil (now known as virgin oil) was the best kind and was used when it was important to have the best oil.

A special use for oil was "anointing". Priests, kings, and prophets were anointed. To anoint someone, oil was poured on their head (Ex. 29:7). Kings were set apart through the ritual of anointing, which was performed by a prophet who acted in God's power and authority (1 Sam. 15:1). People were also anointed with oil when they were sick. The apostle James told the elders of the church to anoint the sick with oil (James 5:14).

When people needed oil for lamps, they used less expensive oil because it worked just as well. When they needed oil for cooking, they used whatever quality of oil they could afford. The rich people used pure oil and the poor used cheaper oil.

When the oil miraculously appeared for the widow in today's Bible event, it gave the widow and her son enough for themselves and enough to sell for the money they needed. We don't know what kind of oil it was, but we do know that God gave them exactly what they needed! ☺

Memory Verse: Phillipians 4:19 ICB

My God will use his wonderful riches in Christ Jesus to give you everything you need.

Alternate version (New King James)
And my God shall supply all your need according to His riches in glory by Christ Jesus.

April 11 Easter

A Toy that Won't Quit
By Judy Comstock

Scripture:
2 Kings 4:1–7

Lesson Aim:
Recognize that God's power can supply what you need and keep supplying even more than you need.

Bible Skill:
Children will know that they can rely on the power of God.

Bible Lesson: The Toy that Won't Quit

Needed: A pink bunny toy or any battery-powered moving toy, an alkaline battery, and a small tray on which the mechanical toy can move

Turn the switch of the toy to the "on" position. As the toy begins to move across the tray, ask for a show of hands from those who have seen a bunny like this on television.

Explain that the battery bunny is advertised to show the power of the battery that was placed inside the toy to make it work. What happens when the battery runs out of power? (Allow a child to describe the result.) You're right! The bunny quits beating the drum and just stands there. Without the battery the bunny does nothing. (Turn toy to "off" position.)

Say: In the Bible there is a story about God's power to supply what we need. The story is quite sad at the beginning. One day a widow—that's a woman whose husband died—had many bills to pay. Unfortunately, she didn't have any money. The man to whom she owed money said, "I will make your two sons my slaves, if you don't pay your bills." The widow wanted Elisha, the prophet, to help her.

Elisha knew the widow could sell oil to get the money she needed to pay her bills, but she only had one jar of oil. Olive oil was very valuable in Bible times. People used oil as an ingredient in their food. They used olive oil to create light inside their houses. They even used olive oil as a lotion. Elisha told the woman to gather jars. She obeyed Elisha's instructions. She sent her sons to borrow all the empty jars they could from their neighbors. Then, she started pouring oil from her one jar into each of the borrowed jars. The first jar soon was full and she began pouring into another jar. God caused the oil to multiply. The woman kept pouring into more jars until all the jars were full of valuable oil. Now, she could sell the oil, pay her bills and have money left over.

(Hold battery before the children.) Will this battery last forever? (Wait for a child's answer) Then say: Of course not, a battery eventually runs out of power and we throw it away or recharge it. Here is an exciting way God is different from a battery. God does not run out of power. He does not run out of ways to meet our needs. God's power keeps going and going and going. His power can meet our needs in many creative ways. All we must do is stay obedient to his instructions.

 Song Suggestions:

Little Is Much by Mary Rice Hopkins from "15 Singable Songs" (Big Steps 4 U 1988)

You Got Game (It's In the Name) by Dean-o from "Game Face" (BibleBeat Music, 2003)

We Will Shout for Joy by Cindy Rethmeier from "I Want 2 Be Like Jesus" (Mercy/Vineyard 1995)

Take My Heart by Kurt Johnson, a.k.a. MrJ, from "Kid Possible" (Kurt Johnson Music 1995)

Good News Songsheets published by CEF Press, P.O. Box 348, Warrenton, Mo. 63383

Craft for Younger Children: Mighty Muscles
Needed: For each child bring a straw and two 4" circles cut from cardboard or fun foam. Create weightlifting equipment by filling up plastic jugs or small plastic containers with water or sand. Include some small barbells or other items that are heavy such as books.

Set up a weightlifting center and let children "build" their muscles by lifting the weights. As children play, say: You are so powerful and strong! Today we are going to hear about God who is stronger and more powerful than anyone!" First we will make some weights. Give each child two circles and one straw. Show them how to push the straw through the circles (you may have to "start" the hole by cutting a small hole).

These are pretend weights. We can use them to show how strong we are. Did you know that God is stronger than the strongest man could ever be? Aren't you glad that God loves you?

 Craft for Older Children: Special Perfumed Oil
Needed: For each child bring one baby food jar, baby oil (cheaper kind is okay), cloves or potpourri, crayons, and paper cut the right size to be a label for the jars.

Pass out baby food jars. Say: We are going to make some very special oil. In Bible times, the people used perfumed oil for many different reasons. Sometimes they used it like we use lotion and sometimes they used it to cover up bad smells. To make perfumed oil, they began with the finest and most pure oil. Then they added spices to the pure oil to make it perfumed oil.

Squirt some oil (about 1 T) into each jar (Do not fill the jar—it becomes too messy). Let each child add a clove to the oil. Put the lid on the jar and shake until oil absorbs the clove smell. Let children smell the oil.

Say: Do you think that this oil smells good? How would you like to use this all the time? It sure was different to live in Bible times, wasn't it?

Pass out paper for labels and let children decorate them with crayons. Put label on the jar. Encourage the children to give the oil as a gift to someone.

Barbells and Power

Needed: Large marshmallows, pretzel sticks (thick ones)

Guide the children to make edible barbells by pushing a marshmallow onto the end of each pretzel stick.

Say: This is kind of a silly snack, isn't it? These are just like barbells in a gym, but they aren't heavy at all. What would you think if you saw someone lifting very heavy barbells? Where would they get their strength? Could they lift the heavy ones when they were children? What did they do so that they could lift something so heavy?

Explain: We have a God who is stronger than the strongest man could ever be. Not only is God strong, but He also loves us. Aren't you glad that you have a God who is both strong and loving?

Special Easter Snack: Empty Tomb Cakes

Needed: For each child bring a round snack cake, a small round cookie, and a "He is risen" sign.

Show the children how to cut the end off the snack cake to open the "tomb". Then guide them to put the round cookie in front of tomb (as though it was the stone that rolled away).

Write little signs for the front of the tomb that say, "He is risen, he is not here!"

Prayer Focus:

Dear God, we thank you and praise you for always giving us what we need. Thank you for knowing us so well, and loving us so much. We praise you and we love you. In Jesus' name, Amen.

Memory Verse Activity:

Print the verse on a white board. Let children chant the verse with you several times, each time delete one or more words. Keep chanting until they can say the verse without reading it at all.

Memory Verse: Phillipians 4:19 ICB

My God will use his wonderful riches in Christ Jesus to give you everything you need.

Alternate version (New King James)
And my God shall supply all your need according to His riches in glory by Christ Jesus.

April 14

The Key to Heaven, Midweek
By Karl Bastian

Scripture:
John 14:6

Lesson Aim:
Jesus is the key to getting into heaven.

Life Skill:
Children will follow Jesus into heaven.

 Bible Learning Activity for Younger Children: Keys of Life!
Needed: Beanbags, paper.

On paper write the following words or phrases:

Prayer, Bible study, go to church, love God, trust Jesus, be kind, help others, give to God, obey your parents. Put the papers on the floor within easy throwing distance of the children.

Play a beanbag game. Call out one of the "keys" written on the papers and let children take turns trying to throw a beanbag to that square. While they throw beanbags explain what each key means and how to do it. Invite children to add even more examples of how to do it.

Say: That was hard to do! But you did it! The Christian life can sometimes be hard, but you can live it well because Jesus will give you strength!

Bible Learning Activity for Older Children: Keys of the Kingdom Twist-up

Preparation: Mark a grid on the floor with masking tape for every few children. Letter the "keys of the kingdom" (prayer, Bible study, go to church, love God, trust Jesus, be kind, help others, give to God, obey your parents) on paper and tape into squares.

Play the game similar to "Twister®," calling out instructions to the kids. Left hand Bible study, right foot prayer, etc. Continue calling out instructions as a few kids on each grid try to position and reposition themselves. Be certain to have enough grids for all children to play.

After playing the game ask: How hard was that? The Christian life can also be hard sometimes, but the reward is great—eternal life with Jesus Christ!

Enrichment for Younger Children: The Way to Heaven!

Needed: blocks, cotton balls

Guide children to move where the blocks are and build a model of earth with the blocks! Then ask them to build heaven with the cotton balls.

Ask: How can we get from earth to heaven? Can we build a bridge there? Can we build a plane that will get us there? Let children brainstorm; then stress: You will go to heaven if you love Jesus and accept Jesus as the Lord in your life! Then you will follow him to heaven! ☺

Memory Verse: John 14:6 ICB

Jesus answered, "I am the way. And I am the truth and the life. The only way to the Father is through me."

Alternate version (New King James)
Jesus said to him, "I am the way, the truth, and the life. No one comes to the Father except through Me."

Enrichment for Older Children: One Way To Heaven!

Needed: A map of the world, a map of your city, large blank paper

Show the map of the world to the children. Ask children to locate certain places on the map that they know about and tell you what they see. Discuss how you might get there such as by airplane, boat, or car.

Say: There are lots of ways to get to California (Africa, etc.) How can we get there? What would be the best way to go? Would the fastest and best way to get there be to fly? Is there more than one way to get there?

Show map of your city to the children. Say: How do each of you get to church? Discuss the different routes that they take and whether they come in a bus, car, boat, or whatever. Agree: There are many ways to get to church, aren't there?

Get out blank paper. Write "Earth" on one end and "Heaven" on the other end. Ask "How can we get from our life now to our life in heaven? How many ways are there to get to heaven?

Explain: The best way to get there would be to find someone who knows the place and follow him there. That's Jesus! In the Bible, Jesus says "I am the way to heaven, no one gets to heaven except through me." What do you think that means?

It means that there is only ONE way to get to heaven, there are not lots of ways. Yes, just one way. That way is through Jesus, or to believe in Jesus and accept him as the savior in your life. When you do that, you will have eternal life with Jesus in heaven. ☺

April 18

The Key to Heaven
By Karl Bastian

Scripture:
John 14:6

Lesson Aim:
Jesus is the key to getting into heaven.

Life Skill:
Children will follow Jesus into heaven.

Bible Lesson: The Key to Heaven

Needed: Assortment of props such as a chest/toolbox that can be locked with a padlock, the padlock that locks it, one or more keys that open the padlock, and a lot of extra keys that don't open the padlock. Bring enough keys so every child can hold one. It is best if the extra keys will actually fit into the lock, but is not necessary. A locksmith can provide you with a great set of keys that look real but will not open the lock.

Fill a large chest/toolbox with candy. If you can find gold chocolate candy, that is best! Put on and lock the padlock. Have the keys that open the padlock where you can find them easily, such as in your pocket. Put all the other keys in a bag or smaller box.

This is a fun, interactive lesson that will engage kids and help them experience both the delight of believers being received into heaven and the disappointment of those who do not get in.

Ask: What do we use keys for? Talk to the kids about keys, let them handle some keys, and discuss what keys are for.

Explain that keys are used to open many things. Talk about why we use keys, and what kind of things keys open. Guide the children to look at their keys and then compare your key to other keys that your friends are holding. Have them compare their keys to each other and look for differences.

Today a few of you have special keys in your hands. The special keys will open the treasure box right here. Someone or several someones has in their hand the key that will open this treasure box. If a key opens the box, the holder of the key can take a handful of candy from the box.

Demonstrate with your own key, which does NOT open it. (Bummer!) This is good, so that you can say to kids whose key does not work, "Neither did mine!") If you have the key that will open it, you will get to have a handful of the candy that is inside! Let me show you what I mean, I will try my key. Oh, look, it didn't work! Maybe yours will work!

Choose groups, teams, grades, or rows of kids to take turns coming up to the front and trying their keys in the lock. You can choose the group that is sitting the most quietly. Whenever a key opens the box, guide everyone to cheer for that child. Console those whose key will not open it. (You will later give them all some candy, but don't tell them that now!) Some will get to open it, but most will not.

Ask the children who were able to open the box to stand. Interview a few of the winners and ask how they felt when the lock opened. Ask the kids who didn't win to show their sad faces. Ask a few to describe how they felt when their key did not work. Now is the time to say, "If you listen very carefully to what I'd like to share with you, every one of you will go home with some gold candy, so don't be sad anymore."

Ask the kids if they can think of a place that many people would like to go, a place where the streets are made of gold, but that you have to have a special "key" to get in. (They will guess heaven.)

Demonstrate how many keys look the same, and if you have keys that fit the lock but do not open the lock, talk about how while they look like the

---

 Song Suggestions:

He's the One by Dean-o from "Soul Surfin'" (1999 FKO Music 1999)

Happiness Is the Lord Songsheets by CEF Press, P.O. Box 348, Warrenton, Mo. 63383

Faith Will Do by Dean-o from "You Got It All" (1997 FKO Music, 1997)

I Will Follow You by Mary Rice Hopkins "15 Singable Songs" (Big Steps 4 U 1985)

right key, they aren't. A lot of people look and act like Christians, but that doesn't mean they will go to heaven.

To get into heaven, we need a key, and guess what? Jesus is offering the key to heaven to us!

Explain that Jesus offers the salvation key to everyone, but most people would rather try their luck at making up their own way to heaven. But Jesus is the only way to heaven; he is the key to heaven!

Now you may do a salvation invitation and invite children to accept Jesus as their Savior, so that they can find forgiveness and someday go to heaven to be with Jesus, who loves them enough to hold out the key to them.

 Craft for Younger Children: Keys of the Kingdom
Needed: For each child bring three key shapes cut from cardboard or construction paper or thin sheets of colored craft foam, and cord for necklace. Write on each set of three keys: Pray, Go to Church, Read the Bible.

Say: Jesus wants all of us to go to heaven to be with him. There are some things that we can do to make life easier here on earth. These things also help us grow closer to God.

Give each child the three keys and help them string them on the cord. Invite them to read or memorize the three words. Say: These keys will help you remember how to grow in your Christian life, and will remind you that Jesus is THE key to getting into heaven.

Craft for Older Children: Keys of the Kingdom
Needed: For each child bring three key shapes cut from cardboard or construction paper or thin sheets of colored craft foam, and a key ring for each child. Leave the keys blank. Bring markers.

Say: There are many things that we have to help us with our Christian life. These can be called "keys to the kingdom." These are things that make our lives on earth easier and help us to be closer to God.

Have children write things on the keys that help them such as prayer, reading the Bible, going to church, being kind, loving God, having faith. Remind them that they played a game with these during the midweek service.

Put the keys on the key ring. Say: These keys will help you remember how to grow in your Christian life.

Heavenly Pie

Needed: Pudding, whipped topping, cups

Let children make "heavenly pie" by layering pudding and topping.

Prayer Focus:

Dear God, thank you so much for giving us a way to get to heaven. We praise you for your plan that is for everyone. Help us do what you want us to do. Amen.

Memory Verse: John 14:6 ICB

Jesus answered, "I am the way. And I am the truth and the life. The only way to the Father is through me."

Alternate version (New King James)

Jesus said to him, "I am the way, the truth, and the life. No one comes to the Father except through Me."

Memory Verse Activity:

Needed: Large box with "Heaven" written on it and a hole in the top, balls or beanbags

Say: "Each of you will get several chances to throw your ball into "Heaven". Each time that you try, you will say the verse. You will keep saying the verse until you succeed in getting your ball into heaven.

Say: "What did you learn from this game? Did you notice we can have lots of chances, but there is only one way to get in. You can't get in through the side or through the bottom—only through the top. There is only one way to get into heaven also—to follow Jesus in! ☺

April 21

Pistachio-Nut Faith, Midweek
By Barney Kinard

Scripture:
Romans 10:14–15

Lesson Aim:
Children will accept God's word and not doubt God.

Bible Skill:
Children will realize that God wants us to respond to him with faith.

 Bible Learning Activity for Younger Children: Where's Your Faith?

Say: When you wake up in the morning, what happens? Do you get up? Do you eat breakfast? Or what? Let children tell about their mornings.

Then say: Do you ALWAYS have breakfast? How do you know that you will have breakfast tomorrow? Do you ALWAYS get up? How do you know that you will get up tomorrow? Let children brainstorm about why they are sure that those things will happen.

Clarify: You know they will happen because you have seen them happen every other day of your life. Faith is like this. We know God has acted consistently in the past and so we know we can trust him to keep on doing good and caring things in the future. We can count on God. God watches over us, God cares for us, God helps us, and God loves us. We can have faith in God because we know God is there for us. We can believe in God and trust in God—and that equals FAITH in God!

Bible Learning Activity for Older Children: Which Comes First?

Needed: For each team of 2–5 children prepare a set of memory cards. Do this by writing two or three words from the following verse on each index card. Then photocopy the sheets so each team will have a complete set:

Before people can trust in the Lord for help

They must believe in him.

Before they can believe in the Lord

They must hear about him.

And for them to hear about the Lord

Someone must tell them.

Shuffle the cards and place them face down on the table with the words hidden. After your signal to begin, children turn over the cards and use Romans 10:14 in their Bibles to arrange the words in the same order as the memory verse. Encourage teams who finish first to help the other teams.

Let children say the verse to you several times, then ask:

What do you have to do first if you want to TRUST in the Lord? (Believe)

What do you have to do to BELIEVE? (Hear)

How can people HEAR about God? (Someone tells them)

Who can TELL them? (Me!)

Stress: God gave us the Bible so that we would be able to learn all about him and tell others what we know about him!

Enrichment for Younger Children:

Where is God? (Have children point up)

Where are you? (Have children point to themselves)

My faith in God (Have children point up)

will see me through! (Have children point to their eyes) ☺

Bible Learning Activity All Ages: Blind Faith
Needed: One soft bag or pillowcase and several toys or other objects that children will recognize by touch.

Put one toy in the pillowcase without children seeing what you put in. Say: We are going to play a guessing game. Can you figure out what this is without seeing it? Let children feel the objects one at a time without seeing them. Give every child a chance to guess one object.

Each time discuss the evidence that they have found. Ask: Why did you guess what you guessed? (*For example—I could feel the hair and face; I could tell that it had arms; so I guessed it was a doll.*)

Explain: The reason that you knew it was a doll is that you found evidence that it was. You believe the evidence and you know that it is true. When you saw the doll, you realized you were right. You were sure that it was a doll even before you saw it. You believed that it was true because of the evidence. You had faith that it was true because of the evidence. Let children continue to touch and guess objects, repeating the faith illustration.

Say: Faith in God is similar. We cannot see God. But God has given us evidence that he is real. He has created a beautiful world that couldn't come on its own. He has made each person an individual with a different face—no cloning or impersonal force could do that. And much more. God exists, and we can know that even without seeing God. What other evidence do we have that God is real? Lead children in a discussion of the things that we can see that lead us to believe in God.

Repeat: We believe in God, even though we can't see God. We have faith that God is real!

Enrichment for Older children: Who Has Faith?
Play this game like London Bridge. Children form a bridge by holding hands and holding their arms up. Have the other children walk under the "bridge" while you sing:

Do we have faith? Yes we do!

Yes we do! Yes we do!

Do we have faith? Yes we do. Who has faith?

As a child is "caught" in the bridge, say "Do you have faith, Becky?" Prod the group to say: Yes, she has faith! ☺

Memory Verse: Romans 10:17 ICB

So faith comes from hearing the Good News. And people hear the Good News when someone tells them about Christ.

Alternate version (New King James)
So then faith comes by hearing, and hearing by the word of God.

April 25

Pistachio-Nut Faith

By Barney Kinard

Scripture:
Romans 10:14–15

Lesson Aim:
Children will accept God's word and not doubt God.

Bible Skill:
Children will realize that God wants us to respond to him with faith.

Bible Lesson: See the Evidences

Needed: Small bag of pistachio nuts. (You will use one nut in the lesson and the rest in the snack.) Please note that if not partially opened, pistachio nuts can be hard to open, so be sure to separate and use the "easy to open" ones.

Hold a pistachio nut in your hand and tell this story: I have something in my hand that no one here has ever seen before. In fact, I have never seen it myself. Let me tell you something more about it. I got this from a man who never saw it. He got it from a man who never saw it. Although I put it in my pocket, I have never seen it.

What I have in my hand is round. It is tan. It makes a noise. Once you see it, you will never see it again. Besides that, it is also green!

Now, you are wondering if I have anything in my hand at all! Well, there are three ways to think about this. Either, there is really nothing in my hand and I am lying, so you don't believe me. Or there really is something in my hand, but you still don't believe that I haven't seen it. Or you are just not sure if there is anything in my hand and you doubt that I haven't seen it. We are going to take a vote to see what most of you think.

Prompt children to vote only once. Say: Raise your hand if you believe that I am lying and that I actually have nothing in my hand at all.

(Let children "vote.")

Now raise your hand if you believe that I have something in my hand.

(Let children vote.)

Now, the rest of you raise your hand if you doubt that I have anything in my hand, but you want to see the evidence to confirm or deny your doubt.

(Let children vote again.)

Ask: Would you like me to show you what I have in my hand? (Dramatically reveal the nut in your hand.) Well, it is a real pistachio nut! I was not lying!

"The shell is tan and it is round.

"I got if from a grocer who never saw inside the shell.

"He got it from a farmer who grew it on the tree.

"He never saw inside the shell.

"Even though I put it into my pocket, I never saw inside.

"It does make a noise. (Open the shell near a microphone.) Hear it?

"It is green! (Show nut without shell.)

"I told you that once you see it, you will never see it again. (Pop it into your mouth!)

Why did I do this? I wanted to tell you about three kinds of people who hear the Bible.

Some people just do not believe God's word when they hear it. They might be called "unbelievers" or "nonbelievers".

There are other people who believe God's word when they hear it. They are called "believers". They have faith based on evidence God has given.

 Song Suggestions:

Up for the Word by Dean-o from "Soul Surfin'" (FKO Music, Inc. 1999)

Little Is Much by Mary Rice Hopkins from "15 Singable Songs" (Big Steps 4 U 1988)

Do You Know About Jesus? Songsheets published by CEF Press, P.O. Box 348, Warrenton, Mo. 63383

Get It Read by Janna Alayra from "Believin' On" (Montjoy Music 2002)

There are also people who hear God's word and they are just not sure about it. They "doubt" it. They could be called "doubters". But when they see God's word lived out in someone else's life, they believe it! This is faith too.

All of us responded when we first heard God's word. Some of us were believers, some were unbelievers, and some were doubters. Whether you needed evidence to believe or not, your chosing to have faith in God is the important point.

Craft for Older Children: Faith Light Catcher

Needed: Old or promotional CD's (two per child), pretty ribbon or lace, assorted beads or sequins. Glue the CD's back-to-back so that the shiny side faces out and ribbon is looped as hanger between CD's.

Give one of the CD light catchers to each child.

Say: Faith is something that you cannot see. Just like we've seen what CD's look like on the inside before, we know God will be there for us and show us what to do in any situation. He will help us use our faith when we are afraid, lonely, or sad. Let's make a light catcher to remind us of our faith.

Show children how to write "FAITH" on the CD. Then stream a line of glue over the letters and decorate the letters with beads or sequins. Let it dry so it is ready to hang. Say: When you look at this remember to have faith.

Craft Simplification for Younger Children:

Prepare CD's as instructed but letter FAITH for the children with glue. Let them fill in the letters with sequins and beads.

Say: Faith is something that you cannot see. Just like we've seen what CD's look like on the inside before, we know God will be there for us and show us what to do in any situation. He will help us use our faith when we are afraid, lonely, or sad. Let's make a light catcher to remind us of our faith. When you look at this remember to have faith.

Pistachio Nut Butter

Needed: Rest of bag of pistachio nuts used in the Bible lesson, blender or food processor

Snack

Say: Today we are going to make pistachio butter. It's kind of like peanut butter, except that instead of making it from peanuts, we will use pistachio nuts.

Guide the children to shell the rest of the bag of nuts. Blend the shelled nuts in a blender or food processor. Add a little oil or butter, if needed.

Spread on crackers and eat!

Prayer Focus:

Dear God, thank you for your word. We praise you and love you for giving it to us. Help us to accept your word and not doubt it. Help us as we grow in our faith. Amen.

Memory Verse: Romans 10:17 ICB

So faith comes from hearing the Good News. And people hear the Good News when someone tells them about Christ.

Alternate version (New King James)
So then faith comes by hearing, and hearing by the word of God.

Bible Verse Activity: Memory Verse Mix-Up

Needed: Several index cards with words of the verse written on them, one or two words per card. Give each team a set of cards.

Say verse out loud to the children. Pass out cards and let children put the words together in the correct order using their Bibles.

Where does your faith come from? What is the Good News? ☺

April 28

Red, White and Blue Paint and Chocolate Chip Cookies, Midweek
By Pat Verbal

Scripture:
1 Timothy 2:1–4

Lesson Aim:
To help children know that God wants us to pray for our leaders.

Bible Skill:
Children will realize that they can change the world by praying for their leaders.

Bible Learning Activity for Younger Children: Prayer Book
Needed: A small photo album, colored construction paper, white typing paper, colored markers, and glue

Help students write or draw prayer concerns onto the white paper. Cut it out with decorative scissors and glue it to a 3x5 colored background paper. Slip it into a photo album to fill the pages.

As prayers are answered, let children write what happened and add to the book. This will show the practical way that God answers our prayers.

Bible Learning Activity for Older Children: All Star Leaders
Needed: Yellow construction paper

Teach children to make a five-point star. While they cut their stars ask: What would it be like to live in a country where there were no churches? How would life be different? (Make a list of changes.)

There are many leaders in the Bible. Who can you remember? Give their names and I'll help you name what they did. Encourage children to leaf through their Bibles to find these leaders. Examples include:

Abraham was the father of the Hebrew people

Moses led the Israelites to the Promised Land

Joshua led the Israelites into the Promised Land

David was a great king who God loved

Solomon was a leader who built a temple for God

Peter was the founder of the church

Paul led many Gentiles to Jesus.

Let's write the names of these Bible leaders on these stars. On the other side of the star, write the name of a local or national leader's name. We will use them to help us remember to pray for our leaders. When you are finished, hang them on a "prayer tree" (made from branch or Christmas tree).

Memory Verse: 1 Timothy 2:1–2 ICB

First, I tell you to pray for all people. Ask God for the things people need, and be thankful to him. You should pray for kings and for all who have authority. Pray for the leaders so that we can have quiet and peaceful lives—lives full of worship and respect for God.

Alternate version (New King James)

Therefore I exhort first of all that supplications, prayers, intercessions, and giving of thanks be made for all men, for kings and all who are in authority, that we may lead a quiet and peaceable life in all godliness and reverence.

Enrichment for Younger Children: Pray for Godly Heroes

Ask: Do you have any heroes? Why do you like them? Why are they your heroes?

Explain that a hero is an authority figure you try to imitate.

Clarify: We have heroes that work for our country. Some of these are policemen, firemen, and even the President of the United States! Can you draw pictures of these heroes? As children draw pictures, talk with them about these good heroes. Say a prayer for each one. ☺

Enrichment for Older Children:

Tell this true story:

To observe the National Day of Prayer a fourth-grade teacher in Texas asked her students to write a prayer for America and our leaders. The teacher then asked a local pastor to choose several prayers to be read at a school assembly. The pastor carefully read each child's prayer and returned the packet to the teacher with these words: I could not choose only a few prayers. So, I've taken all the prayers and combined them into one prayer. With only a few exceptions, every word comes from the heart of your students. Here is the prayer that was read at the assembly.

Dear Awesome Lord God, Our Heavenly Father,

I've written this prayer so that You can not only solve my problems but so that You could hear many other people's prayers, too. Forgive us for the sins we have done and help us to not do them again.

Please help the major problems with drugs. Please change people's minds about doing and using drugs so we won't have more people in hospitals. Help all our people who are sick or hurt. We would like for You to heal the people who have diseases or who are sick. Help people who are killing other people. Touch them with Your heart so they will think of You, Lord, and think of what they are doing. Help the prejudiced people to respect people for how they are, not for what they look like, and for what their color is.

Bless all the children here at our school and at all the other schools in the world. Please let us have strong families and less divorcing. Also help some of the families that are split up. Help the people who are living on the streets to get food and a house. I'd also ask for help to feed and clothe the homeless and unemployed.

Please help our country get out of debt and pick good strong leaders to lead our country. Those who are in the army don't let them get hurt. And one last thing, help stop pollution, because this is the only place we've got, so let's save our planet.

Lord we need You to help us through our times of trials. We can't survive without you.

Yours with love, Amen.

A Fourth Grade Class in Texas

Action: Help children look up the names of public officials in your area using the phone book or Internet. Write a sentence prayer for each leader. Print them on a bookmark and hand them out at your church. ☺

May 2

Red, White and Blue Paint and Chocolate Chip Cookies
By Pat Verbal

Scripture:
1 Timothy 2:1–4

Lesson Aim:
To help children know that God wants us to pray for our leaders.

Bible Skill:
Children will realize that they can change the world by praying for their leaders.

Bible Lesson: Who Taught You to Pray?
Tell this story:

With the sound of the bell a flurry of excitement erupted throughout Brown Elementary School. Colin and Dusty headed to the bike racks dreaming about spring break.

"Get your roller blades and come to my house," yelled Colin.

"I can't," Dusty said, "I promised to go to Mrs. Cassidy's house to make posters."

"Why in the world would you want to do something like that?"

Dusty reminded Colin of the class discussion they had about the President's power to issue special proclamations.

"May sixth is our National Day of Prayer and Mrs. Cassidy wants some of us to put posters around town," said Dusty.

"Come help us, Colin. You're really good at art," said Dusty.

"I like art okay, but I don't know anything about prayer," responded Colin. Then Colin took off like a bullet towards Mrs. Cassidy's house.

They both arrived out of breath and joined several kids at tables set up in the garage. Lemonade, chocolate chip cookies, and cans of red, white, and blue paint were everywhere. Colin jumped right in drawing a picture of a bald eagle from a picture of the Presidential Seal.

"Colin, tell me what you think about America?" Mrs. Cassidy asked.

"America is great, but our country has a lot of problems too," said Colin.

"Do you know what made America great?" said Mrs. Cassidy.

"Probably the people who fought for our freedom," Colin answered.

"And the people who prayed for our country," Dusty chimed in. "My mom says our Founding Fathers asked God to bless our nation," said Marcie, "and that's why we stay strong."

Mrs. Cassidy reminded the children that National Days of Prayer have been a tradition since the first Continental Congress in 1775. President Harry S. Truman declared it an annual event in 1952.

"Doesn't the Supreme Court and the Congress open their sessions every day with prayer?" asked Dusty.

"Yes!" said Mrs. Cassidy.

"But what if you don't know how to pray?" said Colin.

"Prayer is just talking to God and believing that he hears you," Dusty answered.

"My mom says prayer is one of our most precious freedoms and if we don't use it, we'll lose it," said Marcie, stepping back to admire her colorful flag poster.

Dusty passed Colin another chocolate chip cookie. "We can put these posters up around town tomorrow while we've cruising on our roller blades," said Dusty.

"Sounds good to me!" cheered Colin and the other kids.

Ask: What are some things you could tell Colin to help him learn to pray? Have you ever participated in a National Day of Prayer event held the first Thursday of May? How?

Then continue the story: Pretend you are a young pastor about to start a new church in a town that doesn't know about God. Who would help you? The apostle Paul!

When Timothy started a new church, Paul wrote him two important letters. Timothy was a young preacher who often traveled with the letters. In the first one, Paul urged Timothy to pray for kings and all those in authority. Why? God wanted Timothy to pray for the leaders.

In his teen years, Timothy traveled with Paul on his missionary journeys. Perhaps they sat around campfires talking about great leaders like King Solomon.

King Solomon took his father David's place as king. He was famous for building the Temple of Jerusalem. God gave Solomon wisdom and very great insight, and a breadth of understanding as measureless as the sand of the seashore. Solomon's wisdom was greater than the wisdom of all men (1 Kin. 4:29–30a).

So, what went wrong? Was King Solomon so successful that no one in his kingdom thought he needed prayer?

King Solomon took his eyes off of God. He tried to be like other kings. He married foreign wives and worshiped their pagan gods. He became greedy and required forced labor from his citizens. Then the Lord said to Solomon, "Because you have not kept My covenant and My statutes, I will tear the kingdom away from you and give it to your servant" (1 Kin. 11:11 NKJV).

Paul understood what could happen to Timothy if he failed to follow God in every way. Paul promised, however, that if he prayed for those in authority, he would live a peaceful and quiet life in all godliness and holiness (1 Tim. 2:2). Prayer leads to good actions from both leaders and subjects. Good actions lead to peaceful and quiet lives.

That's what we want for America's leaders!

 Song Suggestions:

Pray, Pray, Pray by Mary Rice Hopkins from "Good Buddies" (Big Steps 4 U 1994)

Generation Filled with Righteousness Joy by Cindy Rethmeier from "I Want 2 Be Like Jesus" (Mercy Vineyard 1995)

Around the Corner, Around the World Songsheets published by CEF Press, P.O. Box 348, Warrenton, Mo. 63383

God Bless America Traditional

Craft for Older Children: Prayer Reminders

Needed: Information about local Christian leaders including who they are and what some of their important views are, poster boards or construction paper, markers

Say: Today we are going to make posters to honor local and national leaders and remind others to pray for them. Together with the children decide: What could be on the poster? Who would you like to choose? What would you like to say? Let children draw their posters and post them around the church on the National Day of Prayer.

 Craft for Younger Children: Tear Paper Art Flag

Needed: Red, white, and blue construction paper, American flag or picture of one.

Show the children a picture of the American flag. Explain that they will make their own copy of the American flag. Show the children how to tear the paper into shapes and make a flag.

Say: These are beautiful! Let's post them around the class to honor the National Day of Prayer!

Alternate Craft: Stars and Stripes Collage

Needed: Blue construction paper, Red and white construction paper cut into 1"strips, Silver star stickers, glues

Set out all of the materials and let the children create patriotic posters. Explain that posters look patriotic when they use red, white, and blue and include star stickers.

Urge children to use the posters to pray for their leaders.

Special Holiday Activity: National Day of Prayer Activity

As a teacher, you play a critical role as leader of your class. Just as a pastor shepherds a congregation, your students are your little flock. Someone once said, "First, I love my teacher, then I love my teacher's God."

Always be mindful that children are watching your attitudes and actions. Watch your conversation because little ears are sharp.

When children bring you flowers, apples, bugs, or pictures, accept them graciously. They learn to honor you before they can honor God. Let them see you prepare for participation in the National Day of Prayer, and perhaps see you pray on that day. ☺

Chocolate Chip "Leadership" Cookies

Let the ingredients represent all the *right stuff* to make a person a good leader.

Let children decorate cookies to look like flags. Say: This week we need to remember to pray for our leaders. These flags will remind us to do just that!

Alternate: Decorate a rectangle cake prior to class to look like a flag. Use icing, or a combination of icing, red licorice, mini marshmallows and blue candy or blueberries.

Prayer Focus:

Dear God, thank you for our faithful leaders who serve you around the world. We ask you to give wisdom, guidance, protection, and awareness of His presence to leaders of governments and of churches. We thank you and we praise you for your protection. Amen.

Memory Verse: 1 Timothy 2:1–2 ICB

First, I tell you to pray for all people. Ask God for the things people need, and be thankful to him. You should pray for kings and for all who have authority. Pray for the leaders so that we can have quiet and peaceful lives—lives full of worship and respect for God.

Alternate version (New King James)

Therefore I exhort first of all that supplications, prayers, intercessions, and giving of thanks be made for all men, for kings and all who are in authority, that we may lead a quiet and peaceable life in all godliness and reverence.

Memory Verse Activity:

Read this verse to the children. Talk about kings and leaders. Say:

Who are these people?

What can we pray?

How do our prayers impact the world?

How do they impact our country?

Who are some of the leaders we can pray for?

What should we pray for them?

May 5

Security Blanket Mom (Mother's Day), Midweek
By Vicki Wiley

Scripture:
John 14:16

Lesson Aim:
To teach children that the Holy Spirit is a comforter for them.

Bible Skill:
To learn to ask the Holy Spirit for comfort.

Bible Learning Activity for Younger Children: Mommy Says
Play like Simon Says, with the leader leading a series of activities that a mom often asks a child to do such as: take out trash, take care of sibling, read a story to baby brother, etc.

Bible Learning Activity for Older Children: What Does the Bible Say?
Explain that the Bible says many things about mothers.

• One of the Ten commandments says to "honor your father and mother."

• The book of Proverbs says a woman's family can be held together by her wisdom, but it can be destroyed by her foolishness.

• Luke tells a story about Jesus when he was lost and his mother was searching for him. When she found him she said, "Son, why have you done this to us? Your father and I have been very worried, and we have been searching for you!"

• And Paul talks about a woman who was "like a mother to him." We don't know her name, we only know that her son was named Rufus. Rufus was a special servant of the Lord, so his mother was probably very special too, and she treated Paul like a son.

The Bible talks about the importance of motherhood and how children should respect and be kind to their mothers. Ask: How do you treat your mother? Are you kind even when she wants you to do something you don't want to do? True respect will come when you always obey, even when you would rather do something else.

Enrichment for Younger Children: Are You My Mother?

Needed: Game in which you match mommies and babies, or make a similar game out of magazine pictures.

Place game pieces face down on a table.

Each time a child guesses which is the mommy to the baby on their card they say, "Are you my Mother?" and give the card to the child.

If the card is not the mother, the child and other children can say, "You are not my mother" and the card stays. ☺

Enrichment for Older Children: History of Mother's Day

We have been celebrating Mother's Day since 1914 when the U.S. Congress decided that the second Sunday in May should be called Mother's Day. The founder of Mother's Day was Anna Jarvis.

Anna was a mother of four children. She was also a Christian and a Sunday school teacher. She also loved her own mother very much and decided to find a way to honor her after she died. She wanted a special day to honor her mother and other mothers that served their families and worked hard for their countries. She felt Memorial Day honored the sacrifices of men and Mother's Day would honor the sacrifices of women.

Today, though, Mother's Day isn't considered a patriotic holiday at all. Instead, it is a time to think of our mothers and what they do for us. We can thank them and tell them how much we love them. Ask children to tell ways they thank their mothers.

Anna Jarvis encouraged people to wear and give white carnations on Mother's Day because they were her favorite flowers. We still follow that tradition today, but now we give all kinds of flowers.

Be sure to thank your mom today for all that she does for you and tell her that you love her. ☺

Memory Verse: John 14:16 ICB

I will ask the Father, and he will give you another Helper. He will give you this Helper to be with you forever.

Alternate version (New King James)
And I will pray the Father, and He will give you another Helper, that He may abide with you forever.

May 9

Security Blanket Mom (Mother's Day)
By Vicki Wiley

Scripture:
John 14:16

Lesson Aim:
To teach children that the Holy Spirit is a comforter for them.

Bible Skill:
To learn to ask the Holy Spirit for comfort.

Bible Lesson: God Comforts You Like a Mother

Needed: A teddy bear or Blankie (well worn, maybe even your own security blanket)

Look what I brought with me today? What is it? (A Blankie!) Okay, be honest… How many of you have one of these?

Well, if we were honest, most of us would say that we have one. What do you use it for? (let children respond) A Blankie is great when you need to feel better, when you are sick or scared. It is great when you are in a new place without your mom.

Did you know that when children are little, mothers love them so much that they want to be with them all the time? For those times the mothers can't be with their children, some mothers give a security blanket or other soft toy. These mothers know that if you had your "Blankie" or "Lovey" you would feel better.

Now that you are older, it might be a little embarrassing, to carry a Blankie or Lovey. But there is no reason to be embarrassed. Almost everyone had something to comfort them when they were little.

That is how it is with the Holy Spirit! What is the Holy Spirit? Let me tell you.

When Jesus was here on earth, he helped and gave comfort to those who needed it. But when it was time for him to go back to heaven, he wanted to leave a comforter here for us. He knew that there would be times when his disciples and those who loved him would miss him and would need help and comfort. He would not be there to give it to them.

So, he told his disciples that he would ask his Father to send them another comforter who would stay with them forever. That is exactly what he did. He asked God and God sent us the Holy Spirit. God's Holy Spirit is with us all the time.

Jesus said, "I will ask the Father, and he will give you another Helper. He will give you this Helper to be with you forever. You can know him, he lives with you and he will be in you." The Holy Spirit is always here to comfort and to guide us in times of trouble. You might not need your Blankie anymore, but you will always need the comfort and help that the Holy Spirit can give you.

Whenever you are lonely or afraid, you can ask the Holy Spirit to be with you and comfort you. The Holy Spirit will fill you up and you won't feel lonely anymore! He is like a good blankie or a good mother.

 Song Suggestions:

Fingerprints by Mary Rice Hopkins from "Juggling Mom" (Big Steps 4 U 1999)

Jesus Loves the Little Children Traditional

Turn It Over by Dean-o from "God City" (BibleBeat Music 2001)

Faith Is Just Believing Songsheets published by CEF Press, P.O. Box 348, Warrenton, Mo. 63383

Mother's Day Craft For Younger Children: Fingerprints
Needed: Tempera or other non-toxic paint, paintbrush, clean up cloths, and for each child a printout of the following poem.

Paint the child's hands with a paintbrush and paint. Press onto a piece of paper with these words of "Fingerprints" (by Mary Rice Hopkins) printed on it:

When you find my little Fingerprints all over your bedroom walls

And you want to yell a bit cause they're even in the halls

Well I know it's hard to believe, but once you were a kid like me

And someday I'm going to grow up, so remember me while I am small

I get in the way a lot of the time though I'm only 3 feet tall

I make you forget what's on your mind and trip over my toys in the hall

Well I know it's hard to believe, but once you were a kid like me

And someday I'm going to grow up, so remember me while I am small

I've heard that where your treasure is, that's where your heart will be

I don't know much about hearts and things but I'm glad you treasure me

I'm gonna make great fingerprints, but I promise not on your walls

I'm gonna touch those around me though I'm only three feet tall.

Mom's Favorite Cookies

Needed: Heart shaped cookies (at least one per child), red icing, sprinkles.

Let children decorate cookies for their moms as they wish. Have them write "Mom" on them with the icing.

Special Snack: Mom's Cookie Mix

Needed: For each child a quart sized jar, a preprinted label with the following words, measuring cups and the following ingredients. Combine and set aside, one batch for each child.

1 3/4 cups all-purpose flour

1 teaspoon baking powder

Mother's Day Craft for Older Children:
Hand-shaped Flowers

Needed: Paper: Obtain a photo of each child, and bring for each child a flowerpot, craft sticks, paper, green paint, white or green thick craft foam. Place craft foam into each pot, and paint the craft sticks green.

Have children trace their hands onto paper and cut them out. Place a picture of the child in the center of the handprint that matches.

Guide children to glue the hand shapes onto a craft stick that you have painted green. Direct them to put it into the pot as a flower.

Say: This will make a great Mother's Day present for your mom today! Why do you think your mom will like this? (*Samples: because it is my handprint, my picture, more*)

Moms like this kind of present because they love their children so much!

Jesus loves you so much that he sent a special comforter to you—the Holy Spirit! He is like a good mother. Whenever you are afraid, you can ask the Holy Spirit to comfort you and you won't be afraid anymore.

Are you my Mother? Game II: (played like Doggie, Doggie, where's your bone?)

Needed: One block or bone

Choose one child to be a baby bird.

This child sits in the middle of the circle. Give the block to a child and that child will be the "mommy".

The Bird points to a child and asks "Are you my Mother?" the child answers "Yes" if they have the block or "No I am a ___"; fill in the ___ with cat, dog, boat, etc. On the third guess if the child guesses incorrectly, the child can point to the "Mother."

Play enough rounds that every child gets to be baby.

1 teaspoon baking soda

1/2 teaspoon salt

Line ingredients up in a line in the proper "stacking" order. Guide the children to put the into ingredients their jars and then label the jar.

In the jar layer 3/4 cup dark brown sugar

1/2 cup white sugar

1/4 cup cocoa

1/2 cup pecans

and 1 cup chocolate chips

Pack everything down and then guide children to pour the flour mixture on top.

As they put on the lids, distribute tags with the following instructions:

Preheat oven to 350 degrees

Empty cookie mix into large bowl

Blend mixture with hands

Mix in 3/4 cups softened butter or margarine, 1 egg and 1 teaspoon vanilla.

Shape into walnut size balls and place 2 inches apart on baking sheet.

Bake for 11–13 minutes.

Prayer Focus:

Dear God, thank you so much for my mother. Thank you also for the Holy Spirit which you gave us to comfort us when our mothers are not with us. Thank you for thinking of us. We love you and we praise you for you are a wonderful God. Amen.

Memory Verse: John 14:16 ICB

I will ask the Father, and he will give you another Helper. He will give you this Helper to be with you forever.

Alternate version (New King James)

And I will pray the Father, and He will give you another Helper, that He may abide with you forever.

Memory Verse Activity: Clothespin Relay

Needed: Verse written on regular paper, a few words on each paper (you will need one set per team) clothesline stretched across room, clothespins

Divide into teams. Say: Moms used to have to hang out the laundry to get it dry. Most of the time now, they just use a clothes dryer, but some still like to use the clothesline. Today we are going to "hang our laundry" as we learn this verse. One at a time, run with your words to the clothesline and clip your part of the verse onto the clothesline. Run back and the next child will have their turn. Be sure to put the words in the right order!

Ask: Who is this helper in the verse? What does the helper do?

Using children's words, explain that this "helper" is the Holy Spirit. The Holy Spirit comes from God to help us understand God, comfort us when we are sad or afraid, and helps us learn all about Jesus. When Jesus went back to heaven, he sent the Holy Spirit to stay with us forever. The Holy Spirit is always there. When you need comfort or help, just pray and ask God to send the Holy Spirit to you. You will feel his comfort.

May 12

Joy in the Yucky Places, Midweek
By Ivy Beckwith

Scripture:
Philippians 4:4

Lesson Aim:
God shows us how to be joyful.

Bible Skill:
Kids will understand what joy is and how God helps us be joyful.

Bible Learning Activity for Younger Children: I've Got the Joy!
Teach children the song "I've Got the Joy, Joy, Joy, Joy down in my heart."

Ask: "What do you think joy is?"

Explain that joy is different from happiness because it stays even when things go badly. Joy is deep in your heart where events of life cannot shake it. It is the confidence that God will find a way to take care of you no matter how good or bad things go.

Bible Learning Activity for Older Children: Jail Talk
Guide children to pretend they are in jail. Explain that a man named Paul was in jail and while he was there he wrote letters to people. This was better than feeling sorry for himself because he was actually able to help people. Invite the children to pretend to be Paul and to write a letter that makes someone happy.

After children read their letters, invite each to tell about a time they felt really yucky, and how God helped (*Example: My mom died when I was young and God sent other people to give me hugs; he also held me while I cried; more).*

Explain: Letting God help whether times are happy or sad is the essence of joy.

Enrichment for Younger Children: Joy Bubbling Up!

Needed: small container of bubbles

Say: What is joy? Is joy the same as happy? Joy is feeling happy down deep in your heart! When you feel "joy" you feel like something is bubbling up inside you!

Blow bubbles up into the air and encourage children to catch them.

As they catch one, guide them to say, "I've got joy!" ☺

Enrichment for Older Children: Elementary Enrichment: Slime!

Needed: Ahead of time, prepare slime with this recipe:

2 Cups Water

1/2 Cup Cornstarch

Food Coloring

Boil 2 cups water in a medium saucepan. Add cornstarch while stirring. After that is mixed well, add food coloring and stir. Remove from heat and cool to room temperature.

Give each child a section of slime and encourage them to play with it. Make sure they play with it on a plastic covered surface.

Say: This stuff is sure slimy, isn't it? What can you do with it? Believe it or not, you can take this yucky stuff and make "joy". Want to see? Show children how to form the word "Joy" with slime.

That doesn't really make us joyful, does it? But God can move past the bad or yucky things in our lives and create joy anyway. Would anyone like to share a time that something was really bad and God brought in joy? ☺

Memory Verse: Philippians 4:4 ICB

Be full of joy in the Lord always. I will say again, be full of joy.

Alternate version (New King James)

Rejoice in the Lord always. Again I will say, rejoice!

May 16

Joy in the Yucky Places
By Ivy Beckwith

Scripture:
Philippians 4:4

Lesson Aim:
God shows us how to be joyful.

Bible Skill:
Kids will understand what joy is and how God helps us be joyful.

Bible Lesson: Surround Unhappiness with Happiness

Gather children together and ask "Can you tell me what kinds of things make you really unhappy?" Ask: "Why do these things make you unhappy? Tell me how being unhappy feels. Maybe you feel sad or tired or crabby or cranky. Do you like being unhappy? I know I don't like feeling unhappy."

There was a man in the New Testament who was named Paul. He traveled to many places telling people about Jesus and God. And he helped these people start churches. But not everyone was happy to see Paul come to town. Some people didn't want others to hear the Good News about Jesus. They were jealous of the attention Paul got. So they plotted to hurt Paul and the people who traveled with him. Sometimes they chased him out of town. But other times they arrested him and put him in jail even though he hadn't committed any crime.

Ask: How do you think you would feel if you were put in jail? I think I would feel unhappy. Jail isn't a very good place to be and it really wasn't a very good place to be when Paul was alive many years ago. So, how do you think Paul felt when he was put in jail because he was telling people about Jesus?

Explain that at first he might have been unhappy and maybe even angry with the people who had put him in jail. But then he realized that God was still with him in jail and that God would help. So Paul began to feel better about being in jail and he even started to talk to the guards about Jesus. Some of the guards came to believe in Jesus. In fact Paul started to feel downright joyful while he was in jail.

Ask: What do you think it means when someone is joyful? It means they are finding deep down contentment or they are finding security in something or someone. So Paul was finding great contentment or security even though he was in jail. Some people probably thought he was crazy because nobody is supposed to be that happy in jail.

Ask: Now, do you really think it was jail that made Paul this happy? No, jail was still a really yucky place to be. What made Paul really happy was knowing God was with him, even in jail, and that God would take care of him even if Paul had to stay there a really long time.

While Paul was in jail he wrote a letter to the people at one of churches he started. He wanted them to know how he learned to be joyful even while he was in jail. So he told the people at this church they should "Rejoice in the Lord always, again I will say, Rejoice." When the people at the church heard this from Paul what do you think they thought he meant?

I think they thought Paul was telling them that people who love God and Jesus will find a reason to be happy because God is always with them. God will help them, even when they are in places that can make them unhappy.

Can you think of some ways you can make someone else happy even when yucky stuff is happening to you? How will this help you "rejoice in the Lord always"?

 Song Suggestions:

It's Gonna Rock! by Dean-o from "God City" (BibleBeat Music 2001)

Little Is Much by Mary Rice Hopkins from "15 Singable Songs" (Big Steps 4 U 1988)

Less of Me by Mister Bill from "When I Grow Up" (Mister Bill Music 1997)

G-O-S-P-E-L Means Good News! Songsheets published by CEF Press, P.O. Box 348, Warrenton, Mo. 63383

I've Got the Joy Traditional

Craft for Older Children: Joy Frame

Needed: Shapes cut from colored craft foam or construction paper, plain paper, markers or crayons, glue, and a ruler. Before class prepare a frame for each child. Fold a piece of construction paper in half so that each half measures 6" x 9". On one of the halves measure and mark one inch all the way around the edge of the paper. Cut out the inside square so that you have a frame on one side of the paper. Cut up different colors of foam or construction paper into small pieces to use to decorate the frame.

In class give each child a piece of drawing paper 6" x 9" with a square the size of the inside of the frame marked on it. Guide children to write "Joy" on the paper and to decorate the frame with the shapes.

Explain: When you build your life around Jesus, like this frame is around the picture, your life will fill with joy.

Craft Simplification for Younger Children:

Give preschool children *pre-made* frames. Let them decorate as they wish. Write "Joy" for them and let them color or glue shapes onto the word.

Say: Joy is a very special thing to have. Joy means that you are "deeply" happy and satisfied. When we know Jesus, we can have joy because we know that God and Jesus love us.

Yucky or Joyful?

Needed: Graham crackers, yucky colored icing (mix colors until it looks ugly), pretty colored icing in a tube for writing, sprinkles

 Say: I want each of you to write "Joy" on your cracker with this icing tube. Wait until everyone is finished. Then say: Now I want you to cover it up with the ugly, yucky icing and the sprinkles. Kids will really get into this as they "ruin" the way their cracker looks.

Is the joy still there? (Yes, but now it is under the yucky stuff.) But is it still there? Yes!

Our joy is always there because God is always there.

Explain: True joy comes from knowing Jesus Christ and knowing that

God loves us. True joy may be covered up for a little while like this joy was on your cracker, but it is still there. Sometimes when you are having yucky times you may not be able to feel joyful, but the joy is still there and it will come back to you.

Prayer Focus:

Dear God,thank you for being my joy. Thank you that you are an awesome God who cares about me and loves me and gives me joy. Please help me to always know that my joy is due to you, and to help others feel their joy. Amen.

Memory Verse: Philippians 4:4 ICB

Be full of joy in the Lord always. I will say again, be full of joy.

Alternate version (New King James)

Rejoice in the Lord always. Again I will say, rejoice!

Memory Verse Activity:

Say: Let's see if we can spell JOY. Have three children stand up and form the letters JOY with their arms (similar to how a cheerleader would do it). If you have more than three children, spell joy again and again, once for every three children.

Paul told us to rejoice in the Lord always. Let's learn the verse a new way. Everyone stand up and let's say the verse together. When we say "JOY" you must form one of the letters with your arms. Ready?

Say verse a few times, letting the students form the letters JOY.

Repeat: Real joy comes from Jesus and no one can take it away from us!

May 19

Miracle Mud, Midweek
By Mary Rice Hopkins

Scripture:
John 9

Lesson Aim:
Jesus can make anything become important and special, even mud.

Bible Skill:
Kids will realize that they are special to Jesus and they can treat others as special too.

Bible Learning Activity for All Ages: Being Blind
Needed: Braille book (if possible) or use this sheet. Teach these letters in Braille by copying the positions of the dots. Poke pin holes in each bold dot to form Braille book.

    A ..   B ..   C ..   D ..   E ..   F ..   G ..
    ..   ..
    ..   ..

Explain: When someone is blind, they can't see anything at all, or see very little. It's like having your eyes closed all the time.

Do you want to know what this is like? Guide children to form pairs. Let each group have a copy of the Braille sheet and try to learn to recognize the letters by touch.

Ask: How does it feel to not be able to see? How does it feel to read by touching? How could you be friends with someone who is blind? (*The same way you would anyone else. They can still talk, share ideas, play on the playground, and more.*) Ask: If you had a blind friend, would you want to help him or her to see? If you were blind, would you want to see? IMPORTANT:

Because you may have a blind child in your group, or your group members may know a blind child, avoid communicating that blindness is cool, or that children with blindness are different or distant.

Explain: You and I can't help people see, but Jesus could. Jesus miraculously cured the blind man. You might become a doctor so Jesus could heal blindness through your hands.

Enrichment for Younger Children: Jesus' Miracle Mud

Explain: When Jesus healed the blind man, he used something very simple: mud. The mud wasn't special, but when Jesus touched it it became "Miracle Mud!"

The man felt so good when he could see the light, he wasn't blind anymore! Now he could see, he could see the light and the people and more!

Ask: How can you help someone like Jesus did? Is there a way that you can be like this "miracle mud?" (*Samples: Be kind; ask a blind friend if you can take notes for her at school; study to become a doctor who might cure blindness*). ☺

Enrichment for Older Children: Light and Dark

Jesus told the Pharisees that he was the "Light of the World". Right after he told them that he was the light of the world, he chose to heal a blind man. Do you think that the blind man felt like he lived in darkness? What would he like about seeing the light?

Jesus wants all of us to live in the "light", live with Him. He doesn't want us to live in the darkness. When Jesus healed this blind man, he took him out of the dark and led him into his light! ☺

Memory Verse: John 9:38 ICB
He said, "Yes, Lord, I believe!" Then the man bowed and worshiped Jesus.

Alternate version (New King James)
Then he said, "Lord, I believe!" And he worshiped Him.

May 23

Miracle Mud
By Mary Rice Hopkins

Scripture:
John 9

Lesson Aim:
Jesus can make anything become important and special, even mud.

Bible Skill:
Kids will realize that they are special to Jesus and they can treat others as special too.

Bible Lesson: The Mud Party
Gather children together and ask "Have you ever made mud and played in it?" Well, one of my friends told me this story about her son and lots of mud.

Her son David was having his seventh birthday and he had eight of his friends over for the party. They had set up the slip n' slide in the backyard and the boys started playing on it. The next thing we knew they were sliding down a piece of plastic with water on it with the end being a BIG MUD PILE—much to the boys' delight!

This little mud pile turned into a big one and the boys were having the time of their lives! When their moms picked them up, they had a look of disbelief! They were covered in mud! My friend shrugged her shoulders trying to apologize. She hosed them off before they left to go home.

Ask: Have you ever been covered head to toe in mud like these boys? Have you played in a little mud? Have you made mud pies? What else have you done with mud? No question about it, mud can be really fun!

Sometimes adults use mud for things like building bricks or making their skin feel soft. Did you know Jesus liked mud too? He used it one day to do something very important. He used mud to heal a blind man and give him sight. Let me tell you about it.

There was a man who had been blind from birth. As Jesus was walking along one day, he saw this blind man. Some people thought he was blind because of sin in his life and they asked Jesus about it. Jesus said, "No, that's not why he's blind." Jesus knew that he was blind for another reason, a very special reason. Jesus said that he was blind so that he could show how powerful God is!

I don't know why Jesus chose MUD to heal the man. He could have just touched the man with his hand and he would have been able to see. But he didn't. He used MUD! I think Jesus may have used mud to show us that He can use anything at all—anything to heal people. Mud is just mud. But in the hands of Jesus, it is MIRACLE MUD!

Our lives are like that mud. Jesus works through us to do great things. Later on in the book of John, (John 15:5) Jesus said, "Without me you can do nothing." As we obey Jesus, He will show his power through us to others. He will show kindness to friends through you. He will give hugs to parents through you. He will get chores done for people through you. Today people are healed when God uses people just like you, people who grow up to become doctors or nurses or researchers. You may think you are not anyone special. Well, remember that the mud wasn't special either until Jesus got hold of it!

 Song Suggestions:

Miracle Mud by Mary Rice Hopkins from "Miracle Mud" (Big Steps 4 U, 1995)

Do You Know About Jesus? Songsheets published by CEF Press, P.O. Box 348, Warrenton, Mo. 63383

He Is Really God! by Dean-o from "You Got It All" (For Kids Only, Inc. 1997)

Can You Hear My Heart? by Jana Alayra from "Dig Down Deep" (Montjoy Music 1997)

Did you know that even though you are a child you can be the MIRA-CLE MUD in someone's life? Speaking kindly to someone who had their feelings hurt will help heal their hurt and make them feel better. Helping your friend who just fell down will make them feel better. Being a friend to someone who doesn't have a friend will make them feel better. That is how God can use you to be MIRACLE MUD! So, all of you little Mud Pies out there, today when you leave try to be MIRACLE MUD. Try to help someone feel better. Let God show his power through you!

Dirt Pie
Needed: Sandwich cookies, gummy worms, and chocolate pudding.

Guide children to place the sandwich cookies into a sandwich bag and break into crumbs. Place the crumbs into bottom of a small cup. Fill with pudding and add the worm.

Say: We don't usually eat dirt, but today we are going to eat pretend dirt. Enjoy yourself—but don't eat real mud!

 Craft for Younger Children: Mud Clay
Needed: Prepare mud clay with this recipe:
  1 cup flour
1/2 cup salt
2 teaspoons cream of tarter
1 cup water
1 tablespoon vegetable oil
Red, yellow, and blue food coloring to make brown clay

Mix oil, water and food coloring in heavy sauce pan. Add flour, salt and cream of tarter. Mix over low heat stirring constantly. Play dough is done when dough forms around the spoon. Knead when it is touchable. Let cool.

Give each child a lump of clay. As children play with the clay, explain: Jesus worked a miracle with clay like this. We can't do miracles; only Jesus can! But we can let Jesus work through us. Let's play with this clay and remember that Jesus used clay like this to heal a blind man.

Craft for Older Children: Mud Bricks

Needed: Make mud bricks using this recipe:

      Mix 3 cups of dirt (as clean as possible)

1 cup of water and

1 cup of straw cut into small (about 2 inch long) pieces

Press mud into an ice cube tray and let harden in the sun for several hours.

Bring the ice cube trays full of hardened mud. Release the "bricks" and let children build with them.

Explain: Mud was used for many things in Bible times, including making bricks for buildings. Jesus picked up some mud like this before it was hardened and worked a miracle with it. Today we see what it was like to build with mud bricks. Can you heal someone with this mud? No! Only Jesus can! Can you build with this mud? Yes, that is something you can do. You might learn how to heal as a doctor or researcher. In that way Jesus could work through you.

Prayer Focus:

Dear God, thank you that you are a light in this world. Thank you for healing blindness and other diseases. Please help us to become lights in our world by our kindness to others. Help us to be your followers. Amen.

Memory Verse: John 9:38 ICB

He said, "Yes, Lord, I believe!" Then the man bowed and worshiped Jesus.

Alternate version (New King James)
Then he said, "Lord, I believe!" And he worshiped Him.

Memory Verse Activity: Flashlight Tag

Needed: One working flashlight

Read the verse to the children and have them all repeat it several times together. Let one child be "it". "It" will turn around in the center of a circle of children with his eyes closed. When he stops he will shine the flashlight on a child in front of him, but not in the eyes. That child will say the verse. Continue until most children have been caught in the light!

May 26

Special Story for Special Kids, Midweek
By Becky Howell

Scripture:
Matthew 18:10

Lesson Aim:
Children will understand that God loves them and that they are important even when they are children.

Bible Skill:
Children will begin to develop their gifts while still children.

Bible Learning Activity for All ages: Fear Not!
Play game like "Marco Polo". One person is "it" and is blindfolded. It shouts out to the rest of the group, "FEAR NOT!" The rest of the children respond "I bring good news." It tries to tag children. All children tagged sit down until all children have been tagged. If you have a child who reads lips or a child who cannot hear, take the blindfolds off all children.

Say: Many times when angels talk to people in the Bible, they say "Fear not, I bring good news!" This is another way to say "Don't be afraid, God has sent good news for me to tell you."

Encourage children to look in their Bibles while you ask: What good thing did the angel tell Mary in Luke 1? (that she was going to have a baby) What good thing did the angel tell the shepherds in Luke 2? (Jesus was born.)

Explain: God speaks to us in many ways and one of them is through angels! Angels are not people who have died and gone to heaven. They are God's special messengers. They are specially created for this purpose.

Enrichment for Older Children: What Is an Angel?

Ask: What do people think about angels that may or may not be true? (*Samples: people become angels; people who die young become angels; when you go to heaven you become an angel; I have a guardian angel; more*). Distinguish between biblical images and images that are not biblical. Then ask: So what are angels?

An angel is actually a specially-created heavenly being who has power and intelligence. Angels are spiritual beings (Heb. 1:14). Their nature is superior to human nature but less than God (Heb. 2:7). They have power and knowledge that God gives them (2 Sam. 14:17, 20; 2 Pet. 2:11). They are not like God, though. They are not all-powerful and all-knowing (Ps. 103:20; 2 Thess. 1:7).

Angels do not usually have wings, like they do in pictures, but they were created by God (Ps. 148:2, 5). Two angels are named in the Bible. They are Michael (Dan. 10:13, 21; 12:1; Jude 9; Rev. 12:7) and Gabriel (Dan. 8:16; 9:21; Luke 1:19, 26).

Angels love to praise the Lord continually (Ps. 103:21; 148:1–2). Large numbers of them remain at God's side, ready to do His every command (1 Kin. 22:19).

Angels also protect the people of God (Ex. 14:19–20; Dan. 3:28; Matt. 26:53). They meet a wide variety of human needs, including relieving hunger and thirst and overcoming loneliness and dread (Gen. 21:17–19; Mark 1:13; Luke 22:43). They sometimes deliver the people of God from danger (Acts 5:19; 12:6–11). ☺

Enrichment for Younger Children: If You're Special . . .

Play "Simon Says" with actions such as these:

If God made you special hug yourself

If God made you special touch your head

If God made you special jump on one foot

If God made you special jump on two feet

If God made you special touch your knee

If God made you special say "I'm Special!"

Clarify that children are only to do the action if it is preceded by "If God made you special." In some rounds, leave off "if God made you." ☺

Prayer Focus:
Dear God, thank you for creating angels. Thank you for loving children. Thank you that we can serve you even while we are small. We love you. Amen.

Memory Verse: Matthew 18:10 ICB
Be careful. Don't think these little children are worth nothing. I tell you that they have angels in heaven who are always with my Father in heaven.

Alternate version (New King James)
Take heed that you do not despise one of these little ones, for I say to you that in heaven their angels always see the face of My Father who is in heaven.

May 30

Special Story for Special Kids
By Becky Howell

Scripture:
Matthew 18:10

Lesson Aim:
Children will understand that God loves them and that they are important even when they are children.

Bible Skill:
Children will begin to develop their gifts while still children.

Bible Lesson: Special Story for Special Kids

Have you ever had a day when you felt that you weren't important? When nothing seems to go right? When big people seemed important but kids didn't? You might think: "If only I could grow an inch or two!" Or, "When I get to be ten maybe then I'll be someone special!"

You know that you have important things to say and great stories to tell. You know you have skills that just need a little practice. You know you are fun company. But maybe no one seems to want to listen to you. Or maybe your coach lets you bat only once. Maybe someone acts cruelly or you don't get invited to a party. These events can make you feel bad.

In the Bible, some children understood just how you feel! There is a story about it in the book of Matthew. The children had waited and waited for the day when Jesus would come to their town. Jesus was always so kind to them and he always listened. He made them feel important! With much excitement they went to the place where Jesus was planning to be. As they climbed the hill where Jesus was teaching they dodged in and out of the crowd until they finally got close enough and ran toward their friend Jesus.

Song Suggestions:

All Night, All Day, Angels Watching Over Me Traditional

I'm Not Too Little Songsheets published by CEF Press, P.O. Box 348, Warrenton, Mo. 63383

Little Is Much by Mary Rice Hopkins from "15 Singable Songs" (Big Steps 4 U 1988)

Jesus Loves Me Traditional

Just as they got there a hand reached out and stopped them, "Don't bother the Master. He doesn't have time for you children." With disappointed hearts they turned and began to walk away, but Jesus stopped them: "Don't send my young friends away! Don't you know that their angels are constantly before the face of the Father?"

With those few words Jesus welcomed the children back to the arms of their Savior and Friend. They talked with Jesus and he listened. Jesus told them how important they are to God. Before they went home he said one more thing: He told the grown ups that they should be like kids. Jesus communicated that children are very special.

Do you know that Jesus loves you too? He cares about your thoughts and ideas, your successes and your failures. He loves you so much that he gave his very life for you. The next time you are feeling small, don't forget—Jesus cares personally for you.

 Craft for Younger Children: Angel Puppets
Needed: For each child: old fashioned clothespin, cotton ball and gold chenille wire

Show children how to make an angel with a clothespin body and cotton ball head. Add halo if desired.

Say: "What do you think angels look like? We don't know exactly, but the ones in the Bible looked a lot like grown men, and they had boy names. Let's make angels to show what we think they look like."

Craft for Older Children: Angels
Needed: White paper, markers, gold chenille wire

Say: "What do you think angels look like? We don't know exactly, but the ones in the Bible looked a lot like grown men, and they had boy names. Let's all draw pictures of what we think they might look like.

Let children draw pictures and enhance with chenille wire if desired.

Craft Alternate: Pasta Angel

Glue the wood ball on top of rigatoni. Glue the tiny pasta on the wood ball. Glue two elbow pastas for arms coming toward each other in front of angel. Add bow pasta in back for wings. Paint entire angel white. Add facial features and a gold halo if desired.

Craft Alternate: Clothespin Angel

Place the 2 pieces of 4" wide lace on top of each other. Gather top, pull thread tight leaving a small hole. Knot to form dress. Slip dress onto round part of clothespin, glue. Glue ball on top.

For the wings, join each piece of 1 1/2" lace with glue to make a tube. Overlap the 2 pieces in the center, gather up the middle, wrap thread around and tie tightly. Glue wings onto dress just below the head. Make a halo by forming a small circle from a piece of shiny pipe cleaner. Tie a piece of thread or ribbon through this for a hanger and then glue halo on to head. Decorate with ribbons, etc.

Serve Angel Food Cake

 Ask: "Why do you think this is called angel food cake? (*Because it is light and white like an angel*)

We think of angels as being white and beautiful. Although we don't really know what angels look like, we do know that God created them and that they protect us!

Prayer Focus:
Dear God, thank you for loving little children and sending angels to us. Thank you that we can serve you even while we are small. We love you. Amen.

Memory Verse: Matthew 18:10 ICB
Be careful. Don't think these little children are worth nothing. I tell you that they have angels in heaven who are always with my Father in heaven.

Alternate version (New King James)
Take heed that you do not despise one of these little ones, for I say to you that in heaven their angels always see the face of My Father who is in heaven.

Memory Verse Activity:
Needed: For each child bring one long strip of paper such as adding machine tape.

Write the verse on the strip of paper, or let children write it. Let children illustrate this verse to form memory verse banner.

Say: This is a great verse about children! Did you know that you have angels in heaven? Let's learn this verse. ☺

June 2

Raw Eggs! Yuck!, Midweek
By Judy Comstock

Scripture:
Genesis 37: 28; 39–45

Lesson Aim:
Believe that God can work for your good.

Bible Skill:
Children can do the right thing no matter how bad things get.

Bible Learning Activity and Enrichment for Younger Children: Many-Colored Coat
Needed: For each child bring a grocery bag and markers.

Explain: one of the special things about Joseph when he was young like you is that he had a special colored coat. Let's make one that looks something like his did.

Show children how to cut arm holes in front and an opening in the bag to create a coat. Let them use markers to decorate it.

Let children put coat on. Let children pantomime story while you tell it.

Story: Joseph was his father's favorite son. His father gave him a very special coat to wear. But his brothers were jealous of him. So they threw him into a pit and sold him to some traders. Joseph ended up praying to God and God protected him. Even though his life seemed yucky for a while, good things happened later.

Bible Learning Activity for Older Children: The Shofar

Needed: Bring for each child a toilet paper tube. Bring also a horn or real shofar, and arrange chairs for musical chairs

Tell this story: In Bible times, there was a holiday that was especially for forgiving someone. When someone makes your life hard or yucky, sometimes the only way to find joy again is to forgive them. That's exactly what the Bible people did! They had a special holiday to celebrate this. This holiday was called "The Feast of the Trumpets."

At the Feast of Trumpets, they blew a special horn called a shofar. The shofar was made from the horn of a ram. When they blew on it, it made a loud sound. When they blew the shofar, the people remembered that they needed to be forgiven. Forgiveness gave people a fresh start.

Let's play a game. This game will be like musical chairs, except you will walk around the chairs until the shofar blows. When it blows, the person without a seat will say "I forgive you!" to everyone. Each time the shofar blows and one child leaves the game, also remove one chair. The game will continue until all chairs are gone.

When someone makes you angry, do you feel "yucky"? How does it feel when they say "I'm sorry" and really mean it? God wants us to find this kind of joy and togetherness.

Memory Verse: Genesis 41:39–40 ICB

So the king said to Joseph, "God has shown you all this. There is no one as wise and understanding as you are. I will put you in charge of my palace. All the people will obey your orders. Only I will be greater than you."

Alternate version (New King James)

Then Pharaoh said to Joseph, "Inasmuch as God has shown you all this, there is no one as discerning and wise as you. You shall be over my house, and all my people shall be ruled according to your word; only in regard to the throne will I be greater than you."

Enrichment for Older Children: Other Religions

When you are at school your teacher might talk about a religion or a concept that you don't believe in. What should you do?

Follow Joseph's example: He was cut off from his family. He was part of a culture that worshiped pagan gods. Apparently he alone worshiped the true God. This could have been very lonely for Joseph. He had no one to turn to for godly counsel as he made decisions. His boss, Pharaoh, was considered a god by the Egyptians. Joseph's wife was an Egyptian. His father-in-law was a priest of the sun-god.

So how did he keep his faith? Here are some of the things that Joseph did:

• He did the right thing no matter what. We call that "keeping his integrity." Even though everyone around him was doing things differently, he knew what was right and he did that. What are some right things? (*tell the truth; share; marry only one person*).

• He did his best, even when the situation was really bad. Someone lied about him and he had to go to prison for it. He didn't deserve to go to prison, but he did good things while he was there.

• He did every task he was asked to do, as long as that task was a good one.

• He planned ahead and used his influence compassionately.

Joseph trusted God and obeyed God. God blessed him in return. God gave Joseph wisdom. Joseph became so wise that he ended up feeding the entire Middle East during a seven-year famine (Gen. 41:57). His economic plans helped to revitalize cities and alleviate world hunger in Bible times. ☺

June 6

Raw Eggs! Yuck!
By Judy Comstock

Scripture:
Genesis 37: 28; 39–45

Lesson Aim:
Believe that God can work for your good.

Bible Skill:
Children can do the right thing no matter how bad things get.

Bible Lesson: Do Good Things During Bad Times

Needed: Ingredients to make a cake such as a mixing bowl (clear glass is best), spoon, 2 eggs, cake mix that requires oil, eggs and water to complete it, oil, water and eggs. Consider bringing bite size pieces of a cake that has already been made.

Genesis 37 to 45 in the Bible tells a scary and then exciting story about a man named Joseph. Read the whole story in your Bible sometime. Here are the highlights:

Joseph was sold into slavery by his brothers and then an Egyptian official purchased him.

He was put into prison when he was falsely accused of being mean to his master's wife.

While Joseph was in prison, he was assigned the job of attending to two of Pharaoh's servants who had been made prisoners. Joseph interpreted the dreams of these two servants. Years later, Pharaoh was troubled over a dream and one of the two servants, who had been released, recommended Joseph as an interpreter. The Pharaoh was so impressed with Joseph's skills that he gave Joseph authority to do business in the name of the Pharaoh.

Joseph budgeted grain during plentiful times so there was enough for lean times. During these lean times, Joseph's brothers had no food for their families. They traveled to Egypt to buy food. The brothers did not realize that their brother Joseph, whom they had sold into slavery years before, was now so powerful. Joseph was able to provide food for his brothers, forgive his brothers, and bring all of his family together again.

Genesis 50:19–20 explains: "But Joseph said to them, "Don't be afraid. Can I do what only God can do? You meant to hurt me. But God turned your evil into good. It was to save the lives of many people and it is being done" (ICB).

At this point, mix up a cake while you transition to this part of the story: Ask: What is your favorite kind of cake? *(Allow time for some responses.)* Today, we are going to mix the ingredients for a simple dessert and learn an important lesson. First, I will beat two eggs. *(Break the eggs into the mixing bowl. If available, a clear glass bowl will increase the view of the illustration for the children.)* How many of you think raw eggs look like an appetizing treat? *(String the mixed eggs up and over the bowl as the question is asked. Most children will answer no, but be ready for some teasing agreements.)* Even if it seems disgusting, my cake recipe requires eggs. Now, I blend in some oil. By itself, oil is not considered a tasty snack. In fact, all of the ingredients I am adding are not inviting by themselves, but when mixed together something wonderful happens. *(Add the cake mix.)* Would you like a taste of the flour mixture? *(Allow the children to take a pinch of the dry mixture.)* This ingredient is yucky to nibble as a snack, but without it we will not have a cake. *(Add water.)* Last, let's add the water. Water is good to drink all the time, but it serves a very special role in this recipe.

 Song Suggestions:

He Is Really God! by Dean-o from "You Got It All" (FKO Music, Inc. 1997)

Did You Ever Talk to God Above Songsheets published by CEF Press, P.O. Box 348, Warrenton, Mo. 63383

Purest of Gold by Kurt Johnson, a.k.a. MrJ from "Pure Gold" (Mr. J Music 1995)

Explain: Some days are like the ingredients in our cake recipe. Have you ever had one of those days when everything was bad? Based on the Bible story we just heard, what would Joseph say about that? He had some awful things happen to him when he was still young. He might say that the yucky things blend in with all of life to produce a good result. The events in Joseph's life that were meant to hurt him were turned by God into blessings. God can take the things that are yucky and mix them together to become something good, just as He did for Joseph.

(Option:) Give each child a bite-size piece of cake previously baked from the same recipe. Explain: I knew we would not have time to finish mixing our cake, so I baked one earlier just for you. One small taste will help you remember how the ingredients that are awful alone can become something good.

 Craft for Older Children: Kaleidoscope

Needed: For each child bring a cylindrical potato chip can with one end cut out, a circle of plexiglas, acetate or transparancy, and colorful beads. Prepare each can like this: Poke a hole large enough to see through in the metal bottom of a clean potato chip can. Using a 2 3/8" by 9 5/8" pattern, cut three pieces of plexiglass or acetate, and slide them into the can so that their tops form a triangle. For plexiglas and acetate, slide a matching piece of black construction paper behind each piece; for acetate, add cardboard behind the paper to give it body.

Guide children to:

• Cut out a circular piece of acetate to fit on top of the triangle inside the can.

• Line the inside of the can between the acetate circle and the top of the can (about 3/4") with construction paper to hold the circle in place.

• Fill this area with small, shiny, colorful objects, put on the plastic top, and decorate the outside.

Say: Looking through this kaleidoscope makes the world look different, doesn't it? What do you see? One second, it looks one way and the next, it looks completely different. That is how our lives really are, too. One minute things can look so bad, and then God can completely change everything so that it looks good. When you go through rough times rather than say "poor me" look at it a different way. See it as a challenge that you will not let win. Do the right thing anyway.

Craft for Younger Children: Kaleidoscope

Needed: For each child bring a toilet paper tube, a circle of rose or blue colored food wrap, and a rubber band.

Distribute the supplies and guide children to cover the end of the tube with colored food wrap. Secure with rubber band. Let children look through the kaleidoscope tube.

Say: What looks different when you look through your kaleidoscope tube? What is different about it? Have all the children look at you. Say: How do I look now? Now, look at me though your tube. How do I look different?

Explain: Sometimes the "object" doesn't change but it looks different when we look at it differently. When you go through rough times rather than say "poor me" look at it in a different way. See it as a challenge that you will not let win. Do the right thing anyway.

Jail Bars Cookie

Needed: One graham cracker per child, red licorice strings, icing

 Say: Joseph didn't do anything wrong, but he was put in prison. Today we will make a prison window with bars in it. Show children how to attach pieces of licorice to the cracker to look like a prison.

As they are eating say: What do you think it would be like to be in prison? How would you feel if you were in prison and you hadn't done anything wrong? Even though he didn't do anything wrong, Joseph used his time in prison to help others.

Prayer Focus:

Dear God, thank you for all you do in our lives. Thank you for the bad times and the good times. We know that the hard times in our lives work together for good and we know that you are always helping us. We love you and we praise you. You are an awesome God. Amen.

Memory Verse: Genesis 41:39–40 ICB

So the king said to Joseph, "God has shown you all this. There is no one as wise and understanding as you are. I will put you in charge of my palace. All the people will obey your orders. Only I will be greater than you."

Alternate version (New King James)

Then Pharaoh said to Joseph, "Inasmuch as God has shown you all this, there is no one as discerning and wise as you. You shall be over my house, and all my people shall be ruled according to your word; only in regard to the throne will I be greater than you."

Memory Verse Activity:
This is a long verse and hard to memorize, but great to understand. Write the words on the chalkboard or markerboard and ask the following questions:
- Who was talking to Joseph in this passage?
- How did he know about God?
- What did the king put Joseph in charge of?
- Why did he like Joseph so much?
- Did the king believe that he was greater than Joseph? Greater than God?

Let children ask more questions about the verse.

June 9

Food for Thought, Midweek
By Ivy Beckwith

Scripture:
Exodus 16:11, 12

Lesson Aim:
God gives us what we need and we can trust God for our needs.

Bible Skill:
Kids will understand different ways God meets their needs.

Bible Learning Activity for Younger Children: Find Manna in the Desert
Needed: Small white crackers (such as oyster crackers). Place crackers on the floor all over the room. Role play "gathering the manna" with the children. Have some clean crackers to eat following the activity.

Say: Every morning the manna was on the ground. When the children woke up, they went outside to get some to eat. Let's pretend that we are the Israelite children and we need to go get some manna for our breakfast. Let children pick up crackers. Remind them not to eat those, but that you will serve them some that they didn't pick up off the floor.

Wow, that's a funny way to get breakfast isn't it? How do you usually get your breakfast? God gave the Israelite children all the food they needed. How does God give you the food you need? (*Samples: a parent makes it, grocery store, more*)

Bible Learning Activity for Older Children: God Meets Our Needs
Needed: One posterboard and markers or white board and markers

Gather kids together and ask them to think about ways God has given them something they've needed (*Samples: a classmate came over to talk when you were feeling alone; a teacher taught you a strategy that works for math; you got an idea for solving a problem after praying about it*). Give each child a marker and direct them to write these all at the same time on the poster or whiteboard.

Invite children to share these times with the rest of the group. After all children have had a turn, spend some time in prayer thanking God for meeting these needs by reading them off the board.

Say: Aren't you glad we serve a God that loves us so much that he wants to meet our needs?

Enrichment for Younger Children: Manna Flakes

Needed: Honey flavored flake cereal

Ask: Do you know what manna is? It was a special food God provided to some Bible people called Israelites. No one knows for sure what it was. In fact the word manna means "What is it?"

Pass out the flake cereal. Let children have a small amount to eat. Do you like this? Can you imagine eating it every single day? The Bible says that manna was small and round and tasted like honey. That's sort of like this, isn't it?

Every morning the manna was outside waiting for the people to pick it up. God let them have enough food for each day so they wouldn't be hungry and they would know that God was watching out for them.

People have tried and tried to figure out what this manna was, but they still haven't figured it out. That's because manna was something very special that God gave the Israelite people during a special time in history. It demonstrated God's care for his people. ☺

Memory Verse: Exodus 16:12b, ICB

Then you will know I am the Lord, your God.

Alternate version (New King James)
And you shall know that I am the LORD your God.

Enrichment for Older Children: Manna from Heaven

As long as the Hebrew people wandered in the Sinai Peninsula, they were able to gather manna from the ground each morning (Ex. 16:35). They ate manna until they came to the edge of the land of Canaan—for 40 years.

We read in Joshua 5:11, 12: *The next day after the Passover, the people ate some of the food grown on that land: bread made without yeast and roasted grain. The day they ate this food, the manna had stopped coming.* The Israelites no longer got the manna from heaven once other food was available. They began to eat food grown in the land of Canaan. Once they had eaten the food that was in the Promised Land, the manna stopped coming. God gave them the manna for the exact amount of time that they needed it.

The word manna means "What is it?" (Ex. 16:15). We don't really know what it was, but we do know that it was a "small round substance as fine as frost" (Ex. 16:14), that it looked "like white coriander seed," and that it tasted like "wafers made with honey" (Ex. 16:31).

The manna appeared every morning with the morning dew. The Israelites were instructed to gather only what was needed for one day, because any extra would breed tiny worms and spoil. On the sixth day, however, the Israelites were permitted to gather enough for two days. This fed them for that day and for the Sabbath day. They were forbidden to gather any manna on the Sabbath because that would be work. Miraculously, the two days' supply of food gathered on the sixth day did not spoil.

Manna could apparently be baked, boiled, ground, beaten, cooked in pans, and made into cakes (Ex. 16:23; Num. 11:8). Moses even commanded Aaron to put a pot of manna in the ark of the covenant, so future generations might see the "bread of heaven" on which their ancestors had fed (Ex. 16:32–34). The New Testament records that inside the holy of holies in the temple, the ark of the covenant contained, among other things, "the golden pot that had the manna" (Heb. 9:4).

People have tried and tried to figure out what this manna was, but they still haven't figured it out. That's because manna was something very special that God gave the Israelite people, as a reminder of God's care for his people. ☺

June 13

Food for Thought
By Ivy Beckwith

Scripture:
Exodus 16:11, 12

Lesson Aim:
God gives us what we need and we can trust God for our needs.

Bible Skill:
Kids will understand different ways God meets their needs.

Bible Lesson: Food for Thought
Gather children together and ask, "Do you have a favorite food you like to eat all the time? Tell me what some of your favorite foods are." Let EVERY child answer.

Are there times when you can't have this food? Do your parents only let you have this food once in a while? How do you feel when you can't have the food you like to eat?

God gave us a story in the Bible about some people who weren't able to have the food they liked to eat and they weren't happy about it.

God's people, the Israelites, had escaped from the Egyptians with God's help. But now they were living in the wilderness and they weren't able to have the kind of food they had when they lived in Egypt. In Egypt, they lived in a city and all their favorite foods were available to them, but out in the wilderness there was hardly any food at all.

The people were getting hungry and they went to their leader Moses to say, "We are really hungry. We miss our favorite foods. We wish we'd stayed in Egypt even if it meant we would have died." So God told Moses that he would take care of things. God told Moses a very strange thing. God said that bread would rain down from heaven each morning and the people would be given meat to eat in the evening.

Moses went to his brother Aaron and told him what God told him. He told Aaron to gather all the people together. Aaron did this and told the people God heard their complaining. Aaron told the people God would give them bread in the morning and meat in the evening. And, Aaron told the people that when they saw this happen they would know God was God and God was with them.

And what do you think happened? Did God keep the promise to the Israelites? Of course, God did because God always keeps promises. The Bible tells us in the morning small, flaky bread was on the ground and in the evening small birds called quail covered the ground of the camp. At first the people didn't know what the small, flaky bread was or if it was safe to eat. Moses said: "It's the bread God promised you. Gather as much as you need for today."

The people had all they needed to eat and not only did they have enough —it was good food, too! God gave us this story to demonstrate that he will always give us what we need. The Israelites didn't ask God nicely either, and God still gave them what they needed. Its better if we ask God nicely for things but he still hears us and meets our needs even when we don't ask nicely.

 Song Suggestions:

Believe His Promises by Dean-o from "Soul Surfin'" (FKO Music, Inc. 1999)

Do Not Fear by John J.D. Modica from "Ablaze With Praise" (Revelation Generation Music 2000)

What a Mighty God We Serve Songsheets published by CEF Press, P.O. Box 348, Warrenton, Mo. 63383

History Makers by Kurt Johnson, a.k.a. MrJ from "Kid Possible" (Kurt Johnson Music 1995)

Craft for Younger Children: What Do You Like to Eat?

Needed: Food shapes cut from construction paper or food pictures cut from magazines, and paper plates.

Guide children to make a collage of their favorite foods and thank God for providing them with good things to eat.

Ask: What are your favorite foods? Aren't you glad that God gives you your food? God gives us the food we need each day. Let's put our favorite foods on these plates.

Let's thank God for our food.

Sing:

God we thank you, God we thank you
for our food, for our food.
We are very thankful, we are very thankful;
God is love, God is love.

 Craft for Older Children: Making Manna

Needed: One paper plate per child, small amount of craft dough for each child made from this recipe: Mix:

1 cup flour
1 cup of water
1 Tablespoon oil and
2 tsp cream of tartar (optional, but will last longer)

Cook all ingredients over medium heat stirring constantly until it looks like dough. Knead until cool, soft, and pliable. Give small amount to each child.

Say: We don't know what the manna looked like but we do know that manna in the wilderness could be baked, fried, or boiled. If the dough in your hand was manna, show me what you think it would look like. What would it have looked like if you baked it? What about if you fried it?

Food in the Desert

Provide kids with food that resembles what God provided the Israelites.

Baked chicken can be used to represent the quail and oyster crackers can represent the manna.

Snack

Say: This isn't exactly what God gave the Israelites to eat, but it is similar. I wonder why God chose these foods? I wonder how it would be to eat the same thing for 40 years? Do you think you would grumble and complain, or do you think you would be grateful to God for giving you your food?

Prayer Focus:

Dear God, thank you for the food you gave to the Israelites in the desert and thank you so much for all the food you give us. You are a mighty God and a loving God and we praise you! Amen.

Memory Verse: Exodus 16:12b, ICB

Then you will know I am the Lord, your God.

Alternate version (New King James)
And you shall know that I am the LORD your God.

Memory Verse Activity: Sign the Verse

Say: The Israelites knew that the Lord was God because God met their needs always. How do you know that the Lord is God? How do you know you can trust God for what you need? Let's learn how to say this verse with sign language.

Then you *(point to another person)*

Will know *(pat forehead with fingertips)*

I am *(point hand toward heaven)*

The Lord *(make an "L" with your thumb and first finger, place the "L" at shoulder and then across body to waist*

Your God *(Point first finger in front of you at forehead level, draw it up and back down opening the palm OR point toward heaven).*

June 16

The Golden Bracelet, Midweek
By Vicki Wiley

Scripture:
Ephesians 6:1; Genesis 24:14, 34–67

Lesson Aim:
We can trust God to help us make decisions.

Bible Skill:
We can trust our parents to do the right thing for us.

Bible Learning Activity for All Ages: Fathers in the Bible
Invite children to name fathers from the Bible. Examples include:

Noah (father of Ham, Shem, and Japheth)
Abraham (father of Isaac)
David (father of Solomon and many other children)
Jacob (father of Joseph)
Zechariah (father of John the Baptist)
Jesse (father of David)
Joseph (earthly father of Jesus)

Ask: Why do you think these fathers were so special? Invite comments from each child. Bring out the fact that some fathers were famous for themselves; others were famous for their sons.

Enrichment for Younger Children: Then and Now

Today our fathers do lots of different things. In Bible times, the fathers were also very busy.

Today our dads might mow the lawn. What do you think they did to take care of their homes in Bible times?

Today our dads might work at an office. What do you think they did in Bible times to take care of business?

Today our dads might coach soccer. What games do you think dads helped play during Bible times?

Dads do lots of things! ☺

Enrichment for Older Children: History of Father's Day

Explain: This is how Father's Day came to be:

Sonora Louise Smart Dodd of Spokane, Washington, decided that she wanted to set aside a special day to honor fathers in 1909. She wanted to honor her father, William Jackson Smart, who had raised six children on his own after his wife died. Sonora Dodd drew up a petition recommending adoption of a national father's day, and the Spokane Ministerial Association and the local YMCA supported it.

Through Sonora Dodd's efforts, Spokane celebrated the first Father's Day on June 19, 1910. Over the years, many resolutions to make the day an official national holiday were introduced. Finally, in 1972, President Richard M. Nixon signed Father's Day into law. In the United States and Canada, Father's Day falls on the third Sunday in June. ☺

Memory Verse: Ephesians 6:1 ICB

Children, obey your parents the way the Lord wants. This is the right thing to do. The command says, "Honor your father and mother." This is the first command that has a promise with it. The promise is: "Then everything will be well with you, and you will have a long life on the earth."

Alternate version (New King James)
Children, obey your parents in the Lord, for this is right. "Honor your father and mother," which is the first commandment with promise:

June 20

The Golden Bracelet
By Vicki Wiley

Scripture:
Genesis 24:14, 34–67

Lesson Aim:
We can trust God to help us make decisions.

Bible Skill:
We can trust our parents to do the right thing for us.

Bible Lesson: The Gold Bracelet

Needed: Gold bracelet (hidden for now)

Explain: Today I'm going to tell you the story about how someone found a wife. This is the story of how Rebekah became Isaac's wife. This is a true story. It is in the Bible.

Have you ever been married? (no! ! ! !) Well, one day, you will probably want to build love with someone and get married. But do you think you would ever want your mom or dad to pick your husband or wife? Maybe yes. Maybe no. But that's what happened in this story. Listen.

A long time ago, parents did help their children find someone to marry. One father named Abraham decided that it was time for his son Isaac to get married. But there was a problem; there was no one for him to marry where they lived. Abraham wanted him to marry someone who believed in the one true God, but in the place where they lived the people worshiped idols.

So, Abraham sent his servant to find a wife for Isaac. This is how he did it. The servant went 500 miles away to a place called Nahor. He took ten camels with him. It took a long time to get there and he was very tired and thirsty; he stopped at a well to get some water. When he stopped, he prayed and asked God who to choose for Isaac. Before he even finished his prayer, his prayer was answered.

He had asked God to show him who he should choose for Isaac by showing him a sign. He would ask a girl to give him some water and she would not only give him water but would also offer to give his camels water.

Well, that's exactly what happened. A beautiful girl named Rebekah came to the well. She gave him a drink and then she offered to fill the trough with water for his camels. Rebekah was not only kind but also a hard worker, because ten camels can drink a lot of water! God had prepared her heart for this day. She had no way of knowing that she was an answer to prayer.

Then the servant gave her a gold nose ring and two gold arm bracelets for her kindness and asked for a place to stay the night. [Show children the gold bracelet. Explain that women wore nose rings instead of earrings and gold bands on their arms.]

Rebekah ran home and got her brother Laban to come back with her to the well. They invited the servant to their home to meet her father. While they were there, they listened as the servant told all about what he was doing. He asked Rebekah's father if they would agree to let Isaac marry Rebekah. They had never even met! But her father said yes and she agreed to go.

When Isaac finally met Rebekah, the servant knew that he had chosen the right one, the one that God had picked.

 Song Suggestions:

A Dad Like You by Mary Rice Hopkins from "Good Buddies" (Big Steps 4 U 1994)

One Step at a Time Songsheets published by CEF Press, P.O. Box 348, Warrenton, Mo. 63383

Praise His Holy Name by Norm Hewitt from "Ablaze With Praise!" (Revelation Generation Music 2000)

Craft: Father's Day Tool Belt

Needed: For each child a cloth tool bag that ties around the waist, fabric paint.

Say: Today we are going to make a tool belt for your dad (or grandpa). Lay the tool belt flat and guide children to paint it as they wish. Leave it flat for at least one day while it dries completely. If you don't have that much drying time, use markers for fabric instead.

Simplification for Younger Children:

Use markers instead of fabric paint for younger children.

 Special Holiday Activity: Father's Day

Fathers in Bible times had a very different world to live and work in. The father in the Bible was the head of the family and even sometimes called "lord," He was the ruler of the family, often called "master," or "owner." The father had many responsibilities similar to the responsibilities that fathers have today.

First of all, the father was responsible for the spiritual well-being of the family, as well as of the individual members of the family. The father was responsible to teach his children and family about God.

Socially, the father's responsibility was to see that no one took advantage of any member of his family. He also taught his sons how to work; he taught them the same business or "trade" that he was in.

The father was the wage earner and provided all the money the family needed. Sometimes the wife also helped with his occupation, and she may have helped earn money too. Priscilla and Aquilla are two spouses who worked in the same occupation.

Craft / Activity: Nose Rings and Gold Bracelets
Needed: One toilet paper roll per child, gold crayons or paints, glitter, etc.

Ask: Have you ever seen someone with a nose ring? In Bible times, the women often wore nose rings instead of earrings. They also wore bracelets on their arms. Today, we are going to make a gold bracelet like they had in Bible times.

Cut the toilet paper tube in half lengthwise. Then split the piece so that it will fit over the child's arm. Flatten out the piece of cardboard and decorate. The bracelet will return to its original shape on a child's arm.

Father's Day Yummy Cup
Needed: For each child bring a plastic cup, markers, gum, candy, a small notepad, and tissue paper.

Guide children to decorate the outside of the cup with the markers. Show younger ones how to write "Happy Father's Day!" and sign their names. Let children fill the cup with snacks for dad such as some gum, a small note-pad, candy, etc.

Invite children to tell you the fun way they will give this gift to dad (*Sample: Put it in his room to surprise him; set it by his plate*).

Memory Verse: Ephesians 6:1 ICB
Children, obey your parents the way the Lord wants. This is the right thing to do. The command says, "Honor your father and mother." This is the first command that has a promise with it. The promise is: "Then everything will be well with you, and you will have a long life on the earth."

Alternate version (New King James)
Children, obey your parents in the Lord, for this is right. "Honor your father and mother," which is the first commandment with promise:

Prayer Focus:

Dear God, thank you for our parents. We praise you for what they mean to us and we thank you for giving them to us. We want to obey them and honor them as you tell us to do. Amen.

Memory Verse Activity:

Needed: Roll of butcher, banner, or connected computer paper, markers

Say: We are going to make a mural of this verse. Let child with good penmanship write the verse out first in large letters.

Let children draw pictures to illustrate the verse. Then read the verse several times together.

Say: This verse is so important. How do you treat your parents? How do you treat your father? This verse tells us that if we have honor for our parents we will have a long life!

June 23

EEEK Oh, It's Just a Computer Mouse, Midweek
By Karl Bastian

Scripture:
Ephesians 5:1, 2

Lesson Aim:
As a computer mouse guides the computer's activities, so the Holy Spirit should guide us.

Bible Skill:
To learn to follow God's instructions as the Holy Spirit leads.

Bible Learning Activity for Younger Children: Get Plugged In!
Needed: Light with plug (don't plug in).

Say: "Let's turn on this light!" Turn switch on. "Oh, it didn't turn on. Do you know why? What should I do?" Guide children to notice the plug on the floor that is not plugged in. They will say, "Plug it in!"

Respond: "Oh, yeah, I need to plug it in!"

"The light needs to be plugged in to work. Do we need to be plugged in to anything? How about God? We need to be connected to God like this light needs to be plugged in. It works best when it is plugged in—we do best when we are connected to God."

Bible Learning Activity for Older Children:
Ask: What are things that you plug in at home? (*TV, stereo, games, appliances, etc.*) Can any of them work without their plugs?

Say: Our computer works best when it is plugged in and everything is connected properly. Everything that requires electricity works when it is plugged in and not well at all when it isn't. Our Christian life is like that too.

We can have the best spiritual life when we are "plugged in" to Jesus. How can we do that? What would our "cord" be? Let kids think of ideas on their own (*Samples: Pray, talk to God, read the Bible, go to church*). Then stress: the main cord is the Holy Spirit. He is the expression of God that communicates one-on-one with us.

Enrichment for Younger Children:

Needed: Mice made in craft activity and a computer mouse (does not need to be connected)

Say: A computer mouse isn't alive, but a real mouse is. What else is different about them? What is the same? (*Samples: A computer mouse only works or moves when someone moves it, a real mouse moves by itself; a computer mouse helps with working on the computer, a real mouse doesn't know how; a computer mouse has to stay connected to the computer to live, a real mouse stays with its family; a real mouse is created by God, people made the computer mouse.*)

Say: Today you are going to imitate me by playing Simon Says. I will do something and you do it too, but only if I say "Simon says."

Take children through several actions.

Was it easy or hard imitating me? We are supposed to imitate God. Is that hard or easy? How is it like and unlike imitating a person? ☺

Enrichment for Older Children:

Our Bible sermon this Sunday will be about how we should be "imitators of God." If you were imitating something what would you do? Prompt children to pantomime in answer to: Show me what you would do if you imitated:

Riding a horse

Surfing in the ocean

A very old man

A baby crying

Running in a race

A fish in the ocean

A frog in a hopping contest

Jumping over a stream

What would imitating God be like? Let children brainstorm and then pantomime their ideas. ☺

Memory Verse: Ephesians 5:1, 2a ICB

You are God's children whom he loves. So try to be like God. Live a life of love. Love other people just as Christ loved us.

Alternate version (New King James)

Therefore be imitators of God as dear children. And walk in love, as Christ also has loved us and given Himself for us, an offering and a sacrifice to God for a sweet-smelling aroma.

June 27

EEEK Oh, It's Just a Computer Mouse
By Karl Bastian

Scripture:
Ephesians 5:1, 2a

Lesson Aim:
As a computer mouse guides the computer's activities, so the Holy Spirit should guide us.

Bible Skill:
To learn to follow God's instructions as the Holy Spirit leads.

Bible Lesson: Oh, It's Just a Computer Mouse!
Needed: A computer mouse disconnected from a computer.

EEEEEEK!!!! It's a mouse! Oh, it's just a computer mouse. Wow! What a handy little tool! As I move it around, if the mouse goes up, the arrow goes up. If the mouse goes down, the arrow goes down. If the mouse goes to the right, the . . . O.K., O.K., you get it! The arrow does whatever the mouse does. . . . That is, if it is set up right.

Have you ever had your mouse not work? Or work differently than you expected?

One time I was getting really mad at my computer mouse because no matter what I did to the mouse, the little arrow on my screen did NOTHING! Then I found out that the mouse wasn't plugged in. Another time, though, it WAS plugged in, but it was jumping all over the screen like it was a jumping bean! I had to go into the Control Panel screen and re-do all the mouse settings to get it back to working correctly.

Did you know that our relationship with God is a lot like that little arrow and the computer mouse? We are supposed to follow whatever God says.

Song Suggestions:

He Is God by Jana Alayra from "Believin' On" (Montjoy Music 2002)

Little Is Much by Mary Rice Hopkins from "15 Singable Songs" (Big Steps 4 U 1988)

Faith Will Do by Dean-o from "You Got It All" (FKO Music, Inc. 1997)

God's Power Songsheets published by CEF Press, P.O. Box 348, Warrenton, Mo. 63383

Ephesians 5:1 and 2a says, "You are God's children whom he loves. So try to be like God. Live a life of love. Love other people just as Christ loved us" (ICB).

But sometimes we aren't plugged into God. God is giving the instructions, but we aren't listening. It isn't God's fault that our lives go nowhere, (just like that little arrow that was frozen on my screen). We have to plug into God by having a relationship with him, and by reading God's word! Even when we ARE plugged into God, we sometimes mess up—and that is because we are not perfect.

Kids, if we are willing to let God open up the "Control Panel" of our heart, and show us changes we need to make, then we can get back on track again. Your computer mouse probably won't get stuck in a mouse trap, but we CAN get stuck in Sin Traps, so be careful to be "plugged into" God and follow his instructions!

Craft for Younger Children: Mousy Necklace
Needed: Bring for each child a large gray pompom, two google eyes, and black yarn for a tail.

Show children how to make mice by gluing the eyes on the front of the pompom and the tail on the end.

Say: A computer mouse is different from a real mouse, isn't it? Today we are going to make a mouse that looks sort of like a real mouse. Isn't it cute? (Save the mice to use in the following activity.)

Craft for Older Children: Mouse Pad

Needed: thick foam core board cut into 8x8 inch pieces, markers

Say: Today we are going to make a mouse pad that will remind us to be connected to God. Can you think of some ways to decorate it? Samples: We could write "Stay connected to God" or "Plug into Jesus" on it or "Let the Holy Spirit guide."

Let children decorate the mouse pad with the markers.

Plugged In

Needed: For each child bring a square fruit-filled cookie and small stick pretzels.

Say: Being plugged in is the best way to connect to something. Anything electrical will not work if it is not plugged in. Christians cannot truly know God without being "plugged in" to his spirit. Today we are going to make some "plugs" to remind ourselves to be plugged in! Show children how to push two stick pretzels into the end of a cookie to look like a plug. Eat and enjoy!

Prayer Focus:

Dear God, thank you for loving us so much. Please help us to live a life of love, to love other people and show Christ to them. Amen.

Memory Verse: Ephesians 5:1, 2a ICB

You are God's children whom he loves. So try to be like God. Live a life of love. Love other people just as Christ loved us.

Alternate version (New King James)

Therefore be imitators of God as dear children. And walk in love, as Christ also has loved us and given Himself for us, an offering and a sacrifice to God for a sweet-smelling aroma.

Memory Verse Activity: Copy Cats

Today we have learned to be imitators of God. Let's imitate each other as we learn this verse. Divide children into two groups.

Let one group make up motions to the first sentence of the verse while the other group imitates them and says the sentence with the motions.

Let the other group make up motions to the second part while the first group imitates them.

Repeat until the children know the verse.

June 30

It Doesn't Get Any Better Than This!, Midweek
By Johanna Townsend

Scripture:
Galatians 5:1

Lesson Aim:
To help children discover what true freedom is.

Bible Skill:
To help children practice the freedom that comes through Christ.

Bible Learning Activity for Older Children: Red, White, and Blue Bracelet
Needed: Cord for each child, red, white, and blue beads

Say: Today we are going to make a bracelet to remember the colors of our country's freedom and our freedom in Christ.

Show the children how to put a red bead on their cords and while they do so, say: The red will stand for the blood of Christ. Jesus gave his life for us so we could be free from sin; many men gave their lives so we could be free as a nation.

Show the children how to put a blue bead on their cords and while they do so, say: The blue can stand for loyalty. God is loyal to us; he never leaves us and always watches over us.

Show the children how to put a white bead on their cords and while they do so, say: The white can stand for purity and innocence. When we accept Jesus into our hearts and give our lives to him, we are pure and innocent before God.

Now whenever you see these colors in our flag or other patriotic items, you can remember what Jesus has done for us in giving us true freedom.

Simplification for Younger Children:

Let children make the bracelet as stated, but use simpler words in the narrative:

Red stands for strong people working hard and stands for the blood of Jesus.

Blue stands for being loyal to our country and to God. It also stands for God being loyal to us!

White stands for being pure and clean before God, which we are if we accept Jesus as our Savior.

Enrichment for Older Children: Declaration of Independence

You may have heard these words before in school, but they are very important. They are the beginning of a very important document, the Declaration of Independence. Let's read them together.

When in the course of human events it becomes necessary for one people to dissolve the political bands which have connected them with another, and to assume among the powers of the earth, the separate and equal station to which the Laws of Nature and of Nature's God entitle them, a decent respect to the opinions of mankind requires that they should declare the causes which impel them to the separation.

We hold these truths to be self-evident, that all men are created equal, that they are endowed by their Creator with certain unalienable rights, that among these are life, liberty and the pursuit of happiness.—That to secure these rights, governments are instituted among men, deriving their just powers from the consent of the governed.

John Hancock read this to the congress, and they all signed it because they agreed with it.

Today, we can do the same with Jesus Christ. We already have our free country, but if we also want to be really free in our lives—free from sin— we need to know Jesus Christ. Only Jesus can save us from our sin and make us really free. How can we do this? Do we have to be really, really good? No! That won't free us! Do we have to be really, really nice? No! That won't free us! The only thing that will free us is to accept Jesus Christ as our Savior. You can do that by praying with me.

Dear Jesus, thank you for being my Savior. I know that I am a sinner and I know that only you can save me. Please forgive me from my sins now and come into my heart to stay. I love you and I praise you. Amen. ☺

Enrichment for Younger Children: Symbols

Needed: Pictures of symbols of America and symbols of Christianity

What are some of the symbols of our country? Show pictures of a bald eagle, a flag, the statue of liberty, monuments, the White House. Ask why each one is important to us and what it means to us?

Draw some symbols of our Christian life. Say: These are symbols of our Christian life. These symbols are important to us too! They help us remember what we believe.

Prepare a matching game during which children match these symbols with their meanings:

Dove means (Holy Spirit)

The fish means "I'm a Christian" The manger? (where Jesus was born) The Cross? (where Jesus died) The empty tomb (Jesus' resurrection). ☺

Memory Verse: Galatians 5:1a ICB

We have freedom now because Christ made us free!

Alternate version (New King James)
Stand fast therefore in the liberty by which Christ has made us free, and do not be entangled again with a yoke of bondage.

July 4 Independence Day

It Doesn't Get Any Better Than This!
By Johanna Townsend

Scripture:
Galatians 5:1

Lesson Aim:
To help children discover what true freedom is.

Bible Skill:
To help children practice the freedom that comes through Christ.

Bible Lesson: It Doesn't Get Any Better Than This

Needed: A Bible, a bird cage, and a picture of a woman wearing a burka which is the type of head covering that women wore during the time of the Taliban government in Afghanistan.

Have you ever owned a pet bird? Let the children tell you about birds they have owned. Did you keep it in a cage similar to this one? Wouldn't it be fun to let the bird out of the cage and feel the tickle of little feet as it walks up and down your arm? (Wait for the responses.) Originally God created birds to fly freely throughout the earth but men decided they could make good pets and designed cages to put them in.

Like the birds, God created men to live freely. However men live less free in some world countries than in others. The citizens of the U.S. enjoy much freedom yet in some countries harsh laws make day-to-day living difficult for the citizens there. In America the right to live freely is protected and guaranteed by law. Thank God for the freedoms we have in America!

Have someone model the covering used by the women of Afghanistan or show a picture. As they do so, say: Not long ago Afghanistan was ruled by a group called the Taliban. The Taliban government made unfair laws demanding all women traveling away from home must cover up their entire body leaving only openings for eyes in the headpiece. The coverings called burka looked like individual tents. Women were also forbidden to work and girls were not allowed to attend school. Boys might think these girls were lucky. But girls in Afghanistan wanted to go to school and many attended ones taught in secret by women. Such reports sound unbelievable don't they, but unfortunately they were true!

Ask: Who do you think is the most free: a person living in the U.S.A., a person living in Afghanistan, or a Christian? (Give the children time to discuss this.) The answer is the Christian. Why? (Read the Bible passage Galatians 5:1.) God originally created man to be free to live in a place called the Garden of Eden. Man had perfect freedom living there and was given only one rule to obey which was to not eat the fruit of one tree.

But Adam and Eve disobeyed that rule BIG TIME and were banished from that perfect garden where life was easy and free. They lived outside that garden struggling with problems never experienced before. However God's great love compelled him to give people one more chance to obtain forever freedom. This time God sent his son, Jesus, to be born on earth as a baby, to live a sinless life, to minister to the sick and needy, and to die for the sins of everyone who believed he was the Son of God.

So you see boys and girls those that become believers and followers of Jesus have freedom which lasts forever making them citizens of two places: the country they live in and in heaven.

Today we celebrate the Fourth of July. We remember the freedoms we have in America. Christians in America have the best of the best; a free country to live in and the forever freedom waiting in heaven. It just doesn't get any better than this, now does it!

 Song Suggestions:

America the Beautiful Traditional

God Bless America Traditional

I Will Fight This Fight by Jana Alayra from "Jump into the Light" (Montjoy Music 1995)

Running for the Prize by Mary Rice Hopkins from "15 Singable Songs" (Big Steps 4 U 1988)

Craft for Younger Children: Fourth of July Flag
Needed: Red, white, and blue construction paper, scissors, glue.

Cut out strips of red construction paper and then cut out a square of blue construction paper.

Guide children to glue the blue square onto the top left side of the white construction paper (taking up about 1/4 of the white construction paper).

Next guide them to glue the strips of red construction paper onto a sheet of white construction paper. Then paste stars onto the blue square.

 Craft for Older Children: Patriotic Pinwheels
Needed: For each child bring a 5" square of colored paper, a corsage pin, a new pencil, scissors, and markers.

Preparation: cut the square 3 inches from each corner toward the center, leaving the center uncut. Decorate as you wish, with patriotic designs. Fold an outside point of each cut toward the center, and using the pin, pin the four points to the eraser of the new pencil. This forms a pinwheel.

Alternate Craft for Older Children: Safe Sparklers
Needed: 3 pipe cleaners for each child (sparkly silver ones), glitter, scissors.

Guide children to cut two of the pipe cleaners into fourths and roll in white glue. Sprinkle with glitter, let dry.

When dry twist all eight pieces to a whole pipe cleaner to look like sparkler.

Alternate Craft: Fourth of July Headband
Needed: Stars cut from red, white, and blue construction paper. Head band cut from white construction paper long enough to fit on the head of the child.

Let children decorate the band with stars. Allow to dry. Then encourage children to put it on.

Special Holiday Activity: Fourth of July Flag Craft
Needed: Red, white, and blue paper strips 1" x 4", stapler, 3'
dowel rod.

Guide children to make paper chains from the strips in these configurations:

Begin by stapling 6 blue strips together, followed by 10 red strips. The second row should have 6 blue followed by 10 white. The third row should have 6 blue followed by 10 red. The fourth row should have 6 blue followed by 10 white. The fifth row should have 6 blue followed by 10 red. The sixth row should have 6 blue followed by 10 white. The seventh row should have 6 blue followed by 10 red. The eighth, tenth, and twelfth rows will be 16 white. The ninth, eleventh, and thirteenth rows will be 16 red.

String the first link of each chain onto the dowel rod and let the rest hang to form a flag.

Flag Cake

Needed: One rectangle cake iced white, blue frosting, star candies, red licorice.

Complete the look of a flag by icing the top left-hand section of the cake blue. Add star candy to the blue icing. Use red licorice for stripes on the cake.

Say: Today we are celebrating our freedom! This cake looks like a flag, the flag has seven red stripes and six white stripes. The stars are in a blue square that symbolizes the sky.

Prayer Focus:

Dear God, thank you for the freedom that we have in the United States. We thank you for all those that paid the price for that freedom. We also thank you for your Son, Christ Jesus, who gave us the best freedom that we could ever have. Amen.

Memory Verse: Galatians 5:1a ICB

We have freedom now because Christ made us free.

Alternate version (New King James)
Stand fast therefore in the liberty by which Christ has made us free, and do not be entangled again with a yoke of bondage.

Memory Verse Activity: Being Free!

Rope off a corner of the room large enough for all the children to fit into. Choose one child to be "it". Choose another children to be "Freedom Fighter."

"It" tries to free the children by touching their hands. If "It" can touch their hands and they can run across the room and touch the other wall they will remain "free." However, if the Freedom Fighter touches them, they must go back.

When everyone is free say, "How did it feel to be free? It feels really good to be free! But sometimes Satan tries to take away our freedom, like the Freedom Fighter did in this game. We need to remember to follow only God so that we keep our freedom.

Repeat the verse after each round of the game.

July 7

A Letter from God, Midweek

By Karl Bastian

Scripture:
Psalm 119:15–16

Lesson Aim:
Children will know that God talks to them through the Bible.

Bible Skill:
Children will establish a habit of reading the Bible daily.

Bible Learning Activity for Younger Children:
Sing The B.I.B.L.E. (traditional song)

The B-I-B-L-E. That's the book for me. I stand alone on the Word of God—the B.I.B.L.E.

Say: Why do you think the Bible is so important? Why should we read it?

Use children's responses to emphasize that we read the Bible because it is God's word. He gave it to us so we would know all about him. The Bible is a very special book!

Bible Learning Activity for Older Children: Making a Scroll
Needed: For each child bring two 10" dowel rods, a length of off-white paper or parchment, and glue.

Show children how to make a scroll by gluing the dowel rods onto the edges of the paper.

Practice writing some Hebrew letters:

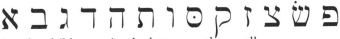

Let the children write the letters on the scroll.

Enrichment for Younger Children: Letters!

Needed: One letter or postcard for each child, made out personally to them.

Ask: Have you ever received a letter? I have one for you today. This letter was written just for you. It is addressed to you and it has special information just for you.

Let children look at their letters and read them if you have time. Say: God's word, the Bible is like this letter. God wrote it just for you! ☺

Enrichment for Older Children: Dead Sea Scrolls

Tell this historical event: In 1947 a very important discovery was made near the Dead Sea. A shepherd boy threw a little rock up into a cave on the hillside. When it went inside the cave, it made a funny noise, a noise that sounded like it hit some pottery. The boy went to investigate and he discovered one of the greatest archaeological finds in history; what is now known as the Dead Sea Scrolls.

The Dead Sea Scrolls contain copies of every book of the Old Testament except Esther. They were older than any other manuscripts that had ever been found and were in very good condition. These scrolls have helped us to know that the writings in the Bible were never changed; they have always been the same. ☺

Memory Verse: Psalm 119:15–16 ICB

I think about your orders and study your ways. I enjoy obeying your demands. And I will not forget your word.

Alternate version (New King James)
I will meditate on Your precepts, and contemplate Your ways. I will delight myself in Your statutes; I will not forget Your word.

July 11

A Letter from God
By Karl Bastian

Scripture:
Psalm 119:15–16

Lesson Aim:
Children will know that God talks to them through the Bible.

Bible Skill:
Children will establish a habit of reading the Bible daily.

Bible Lesson: "A Letter from God"
Needed: A sealed envelope addressed to yourself from a very good friend who lives far away (stamp should be canceled to show it really has been mailed).

Show an envelope that you received in the mail. Show that it is addressed to you and explain how excited you are to get this letter from a good friend that you have not heard from in a long time! Talk about what great friends you are. You can even tell a funny story from the past.

Explain that you wonder what is inside. You are so eager to learn how this friend is doing, what this friend is up to. This friend is so special and important to you! (By now the kids should be telling you to open the letter and read it, if not, ask, "How could I find out what they are up to, or how they are doing?" They will suggest opening the letter and reading it.)

Tease that: Oh, no! You would never open this letter. You like it just the way it is. You like the stamp, and the handwriting is so nice. And you feel so special that you received this letter. Why would you open it? You just want to carry it around with you, not actually OPEN it and READ it!

As you drag it out the children will press you even harder to open it. Ask:

Do you think I am silly to say I love this friend, and desire to know my friend better, but not even bother to open the letter my friend wrote to me?"

They will answer YES! Explain that you did this to point out how silly people are who say they love God, and want to know him better, but they never even bother to open the letter that he wrote to them—the Bible! They may carry it around, but they never bother to OPEN it and READ it!" Explain that the Bible is like a letter from God to us, but it does no good if we don't take the time to sit down, open it, and read it.

Encourage children to establish a habit of reading God's letter every day. Explain that they won't always feel like doing this, but to do so anyway, just like eating or sleeping or brushing their teeth. Explain that this is a daily "DISCIPLINE" and helps them to live well as a DISCIPLE of Jesus.

 Song Suggestions:

The B.I.B.L.E. Traditional

God Wrote Us A Letter by Mary Rice Hopkins from "Come Meet Jesus" (Big Steps 4 U 1990)

G-Mail! by Dean-o from *Soul Surfin'* (FKO Music Inc. 1999)

Craft for Younger Children: The B.I.B.L.E.
Needed: Black and white thin sheets of craft foam, construction paper, thin gold ribbon. Cut for each child book shapes, with the black foam a little larger than the white foam to look like an open Bible with the cover larger than the pages.

Together with the children, write: I will not forget your word on the white pages. Show them how to add the ribbon for a marker.

Say: God's word is so important! We need to read our Bibles every day to really know what God is telling us. Will you read your Bible every day? Show children a book to start with, such as the book of John.

Craft for Older Children: Elementary Craft: The B.I.B.L.E.
Needed: Black and white thin sheets of craft foam, construction paper, thin gold ribbon. Cut for each child book shapes, with the black foam a little larger than the white foam to look like an open Bible with the cover larger than the pages.

Have children write: I will not forget your word on the white pages. Invite them to tell about a favorite Bible verse and add those words to the white pages. Show them how to add the ribbon for a marker.

Say: God's word is so important! We need to read our Bibles every day to really know what God is telling us. Will you read your Bible every day? Show children a book to start with, such as the book of John.

God's Letter

Needed: For each child prepare one white rectangle cake with an icing postage stamp made from a tiny square cookie on the top right hand corner. Bring decorating icing.

Snack

When snack time comes, write with icing each child's name on the snack cake and give that cake to the child.

Say: What does this remind you of? Yes, you're right! It looks like a letter! God wrote us a letter that that we call the Bible. The Bible is full of information that we need to live our lives and be happy. God's word is the Bible!

Prayer Focus:

Dear God, thank you so much for your word! Thank you for sending us the words you want us to know. Help us to read and follow what you have told us to do. Amen.

Memory Verse: Psalm 119:15–16 ICB

I think about your orders and study your ways. I enjoy obeying your demands. And I will not forget your word.

Alternate version (New King James)

I will meditate on Your precepts, and contemplate Your ways. I will delight myself in Your statutes; I will not forget Your word.

Bible Memory Verse Activity:

Make up a chant for this verse using a cadence as follows:

Hit knees twice as you say

I think about (clap twice as you say)

Your orders and (snap three times as you say)

study your ways.

Keep doing it until children can do it without help.

July 14

No Other Gods, Midweek
By Ivy Beckwith

Scripture:
Exodus 32:7, 8

Lesson Aim:
God wants to be our only God.

Bible Skill:
Kids will understand what a false god or idol is.

Bible Learning Activity for Younger Children: Statues or Idols?
Needed: Blocks and cow (or other animal) toy.

Let children build a statue with the blocks and put the toy cow on top.

Say: Have you ever seen a statue? Sometimes there are statues at parks or at museums. This is a silly statue. Some people worship statues like this and then it is called an "idol". Worshiping idols is silly. But we should only worship God, the true God. The Bible tells us not to make gods or idols that we worship.

It's kind of silly to think that people pray to idols, isn't it? We pray to the TRUE GOD! That is not silly at all!

Bible Learning Activity for Older Children: Journal from the Promised Land
Needed: Paper and pencils, pictures of ancient Egypt.

Say: What do you think it would have been like to be an Israelite in Bible times? What do you think you would have done when people around you started worshiping idols? Let's pretend that this is your journal page and you are telling your friends about what happened. What are some of the things you can write? (*Samples: It was scary when I saw the idols; I didn't like it when they started worshiping the idols.*)

Have kids write a journal page from the perspective of the Israelites when they were afraid Moses had disappeared and left them all alone. Give them suggestions if needed.

Enrichment for Older Children: Idol Worship in Bible Times

People that lived in Bible times often worshiped idols. Because of this, God warned his people not to worship idols like their neighbors did. An idol is usually a statue of a person or animal or thing. Idols are easy to worship because they are easy to see. But idols are fake gods. They can't help, or comfort, or rule, or create a world. They are not the true God, but people still worshiped them. Instead of worshiping the true God, they worshiped "idols."

Idols were made in different ways and of various materials. Sometimes they were carved and sometimes they were molded. Some were made of metal or wood, and others were poured into a mold or shaped by hand. The silver or gold idols were poured, but the clay ones could be shaped by hand. The image in Nebuchadnezzar's dream (Dan. 2:32–33) was of gold, silver, bronze, iron, and clay.

Kids your age don't usually worship this type of idol, do they? We don't make things just to worship them. But sometimes we do worship idols. We might worship an expensive toy or another thing that is already made. Ask: Can a Nintendo be an idol? Can clothes be an idol? Can special shoes be an idol? How would you know if something had become an idol in your life? You can tell that something is very important to you and may have become an idol if:

You don't mind if someone else gets their feelings hurt over it.

You think about it often.

It is the only thing that you want to do (or the only thing you want to wear).

Whenever things that we have become more important than God or more important than people, we need to be careful that we are not making idols out of them. If you think something has become an idol for you, pray and ask God to help you change your mind and heart about it. You might want to get rid of that something. Talk to your parents about it. ☺

Enrichment for Younger Children: Idol Worship in Bible Times

In Bible times people worshiped idols but God didn't want them to do that. God knew that the idols were not real and God is real! God told the people to worship only him.

The idols that people worshiped were made of metal or wood, or clay. Have you ever made anything with clay? It's okay to make anything you want with clay. That's okay with God. God just doesn't want you to WORSHIP what you make! To worship is to think that something is stronger and better and more valuable than you are.

God wants us to worship only him, because he is the true God. He is the one that can answer prayers and talk to us. ☺

Memory Verse: Exodus 32:7b, 8a ICB

...Your people, the people you brought out of the land of Egypt, have done a terrible sin. They have quickly turned away from the things I commanded them to do.

Alternate version (New King James)

... For your people whom you brought out of the land of Egypt have corrupted themselves. They have turned aside quickly out of the way which I commanded them.

July 18

No Other Gods
By Ivy Beckwith

Scripture:
Exodus 32: 7, 8

Lesson Aim:
God wants to be our only God.

Bible Skill:
Kids will understand what a false god or idol is.

Bible Lesson: No Other God

Gather children together and say, "Tell me some of the things kids your age just *have* to have." (allow for answers) Ask: "Why do you think it's so important to some kids to have these things?" I think sometimes we want certain things or clothes because we think having these things will make us into someone who other people will like. Or we think having these things will make us happy or make us feel special and loved. But we need to remember our Bible tells us that only by following and loving God and being nice to people will we feel happy, special, and loved.

It hurts God when we worship things, clothes, or other people instead of God.

There is a story in the Bible about how God's people, the Israelites, thought that something other than God would give them what they needed and make them happy and help them be safe. Moses, the people's leader, had gone up to the top of a mountain to meet with God and he was gone for a long time. The people feared something happened to Moses and they felt God had left them. So the people went to Moses' helper, Aaron, and asked him to help them make new gods to worship because they didn't know what happened to Moses. Now Aaron should have known better. Aaron knew God and Moses better than the Israelites and he should have known God was still with the people. But, instead, Aaron went along with what the Israelites wanted.

Aaron told the people to bring all their gold jewelry. He melted all the jewelry and made a statue in the shape of a calf. When the people saw the golden calf they immediately named it to be their god. So Aaron built a place where people could come to worship the golden calf and proclaimed that the next day would be a festival where the people could come to worship this new god. The next day the Israelites had a big party to celebrate their new god.

Well, God, the one true God, was watching all this happen and God was not happy. He called to Moses and said, "Moses, you better get off this mountain right away. Those people who you brought out of Egypt are out of control. They have turned away from trusting and worshiping me for their lives and they have made themselves another god. I'm losing my patience with them. I'm very angry with them and I'm thinking that maybe I need to choose another group of people to make my own." God's reaction to what the Israelite's were doing frightened Moses so he tried to persuade God to give these people another chance. Moses reminded God of the promises God made to the Israelites' ancestors Abraham, Isaac, and Jacob to make a great nation out of their children. So God decided not to turn his back on the Israelites.

Why do you think what the Israelites did caused God to be angry with them? Why do you think the Israelites thought they needed to make another god? Had God really gone away from them?

Explain that idols are easy to worship because they are easy to see. But idols are fake gods. They can't help, or comfort, or rule, or create a world. They are not the true God and when people are giving attention to them they will make wrong choices and hurt both God and people. Today we worship idols when we think that things or other people can give us the things only God can give us. Because God loves us he wants us to depend on him for everything we need.

Song Suggestions:

He's the One by Dean-o from "Soul Surfin'" (FKO Music, Inc. 1999)

He Can Do by Mary Rice Hopkins from "Kids Kamp" (Big Steps 4 U 1999)

Fix No Other God by Kurt Johnson, a.k.a. MrJ from "Kid Possible" (Kurt Johnson 1995)

God's Power Songsheets published by CEF Press, P.O. Box 348, Warrenton, Mo. 63383

 Craft for Older Children: Statue Making

Needed: A variety of construction materials; paper tubes, wooden pieces, paper, springs—whatever you can find. Pictures of Bible times idols.

Display on the table the construction items you have gathered. Bring the children to the table and say: We worship the true God, the only real God. Other people worship "idols" which are gods that they make. What is the difference between an idol and a statue? (people worship idols) Today we are all going to make statues. Let children make statues as they wish.

When the statues are finished say: Some people take statues like this that they make themselves and they worship them. They ask these things for help, they give these things their attention, and they make these things more important than the feelings of people around them. When they worship them, they become "idols."

Ask: If you prayed to this statue that you made, what would happen? Yes, nothing! Nothing would happen! NOTHING! But the idols that people make are not much different than the statues you have made—they might make them out of gold or carve them from stone, but they have no power, just like the ones you made.

Who is the true God? Why is the true God different from these statues? (*Sample: Because he can help you; because he can comfort; because he can create; because no one made him, he has always been here; because our God loves us and is powerful; because our God cares about us and hears our prayers.*) God loves us, God hears our prayers, and God wants us to worship only him.

Craft for Younger Children: Worship Only God
Needed: Colored chalk, construction paper.

Say: Today we have been talking about the true God. We don't know what God looks like, but we all have an idea in our mind. Can you draw me a picture of what God looks like?

Let children draw whatever they want. Invite each to tell you what they have drawn. Say something good about each drawing.

Say: We don't know what God looks like, but we do know that God loves us very much and God wants us to love him too! We don't have to see Him to love him.

Ten Commandments Crackers

Needed: Graham, crackers, alphabet cereal, icing for glue.

 Show the children how to break the graham crackers to make tablets (similar to Ten Commandments). Let children glue the alphabet letters to write commandments on crackers.

Ask: The Ten Commandments tell us not to worship idols. Why do you think that is one of God's rules?

Stress that God wants us to love him and only worship him, and that only he can help and comfort. It is very important to only worship the true God, the only God that watches over you and answers your prayers.

Prayer Focus:

Dear God, we love you and we praise you and we know that you are the only God, the true God. Thank you for loving us and taking care of us. Thank you for answering our prayers and for being our God. Amen.

Memory Verse: Exodus 32:7b, 8a ICB

…Your people, the people you brought out of the land of Egypt, have done a terrible sin. They have quickly turned away from the things I commanded them to do.

Alternate version (New King James)

. . . For your people whom you brought out of the land of Egypt have corrupted themselves. They have turned aside quickly out of the way which I commanded them.

Memory Verse Activity: Scrambled Verse

Needed: Small stickable note paper.

Since this is a long verse, write the entire verse on a poster board or white board.

Then write the words again on stickable paper, one word on each paper. Arrange in scrambled fashion next to correct verse. Let the children reassemble the words correctly as you say the verse together.

July 21

God's Masterpiece, Midweek

By Mary Rice Hopkins

Scripture:
Psalm 139:13–14

Lesson Aim:
We are God's treasure and masterpiece.

Bible Skill:
Kids will realize Jesus treasures them.

Bible Learning Activity for Older Children: Creating You!

Needed: Chenille wires (pipe cleaners), plastic spoons, plastic eyes, yarn scraps, other assorted craft supplies.

Put out all craft items and say: I want everyone to make a little person, a "mini you". Make it look however you want, just so it shows us how you look or think or feel.

Give children time to create their person. Circulate and affirm the children's ideas.

Ask: What makes your person special? Is it the face, the hair, the silly way it looks? Partly. But no matter what anyone says, it is special to you because you made it, isn't it?

Ask: What would you do or feel if someone squashed or bent your person? After several answers, point out that because you made it, you want no one harming it.

God made you and treasures you even more than you treasure the little person you just made. He is proud of you, cares about what happens to you, and wants no one to hurt you. You are so special to God and always will be! [NOTE: Be cautious about saying God made children just the way he wants them because children in wheelchairs will wonder why God created them so they can't run. Such disabilities are from this imperfect world, not from God's hand.]

Simplification for Younger Children:

Needed: Chenille wires.

Show children how to make people out of chenille wires. After each child makes one, ask: "What makes your person special? Is it the face, the hair, the silly way it looks? No matter what anyone says, it is special to you because you made it, isn't it?

Ask: What would you do or feel if someone squashed or bent your person? After several answers, point out that because you made it, you want no one harming it.

God made you and treasures you even more than you treasure the little person you just made. He is proud of you, cares about what happens to you, and wants no one to hurt you. You are so special to God and always will be!

Enrichment for Older Children:

Tell this story and encourage children to shape with play clay a piece of pottery you describe in the story: Back in Bible times the Israelite people made pottery in a place called Canaan. Because pottery does not decay many archaeologists (people who dig up old things to find out about people) are still able to find pieces of pottery.

Israelites made lamps, bowls, saucers, plates, and cooking pots of various sizes. They also made, jugs and decanters for holding and pouring liquids. They made fancy glasses called chalices or goblets. The people baked some types of pottery. This gave it a glossy finish, usually red in color. The people painted some with geometric patterns, while others had pictures of human-headed lions, palm trees, bulls, or fish.

By the time Jesus came along, the pottery was much nicer. The vessels were made of finer clays and gave evidence of better firing techniques. They were masterpieces that were used for eating and cooking!

Invite the children to show the pieces of "pottery" that they shaped from clay. Ask: Why do you treasure what you made? (If children do not treasure what they made, suggest they reshape it so they do treasure it.) Did you know that God finds you special because He made you? ☺

Enrichment for Younger Children: Fingerprints

Needed: Washable ink pad and paper, wet wipes.

Ask: Have you ever made your own fingerprints? Let's make some now. Show children how to put their thumb into a washable inkpad and then press it onto paper to leave a finger print. Clean off every thumb with a wet wipe.

Encourage the children to compare their thumbprints to the others and find two that match. Ask: Are any of them the same?

After several answers, point out that every person's fingerprint is different. Say: When God made you he made you uniquely. You are different from everybody else. Your fingerprint is unique and different from everybody else too. You are God's masterpiece! ☺

Memory Verse: Psalm 139:14 ICB

I praise you because you made me in an amazing and wonderful way. What you have done is wonderful.

Alternate version (New King James)

I will praise You, for I am fearfully and wonderfully made; Marvelous are Your works, And that my soul knows very well.

July 25

God's Masterpiece
By Mary Rice Hopkins

Scripture:
Psalm 139:13–14

Lesson Aim:
We are God's treasure and masterpiece.

Bible Skill:
Kids will realize Jesus treasures them.

Bible Lesson: You Are God's Masterpiece
Needed: A photo or picture of a famous piece of art.

Tell this story: Have you ever been to a museum? There are famous paintings in museums that are hundreds of years old! People will stand in line just to see the paintings. This (show picture) is a famous painting. People come to see it because it is called a "Masterpiece". That means a master artist made it. It is a piece of art from that master. People want to see it because not just anyone could make something like that. It is a priceless treasure. What do you think is special about it? Do you like the way it looks? Sometimes observers don't like or understand the masterpiece, but when the master teaches them about why and how it was created, they like it more.

A masterpiece is a priceless treasure for many reasons. First of all, the artist made the painting very special. The artist may have even signed it or put a special mark on it. It may become even MORE valuable after the artist dies.

Sometimes paintings in museums are so special that guards are posted to protect them. Guards stand near the paintings every hour of every day. If you moved too close to the painting, the guards would stop you. If you tried to touch the painting, the guards would make you leave the museum. They don't want anything to harm the paintings.

Did you know that YOU are a priceless treasure? You are! You are more valuable than those famous paintings. In fact you are an original! You are a masterpiece! There is only one like you in the whole world! Your master creator is God himself.

The greatest artist in the world, God, designed you. He created you and put His signature on you. Every hair on your head, every freckle on your face, the shape of your nose, the color of your eyes, the shade of your skin is special to God. It says so in the Psalms. We are so valuable to God that he watches over us every moment of every day. So, remember who made you and that you are God's Masterpiece! [NOTE: Be cautious about saying God made children just the way he wants them because children in wheelchairs will wonder why God created them so they can't run. Such disabilities are from this imperfect world, not from God's hand.]

 Song Suggestions:

I'm Not Too Little Songsheets published by CEF Press, P.O. Box 348, Warrenton, Mo. 63383

Purest of God by Kurt Johnson, a.k.a. MrJ from "Pure Gold" (Mr. J Music 1995)

Miracle by Mary Rice Hopkins from "Juggling Mom" (Big Steps 4 U 1999)

He's Got Plans by Dean-o from "Soul Surfin'" (FKO Music, Inc., 1999)

Craft for Younger Children: Little Masterpiece
Needed: Baby wipes, chalk.
            Guide children to draw with chalk onto baby wipes. Drawing on baby wipes is a little harder than drawing on paper but the drawings do not smudge. When they are finished say: These are beautiful pictures! Can you tell me what you drew? Let each child describe his or her picture to you.

These are all masterpieces. You are the master who created them. You created a masterpiece! When God created you, God created a masterpiece too!

Craft for Older Children: Uniquely Yours!
Needed: For each child bring about five wide craft sticks, and crayons or markers.

Line up the craft sticks side by side to form a square, tape across the back of all five sticks to hold them together and then turn it over. Guide the children to draw on their squares of wood.

When they finish their creations, remove the tape. They now have a "puzzle" that they have drawn. Encourage them to take it apart and put it back together several times.

Say: Each of you has created a masterpiece! No one else can draw one just like yours, can they? But your masterpiece can get mixed up if the pieces are not in the right order. Sometimes we people mess up God's masterpiece: we aren't as nice as he created us to be, we don't take good care of the bodies he gave us, someone else might even push us down so we skin a knee. But with God's help, we can put things back in the order He created them to be.

Graham Cracker Masterpieces

Needed: Graham crackers, different colors of icing in tubes, and sprinkles.

 Give each child a graham cracker. Let children "create" a masterpiece with icing and sprinkles on their crackers.

Say: What you have created is beautiful and ready to eat! You have made your snack just the way you like it, with the colors you wanted and the amount of icing you wanted. God made you wonderful, too. You can serve God just the way you are because you are wonderfully made! [NOTE: Be cautious about saying God made children just the way he wants them because children in wheelchairs will wonder why God created them so they can't run. Such disabilities are from this imperfect world, not from God's hand.]

Prayer Focus:

Dear God, thank you for making me. Thank you for caring about me in an amazing and wonderful way. I praise you and love you for making me in such an amazing way. Amen.

Memory Verse: Psalm 139:14 ICB

I praise you because you made me in an amazing and wonderful way. What you have done is wonderful.

Alternate version (New King James)
I will praise You, for I am fearfully and wonderfully made; Marvelous are Your works, and that my soul knows very well.

Memory Verse Activity:
Needed: One poster board, markers, scissors.

On one side of the poster board print the memory verse in large letters so that the entire board is covered with letters.

On the other side, let children draw a mural with markers. Say: Today we are going to make a mural with all our pictures on it. Please draw yourself doing your favorite activity.

When children are finished, cut poster board into large pieces creating a large jigsaw puzzle. (Make pieces large.) Let children put together the puzzle first using the mural they made and then turn pieces over and let them put together the memory verse.

Say: God made you in an amazing and wonderful way, just like our verse says. You are good at . . . (comment on each child referencing the action they drew in the picture). Because God made you, you can know that you are WONDERFUL!

July 28

How Many Apples Are in a Seed?, Midweek
By Judy Comstock

Scripture:
Proverbs 3:9; 2 Corinthians 9:6

Lesson Aim:
We receive blessings from God in the measure that we give.

Bible Skill:
Children will learn the concept of tithing (giving 10% of income).

Bible Learning Activity for Younger Children: Apple Printing
Needed: For every child bring one apple cut with a lateral cut so you can see the "star" in the core, red, and green paint, and paper.

Place red and green paint in shallow containers. Show children how to use the apple dipped into the paint as a "stamp" to make a picture with the apple.

Say: Apples are really special, aren't they? They taste good, they make great juice, and they have lots of vitamins in them. God gave us apples and apple seeds to plant. God is good!

Bible Learning Activity for Older Children: Scales and Weights
Needed for each child: Two tongue depressors, two small cups (smaller the better), a six inch length of string, tape, seeds or kernels, and a hole punch.

Show children how to put the tongue depressors together to form one strong piece of wood. Punch holes in the sides of the cups and string the string through the holes, tie a knot and tape across the length of the tongue depressors to form a "scale".

Say: In Bible times, they weighed things with scales like this. They put something in one bucket that weighed a certain amount. Then they balanced the weights by putting the seeds or grains in the other side with the same amount.

Let children try it out. Ask: Do you think this is a good way to do it?

Enrichment for Older Children: Bible Times Coins

Explain that coins were included frequently in the Bible. These are the most common coins:

Talent: It was worth the same as an ox, so the ox-talents were pellets or rings of gold weighing 8.5 grams (.29 oz.).

Sheckel: The story of Joseph tells us that the patriarchs used silver pieces of a shekel weight.

Denarius: A denarius was a soldier's daily wage. It was the wage mentioned in the parable of the laborers in the vineyard (Matt. 20:9–10, 13). It was worth about 44 cents today. This coin was also used to pay tribute to the emperor. Jesus recognized it as being Caesar's due (Matt. 22:19–21). Asked whether it was lawful to pay tribute to Caesar, Jesus said: "Show me the tribute money" (Matt. 22:19). The tax coin or *denarius* was shown to Him. It had the image of the emperor on its face.

Pieces of Silver: Jesus told His disciples to take no money (silver) with them when He sent them out two by two (Luke 9:3). Judas was paid 30 pieces of silver to betray Jesus (Matt. 26:15; 27:3, 5. These references cite Zechariah 11:12–13, which did not refer specifically to coins).

Widow's Mite: One of the most famous givers in the New Testament was the poor widow (Mark 12:41–44). She contributed two mites which were worth about one-sixteenth of a soldier's daily pay. Yet the widow's gift prompted Jesus' highest praise. ☺

Memory Verse: 2 Corinthians 9:6 ICB

Remember this: The person who plants a little will have a small harvest. But the person who plants a lot will have a big harvest.

Alternate version (New King James)
But this I say: He who sows sparingly will also reap sparingly, and he who sows bountifully will also reap bountifully.

Enrichment for Younger Children: Planting the Seeds

Needed: A large variety of seeds, microscope or magnifying glasses, and a watermelon cut into small pieces (one for each child).

Let children look at the seeds and compare the different ones using the microscope, the magnifying glasses, and their own eyes.

Ask: What are the differences between these seeds? What is each one for? Do you recognize any of them? What grows from these seeds?

Focus attention on the watermelon. Let them eat and while they are eating have them place all the watermelon seeds into a single bowl.

Say: Let's guess how many seeds may be in the bowl. Take guesses from children and then count the seeds and then say: "Isn't it amazing that when we planted just one watermelon seed we got this delicious watermelon and all these additional watermelon seeds. If we planted all these seeds, we would have even more watermelon and more seeds!" ☺

August 1

How Many Apples Are in a Seed?
By Judy Comstock

Scripture:
Proverbs 3:9; 2 Corinthians 9:6

Lesson Aim:
We receive blessings from God in the measure that we give.

Bible Skill:
Children will learn the concept of tithing (giving 10% of income).

Bible Lesson: The Rule of Sowing and Reaping
Needed: 1 whole apple and 1 apple cut into 6 wedges.

Explain: The word "sow" in the Bible means to plant seeds. If a farmer plants ten baskets of wheat seeds, he expects to get more than ten baskets when he cuts the wheat at harvest time. If we put money into a savings account, we expect to earn interest on the money. That is the rule of sowing and reaping—planting and gathering. Giving money to God is like planting seeds. Giving to God will result in a reward. It will meet the needs of others.

That may sound confusing. Perhaps this apple can help us understand how God blesses our giving. *(Show the children the whole apple.)* What's inside an apple? *(Accept all appropriate answers including seeds, pulp, white stuff.)* Then say: Yes, an apple has all that, and we will focus on the seeds.

Ask: How many seeds are in an apple? *(The answers will vary. Accept the range of numbers.)* Let's look inside this apple and count how many seeds it holds. *(Using fingernail or pointed pick, release the seeds from the apple core previously cut into wedges. Involve the children in counting the seeds.)*

Ask: Now, I have another question for you. How many apples are in one seed? *(Accept the numbers offered.)* That is a difficult question to answer. The number of apples in one seed is very large because each one of these seeds can become what? *(An apple tree.)* That's right, a tree can grow from each seed and year after year each tree produces hundreds of apples. You can count the seeds in an apple, but you cannot count the apples in a seed.

Jesus described some guidelines about giving. He said that you are not to give money in a big showy way, so that people will notice you. People may clap their hands and cheer because of the amount you give, but that may be your only reward. Instead, give money and gifts secretly to help meet the needs of the poor, to meet the needs of missionaries, to pay for things that will help your church tell others the Good News of Jesus Christ such as rooms and light and paper and books. Giving secretly means you do not tell everyone around you how much you are giving. If we give secretly to God's work, our Father in Heaven will reward us.

God's rewards are better than applause from people. God's rewards are overflowing blessings. He might give you more money so you can happily give it away. His reward might be never running out of food. The reward you receive may be creative ideas that will help you be successful in your work. God has different ways of rewarding our giving and they are all good.

 Song Suggestions:

Good News Songsheets published by CEF Press, P.O. Box 348, Warrenton, Mo. 63383

It Started With an Egg by Mary Rice Hopkins from "In My Garden" (Big Steps 4 U 1995)

Less of Me, Mr. Bill, "When I Grow Up" (Mr. Bill Music 1997)

You're in My Heart to Stay by Jana Alayra from "Dig Down Deep" (Montjoy Music 1997)

Craft for Younger Children: Thank You Treasures
Needed: For each child bring one strong paper plate, variety of nature cones, seeds, and glue.

Place items on table and let children choose which items to use in their collages. As children are designing their collages say: "These are all things that God made. Pick up one thing at a time and ask: Why do you think he made this? Why do you think he made this?

Invite children to glue the items on their plates. As they work, say: God made lots of neat things. Let's say thank you for all the things God made. What is in your collage that God made? (cones, seeds) Yes, you're right! Thank you, God for all the seeds and cones that become trees and plants!

 Craft for Older Children: Seed Mosaic
Needed: For each child bring one strong paper plate, glue, pennies.

Say: "God loves cheerful givers." What does that mean? You're right, that means that he loves people that give to him and do it cheerfully!

We are going to make a plaque to remind us to be cheerful givers.

Write "Cheerful Giver" on your plate with a marker. Let each child glue a few pennies onto the plate.

Crock Pot Caramel Apples

Needed: For each child bring 1–2 apple wedges. Combine in a crock pot a 16 oz. bag of caramel squares and 1/4 cup milk. Cook on low for about 1 hour or until caramels melt and you have a thick dip. Add more milk for a thinner dip. Stir often.
Supervise while the children dip apple wedges in the caramel or drizzle the caramel on top of the apple wedges using a wooden spoon.

Variation:
Cut up apples and drizzle with caramel sauce. Eat!

Prayer Focus:
Dear God, we thank you that you require much of us and that you give back much, much more. We thank you for everything that you give to us. We love you. Amen.

Memory Verse: 2 Corinthians 9:6 ICB
Remember this: The person who plants a little will have a small harvest. But the person who plants a lot will have a big harvest.

Alternate version (New King James)
But this I say: He who sows sparingly will also reap sparingly, and he who sows bountifully will also reap bountifully.

Memory Verse Activity:
Needed: Many kinds of seeds, garden tools.

Form teams based on the last digit of children's phone numbers. Give each team a bucket with seeds in it and a small garden tool to carry the seeds. Have another empty bucket on the other side of the room.

Say: The object of this game is to get the seeds from your bucket to the bucket over there. You must carry them on the tool, you cannot touch them with your hands. The winner will be the team that gets the most in the bucket without spilling them on the floor.

When you get to the bucket you must say the words to 2 Corinthians 9:6 before you run back to your team.

When one team is finished, invite all to sit on the floor together and shout out the verse! ☺

August 4

God Has X-Ray Vision, Midweek
By Mary Rice Hopkins

Scripture:
1 Corinthians 2:9

Lesson Aim:
God sees the best in us.

Bible Skill:
Kids will look at things positively, the way God does.

Bible Learning Activity for Younger Children: Look on the Inside
Needed: X-ray or picture of an X-ray, black paper, white chalk.

Hold up the X-ray and ask if children have seen one. Explain that it is for discovering what is going on inside someone's body. Ask: When might someone need an X-ray? What have you needed one for? Let children discuss their experiences. *(Samples include: to see if a bone is broken; to see if something has been swallowed.)*

Say: Today we are going to make a pretend X-ray. Pass out black paper and white chalk so children can draw an X-ray of their body. Ask: What do you think your bones would look like in an X-ray? Your stomach and heart?

As children draw, explain: An X-ray looks right through us, just like God does. An X-ray doesn't see what we look like on the outside or what kind of clothes we have; an X-ray looks at what is inside of us. God is like that, too! God looks right at our heart and sees who we really are.

Bible Learning Activity for Older Children: How People First Peeked Inside
Needed: X-ray or picture of an X-ray

Show the X-ray and ask: Have you ever had an X-ray? If you did, you were probably hurt or sick or something inside your body wasn't working properly. The doctor used the X-ray to learn what was wrong with you on the inside. How were X-rays discovered and how do they work?

X-rays were discovered by a German physicist named Wilhelm Roentgen in 1895. He discovered that a faint green colored light appeared if he enclosed a glass tube with electrical currents in it (similar to a light bulb) inside a black paper box.

When his hand came in contact with the tube, he saw shadows of his hand and fingers with darker shadows representing the bones. When he moved his hand, the shadow on the screen moved, too. He was so excited because he knew that he had discovered something really important! This shadow became known as the first X-ray picture.

Now doctors use X-rays or another imaging system whenever they need to learn something about you that they cannot see with their eyes. X-rays see through your skin and muscles, right to your bones!

Explain: God can see even deeper than that! When he sees you, he doesn't just see what you look like, he sees what you are inside including your thoughts and motivations and hopes and dreams. He sees who you are and the choices you make. He doesn't just see your appearance. God wants you to look at people the same way. Pay attention to the choices they make, not the appearance they show.

Enrichment for Younger Children: Look Through God's Eyes

Needed: Bring for each child a piece of pink food wrap large enough to look through. Hold this for anyone younger than three to look through. Hold it for anyone who would put it in his/her mouth.

Let children look through the pink wrap. Say: Does anything look different when you look through this? What about the window? What about the hamster? Continue naming things in the room, inviting a comment from each child.

Some people think everything looks better through this color. They call it "looking through rose-colored glasses." What do you think?

Explain that God has an even better way of seeing the great things inside us. He looks for the way we can be and he sees the good things we can do, decide, and say. He especially likes it when we do kind things, say kind things, and think kind thoughts. God loves us so much, he looks at us through "God's eyes."

God cares about everything that we do and he watches us with love. God loves us very much. ☺

Enrichment for Older Children: A Christian View

Needed: Bring for each child a piece of pink food wrap large enough to look through.

Give children pink plastic wrap and guide them to look through it at things in the room and out the window. Say: Have you ever looked at things through this colored wrap? How are they different?

After many children have commented, point out that things look a little prettier, don't they?

Ask: Has anyone ever said to you "You are looking at the world through rose-colored glasses"? When someone says that they mean that you see everything as though it was prettier than it really is, like when you were looking through the rose-colored plastic wrap.

Another way to say that you have a positive outlook is to say, "You always think the glass is half full." If someone says that to you it means you always see the best in things, that things always look positive to you. When you do this, you demonstrate the outlook of God.

These are both good things to be said about you! You should feel great if people say you look at things through rose-colored glasses, or you see the glass as half full rather than half empty. These are another way of saying, "You are looking at things through God's eyes." God loves everyone, sees the best in them, and shows them how to bring this good to the surface. ☺

Memory Verse: 1 Corinthians 2:9 ICB

But as it is written in the Scriptures: "No one has ever seen this. No one has ever heard about it. No one has ever imagined what God has prepared for those who love him."

Alternate version (New King James)

But as it is written: "Eye has not seen, nor ear heard, nor have entered into the heart of man the things which God has prepared for those who love Him."

August 8

God Has X-Ray Vision
By Mary Rice Hopkins

Scripture:
1 Corinthians 2:9

Lesson Aim:
God sees the best in us.

Bible Skill:
Kids will look at things positively, the way God does.

Bible Lesson: Look Through God's Lenses

Needed: Assorted types of glasses including sunglasses, reading glasses, prescription lenses, goggles, a microscope, and safety glasses.

Tell this story putting on the type of glasses you describe in each sentence: The other day it was so sunny outside that I needed to put on sunglasses. People who are farsighted need special glasses every day so they can read things up close. People who are nearsighted need special glasses so they can read things far away. Swimmers use goggles to see clearly under water. Scientists need microscopes because their own eyes can't see the tiny living cells they need to study. Some workmen must wear safety glasses to protect their eyes when they work with dangerous tools. People may need special glasses to see near or far, large or small, on the ground or under the water.

Do you wear glasses? What are these kinds of glasses for? Let children show the glasses they wear and what these glasses do for them.

Explain: Whether you do or not wear glasses, you look at the world through certain lenses. When you look at friends, you choose the lenses of acceptance or clothes consciousness. You look at the personality of the person or the skin color. You look at choices or class. When you look at people to find the nice ones who are happy and have a good personality, you are looking at people with God's eyes. You are looking for good hearts.

When that's the way you look at people, and that's the way you pick friends, you might say you have on "God's glasses." You might say you're looking with God's eyes. When you're wearing God's eyes, you're seeing the best in people instead of trying to find things wrong with them. When you put on God's eyes you see how you can help your friends or mom and dad around the house. When you're wearing God's eyes, you might see a friend feeling sad and you want to make them feel better. Or you notice when someone is happy and you get excited with him or her.

Are you wearing God's eyes today? Are you looking at your friend's heart just like God looks at your heart? Are you responding to your mom and dad the way Jesus would? And God's eyes see the future in a happy way. Nothing that we can ever imagine with our eyes or our minds can compare to what God has prepared for us!

So decide to see through God's eyes. You'll have look-inside vision that is far beyond what any eye has ever seen.

 Song Suggestions:

Little by Little Songsheets published by CEF Press, P.O. Box 348, Warrenton, Mo. 63383

The Family of God by Kurt Johnson, a.k.a. MrJ from "Kid Possible" (Kurt Johnson 1995)

No One Else I Know by Mary Rice Hopkins from "15 Singable Songs" (Big Steps 4 U 1988)

This Is Love by Dean-o from "God City" (BibleBeat Music, 2001)

Craft for Younger Children: Silly Glasses
Needed: Bring for every three children a soda six pack plastic holder. Bring scissors and chenille wires.

Cut the holder into three strips (you will get three silly glasses from each holder). Show the children how to attach chenille wire to each side and bend it over their ears to hold the "glasses" on.

Say: These are silly glasses, aren't they? Let's look at some things through our glasses. Point out several things around the room. Does anything look different? (Let children comment.) No, everything really looks the same, because these are just "pretend" glasses. But if we think about how God sees things, we see them differently. For example I see someone yawning, I know they are sleepy and I wonder what made them miss sleep.

Think about what you see, how God made it, and how you can cherish it.

 Craft for Older Children: The Ojo de Dios, or God's Eye
Needed: For each child bring two craft sticks or twigs, glue, and multi-colored yarn or four different colors of yarn.

Explain: The "God's Eye" is a simple weaving made across two sticks and is thought to have originated with Indians in Mexico. Begin by crossing the two sticks and gluing them together to form an "X". Glue the end of one piece of yarn behind the center of the X.

Show children how to wrap the yarn around the "X" weaving it over and under the sticks. Change colors each time you run out of yarn and continue wrapping until sticks are covered. Tie a loop of yarn on top for hanging your God's Eye.

Agree that God couldn't really "see" through this eye. Then ask: What do God's eyes see? How are they like and unlike what we have made? (*Sample: God sees the future; God sees the best about the present; God likes color, and so on*).

Vanilla Wafer Glasses

Needed: For each child bring two vanilla wafers, one 1" piece of red licorice,

two 3" pieces of red licorice, and a small amount of frosting.

Give children licorice pieces and two vanilla wafers. Let them create a pair of glasses, using icing to hold licorice pieces on.

Say: What are glasses for? Who wears glasses? Glasses are really cool because they bring out-of-focus things into focus. What looks better with glasses?

Ask: Do glasses help you like people more? No, of course not! But all of us can put on "God's eyes" and see people like God wants us to see them.

Prayer Focus:

Dear God, please help me to see people just like you do. Help me to love them with the actions and attitudes you want me to show. Thank you for all that you do for me, thank you for loving me just the way I am. Amen.

Memory Verse Activity:

Needed: Index cards.

Print two or three words from the verse onto each card. Hide cards around the room.

Say: You can't see the verse right now because it is hidden from you on cards. Let's try to find it.

Let children look for verse cards and then sit down with them when they have been found. Explain: Sometimes looking with God's eyes takes a bit of searching. But discovering the good in someone and bringing it out is worth the searching.

Ask: What are the very happiest experiences you have had? Prompt each child to contribute something. Say: Did you know that God has prepared many happy experiences for us. You've had some of these already, maybe a happy family, or a good talk with a sister or brother or friend. Encourage children to watch for God's good plans.

Memory Verse: 1 Corinthians 2:9 ICB

But as it is written in the Scriptures: No one has ever seen this. No one has ever heard about it. "No one has ever imagined what God has prepared for those who love him."

Alternate version (New King James)

But as it is written: "Eye has not seen, nor ear heard, nor have entered into the heart of man the things which God has prepared for those who love Him."

August 11

Raising the Bar, Midweek
By Pat Verbal

Scripture:
Exodus 4:1–5, 17; 7:14–16; 14:16

Lesson Aim:
To help children access God's power.

Bible Skill:
I can do anything God asks because his power will help me.

Bible Learning Activity For Younger Children: Pick-Up Sticks
Needed: A set of pick-up sticks or a bag of pretzels.

Show children how to play Pick-Up Sticks. Play for a few minutes, offering strategies to those who struggle (*such as poking down one side to help the stick rise*).

Say: This game is hard, isn't it? But as you play, you get better at it. At first you will settle for a bad score. Then you "raise the bar" and want a better score. That's how it is to be a Christian. You want to get better and better at serving God!

Bible Learning Activity for Older Children: Raising the Bar
Needed: For each child bring a 4 foot tall stick or wrapping paper tube.

Stand children in a circle about 8 feet apart. Give each child a stick about 4 foot tall to hold out to their right side. On the count of three, children let go of their stick and race to the right to catch their neighbors stick before it hits the floor. If they miss, they step out until the next round. The circle gets smaller until one stick is left.

Say: That was a new skill that took some time to learn, didn't it? Did it get easier the more you did it? Caring for people in God's way is like this. It takes practice. God wants us to set a high standard for ourselves and do everything with excellence.

Enrichment for Younger Children: Impossible Temptation

Explain: One temptation that most children face has to do with a stick. It's sometimes called a "cancer stick" or a "coffin nail." It's a cigarette. Someday an older boy or girl will ask you if you'd like to have a cigarette. They'll say smoking is "cool" and if you smoke, you'll make more friends. Don't believe them.

The truth is that smoking cigarettes will make you weak not strong. It weakens your body and your confidence. Smoking is a dirty habit with long term health risks to you and those around you. It is the leading cause of lung cancer. It can lead to using even more harmful drugs. What other ways can you see it weakening you?

Ask: When you're tempted to try a cigarette, do you think you can resist it? The good news is that you don't have to do it alone. Saying "NO" is possible with God's power. Invite a child to read 1 Corinthians 10:13. Watch Sunday for ways to talk to God as Moses did on the mountain and Rich did on the track field. Watch God work miracles for you. ☺

Memory Verse: Philippians 4:13 ICB
I can do all things through Christ because he gives me strength.

Alternate version (New King James)
I can do all things through Christ who strengthens me.

Enrichment for Older Children: Do Your Best!

Explain: The term "raising the bar" is sometimes referred to as setting a higher standard. The standard might have to do with your character or actions. Maybe you've heard commercials that say, "We're the best!" Sometimes, they say, "We aren't the best but we are trying hard to be the best!" These companies are trying to "raise the bar."

When you ask Jesus to forgive your sins and accept Him as your Savior, you become a Christian. You "raised the bar" in everything you say and do because Jesus is your new standard. Christians don't need to measure themselves by other people, nor prove themselves to others. The world's standards change depending on which group of people you hang around.

Ask: What are some of God's standards for your character? What can you do this week to "raise the bar" in word, thought, and action?

Close with: Jesus is a perfect example of God's character and the only perfect human being. You will never be perfect, but the more you try to be like him the happier you and those around you will be. Also the world will get a better picture of God. ☺

August 15

Raising the Bar
By Pat Verbal

Scripture:
Exodus 4:1–5, 17; 7:14–16; 14:16

Lesson Aim:
To help children access God's power.

Bible Skill:
I can do anything God asks because his power will help me.

Bible Lesson: Miraculous Signs and Wonders

Tell this story: Rich started running track in seventh grade. Because he was a dedicated athlete, his coach suggested he consider the decathlon. In the decathlon, athletes compete in ten events over two days; 4 races, 3 throwing events, and 3 jumps.

Rich eagerly tried everything, except the pole vault. Flying through the air at the top of a 10 foot pole and landing on a hunk of foam rubber, scared him. After months of practice, he barely cleared the bar at 12 feet. This height kept him in high school competition until he qualified for the Junior National Olympic Trials. The top two decathletes would earn a place on the U.S. team and travel to Europe.

Rich praised God for such an opportunity, but his hopes of winning faded when he learned the opening height for the pole vault was 15 feet. He'd have three chances to clear the bar.

After the first day of competition, Rich was in the top five. The second day's events were his strongest, except for the pole vault. A little voice inside kept saying, "It's impossible, I'll never clear it." After missing two jumps,

Rich found a quiet place and prayed. "Lord, give me power to do my best that I may honor You."

On the final jump, Rich carefully counted his steps as he ran, planted the pole in the box and pushed off with his legs as hard as he could. He was as surprised as his cheering audience when he barely cleared the bar and dropped to the mat with a thud, but God wasn't surprised.

Following God is often like pole vaulting. The task can look impossible, until God's power takes over.

God has been beating the odds for a long time. In Bible times a man named Moses didn't have a pole, but he did have a rod. He was holding it in his hand when he climbed the side of a mountain to investigate a fire. Actually, it wasn't a real fire—it was a burning bush. God used the bush to get Moses' attention because he wanted to give him an assignment. God told Moses, an eighty-year-old great-grandfather, to lead thousands of Hebrews out of slavery in Egypt. Sounds impossible, right? Moses thought so, too. So he said to God, "But suppose they (the Egyptians) will not believe me or listen to my voice; suppose they say, 'The LORD has not appeared to you.'"

So the LORD said to him, "What is that in your hand?"

He said, "A rod" (Ex. 4:1–2 NKJV).

God told Moses to throw the rod down on the ground and it instantly became a snake.

Moses jumped back rubbing his eyes, as everyone does when the impossible actually happens. The wooden rod became a hissing snake, squirming in the dirt. As if that wasn't enough, God told Moses to pick it up. Do you think Moses felt like running about that time?

Then God said, "Reach out your hand and take it by the tail that they may believe that the LORD God of their fathers, the God of Abraham, the God of Isaac, and the God of Jacob, has appeared to you" (Ex. 4:4–5 NKJV). It's dangerous to pick up a snake by the tail and Moses likely knew this.

When Moses picked up the snake by it's tail, it became a rod again. Because Moses listened to God, he saw many miracles and became one of the greatest leaders in the Old Testament.

Ask: What might have happened if Moses had run away? What gave him the courage to do what God asked? Tell us something you think is impossible and how God helps you with it.

Song Suggestions:

What a Mighty God We Serve Songsheets published by CEF Press, P.O. Box 348, Warrenton, Mo. 63383

Little Is Much by Mary Rice Hopkins from "15 Singable Songs" (Big Steps 4 U 1988)

He's Got Plans by Dean-o from "Soul Surfin'" (FKO Music, Inc. 1999)

My God Is So Big Traditional

 Craft for Younger Children: "Powered by God" Poster
Needed: Small pieces of poster board, instant camera and film, markers. Write "Powered by God" onto the poster boards.

Take instant picture of each child to put on the poster. Let children decorate the rest of the poster. Say: Each of you has God's power in you. How many of you feel like you have God's power in you? You have it whether you feel it or not. How have you seen this power? You have the power to get along with people, to work for good, to overcome temptation, and much more.

 Craft for Older Children: Powered by God Shirt or Banner
Needed: For each child bring a T-shirt, men's white handkerchief, and markers or fabric paints.

Say: We are going to make a T-shirt (or handkerchief) like the one Rich used in the Junior National Olympic Trials. Show children how to use fabric paints or markers to decorate T-shirts or handkerchiefs that say "Powered by God." Let dry.

Say: How can you get power from God? *(Samples: Talk with God; imitate him)* God wants us to be filled with his power, his Holy spirit. All we have to do is ask!

Stick Pretzels
Needed: Stick pretzels.

1. Play a game of pick-up sticks using stick pretzels.
2. Holding a stick pretzel to represent a "bar" in your life, invite each child to tell what it will take to reach that goal.

Alternate Snack: Praise Treats!
Bring for each child a small package of M&M's or jelly beans.

Let each child choose one candy and tell about something the same color that they are thankful for (*Samples: brown—mountains, green—trees, red apples.*) Let each child have a few turns.

Say: It's easy to thank God for things that we appreciate, isn't it? Let's do it everyday!

Prayer Focus:
Dear God, thank you for sending Jesus to show me how to live and to give me your power. I believe you have special tasks for me. Help me do them with your strength and power. Amen.

Memory Verse: Philippians 4:13 ICB
I can do all things through Christ because he gives me strength.

Alternate version (New King James)
I can do all things through Christ who strengthens me.

Memory Verse Activity:
This is a great acting out and chanting verse. Ask children to help you make up motions and then lead the motions while you all say the verse with the motions. Repeat several times.

August 18

First Place in Friendship, Midweek
By Pat Verbal

Scripture:
2 Samuel 9:1–13

Lesson Aim:
To help children accept weaknesses and appreciate strengths in others.

Bible Skill:
I can honor God by the way I treat my friends.

Bible Learning Activity for Younger children: Friendship Chain
Needed: For each child bring four strips of paper about 1 inch by 6 inches in assorted colors. Bring markers and a stapler.

Let children choose the paper strip they want. Have them write their name on the strip. Make a strip for Jonathan, David, and Jesus, too. Link the strips together into a "Friendship Chain."

Say: David and Jonathan were best friends. They loved each other very much and were willing to do anything for each other. Jesus also loves us very much. He can be our best friend. As we link to him we can do anything. Jesus wants you to be his best friend.

Bible Learning Activity for Older Children: Sharing Pizza
Need: Bring for each child two paper plates, red paper circle to cover one paper plate minus edge for crust, orange circles (pepperoni), yellow long rectangles for cheese, small brown circles for sausage, and a glue stick.

Give each child a paper plate and one type of paper topping. Say: We're making a paper pizza. Have each child "share" his/her toppings in order to create several pizzas. Attach them with glue sticks to make the pizza easier to cut. Cut the "pizza" into slices and glue one slice to each plate.

Discuss:

Why is it good to share?

What happened when we shared?

Why does God/Jesus want us to share?

What are other ways we can share?

Enrichment for Older Children: We're All More Alike Than Different

Have a conversation with the children about boys and girls with disabilities. Ask: How are you just like someone with a disability? How are you different?

Highlight these points as children talk:

• The only way we are different is that I have an ability or disability someone else does not have. We all still play, think, dream, hope, laugh, and have birthday parties.

• When you meet someone differently abled than you, focus on forming a friendship.

• Help, but not so they feel inferior to you, or superior to you.

• Remind children to treat children with disabilities just like they treat others.

• If one of your students has a disability, remind him/her to be a giver rather than expect others to take care of them.

• Ask: How can I help you? Don't assume you know. For example, not all deaf people sign or all wheelchair-bound people need help with moving a wheelchair.

• Remember that any person with a disability has abilities you don't have. So help each other.

• Remember not to:

  • Pet a Seeing Eye dog while he is working.

  • Let anyone (abled or not) withdraw from the group. Instead pull them in.

  • Be embarrassed to have them as your friends.

• Treat a person with disabilities just like you want to be treated: be friends, listen and talk, accept each other, find similarities. ☺

Enrichment for Younger Children: My Friends Booklet

Needed: Paper, crayons, paste, scrap supplies such as ribbon and stickers.

Say: Jesus showed us the secret of sharing when he said to "Love Your Neighbor as Yourself." What is sharing? When is it easy to share? When is it hard to share?

Today we are going to share so that we can make books. There are many materials here to share with each other. Fold for each child several pages and staple them to make a booklet. Guide them to decorate the cover with the art scraps. Affirm each act of sharing.

When the covers are ready, say: Now we will let our friends outline their handprint on the pages of our books. That's another way to share with each other! Guide children to work in twos to trace handprints on the pages of each others' books. Point out how each child is unique, each handprint is different, and each child has something special to share. ☺

Memory Verse: Proverbs 17:17a ICB
A friend loves you all the time.

Alternate version: (New King James)
A friend loves at all times.

August 22

First Place in Friendship
Pat Verbal

Scripture:
2 Samuel 9:1–13

Lesson Aim:
To help children accept weaknesses and appreciate strengths in every other person.

Bible Skill:
I can honor God by the way I treat my friends.

Bible Lesson: First Place in Friendship
Ask: Who are some of your friends? What do you like best about them? Today we'll meet two friends who taught one another a valuable lesson.

Say: This first story is about two friends in a present day school: "Come on, Champ!" my mom called, "You look tired. It's a good thing Field Day is only once a year. How many ribbons did you get?"

"I got five!" It sounded better every time I said it. I loved Field Day better than any day of the year. Almost every boy I knew played sports—except me. I had asthma. So as spring temperatures climbed to 85 degrees, I prayed. Lord, please help me breath right and help me do my best today. It didn't seem right to pray to win. I just wanted to be like the other guys.

"You're awfully quiet," Mom said, turning into the driveway.

"I was thinking about Joel. He entered every race, but got only one ribbon." Joel had been one of my best friends since first grade. He was real smart, but his left arm and leg were twisted, causing him to wobble when he walked. Joel said it didn't hurt and he always tried everything I did.

"It's not fair," I complained. "Joel tried as hard as anybody."

"Tell them to have a special race just for Joel," chimed in my little brother, Ronnie. That gave me an idea.

After my homework, I went to the craft room in our basement. Using pasteboard and silver glitter, I made a list of races that didn't require athletic skill. Instead they required strategy and attention: checker tournaments, spelling bees, mystery games. I called the sports store and ordered some ribbons.

The next day at school, I asked my teacher if we could have an indoor field day. I showed her the poster and we planned for it. We found a way for the whole school to do it. The class added more events.

Joel won a ton of awards as did everyone else. I didn't know he was so good in checkers and chess. It reminded me that we all have strengths and weaknesses.

[NOTE: Avoid communicating that children with disabilities can only succeed in friendship or in things other kids can also do. Instead highlight everyone's strengths.]

Say: This second story took place in Bible times and is told from the viewpoint of David: My test of courage didn't come on Field Day, but it was on a battle field. When I killed the dreaded giant, Goliath, I won the heart of King Saul. He invited me to live in the palace, where I met a life-long friend, Prince Jonathan. Later, when Saul became jealous of me and threatened my life, it was Jonathan who helped me get away.

Jonathan reminded me that we had given ourselves to God forever, and that God would take care of us.

"Yes, he will," I told my friend, "and we'll always be best friends, Jonathan, forever."

It was after Jonathan's death that I finally became king over all of Israel. In those days, kings hunted down members of the family of former kings and killed them. But I had made a vow to protect Jonathan's family. So, I said to my servant, "Is there still anyone who is left of the house of Saul?"

"There is one servant named Ziba," she said. When Ziba was found, I asked him how I might show kindness to Jonathan's family.

"There is still one son of Jonathan yet alive. His name is Mephibosheth, but he is lame in his feet."

I quickly sent for him. Mephibosheth, fearing for his life, came and fell on his face before me. My heart ached for my old friend, Jonathan, and for his son.

Song Suggestions:

I'm Not Too Little Songsheets published by CEF Press, P.O. Box 348, Warrenton, Mo. 63383

Good Buddies by Mary Rice Hopkins from "Good Buddies "(Big Steps 4 U 1994)

Lovin' God Is Livin' Great! by Dean-o from "You Got It All" (FKO Music, Inc. 1997)

I told him not to be afraid. I promised to show him kindness for his father's sake. I restored to him all the land of Saul, his grandfather. I arranged for him to eat at my table from then on. It felt good to keep my promise to Jonathan and to care for Mephibosheth and his household. Now, I think my friend is finally at peace.

Explain: The best way to respond to a friend with disabilities is to treat him like you want to be treated, to be a friend first. How did Richie and David do this? (*Samples: They found strengths in their friends; they found ways to highlight those strengths; they treated them as people first*). How do you think Joel and Mephibosheth felt about their friends? How do you think Joel and Mepisbosheth helped Richie and David right back? How has a friend with a disability been kind to you during a tough time in your life?

 Craft for Older Children: Friendship Buttons
Needed: Bring for each child at least one plastic lid from snack food cans and a craft pin fastener. Bring glue, paint pens, glitter, and ribbons.

Glue the fastener onto the back of the lids while you say: Our friends need to know how much we love them. Let's honor our friends by writing with one of the following sayings: First Place in Honesty, First Place in Trust, First Place in Fun, etc. on the button and decorating it. Then give it to a friend!"

Let children make an extra button for another friend if time allows.

Craft for Younger Children: Best Friends Necklace
Needed: For each child bring beads and cut one craft foam heart about two inches across and then cut it into two halves. Punch a hole in each half and cut a necklace length cord for each.

Give each child both halves of the heart. Say: "Have you ever seen a "best friends" necklace? Today we are going to make one for you and one for a friend. Guide the children to string the heart onto the cord and add beads if desired.

Say: "If you put the two hearts together, you will have one heart. If you wear this necklace and give the other one to a friend, you will be "sharing a heart!" In this way you can show other people what friendship is all about. Caution children against calling this person a best friend so other friends won't feel less important. Assure them: We all have room in our heart for several good friends.

Build a Friendship Sundae
Needed: Bring for each child a clear cup, a plastic spoon, a graham cracker, a banana, and a spoonful of vanilla pudding.

Explain that we will think about friends while we make a pudding sundae. Give each child a small clear plastic cup and talk about friendship while you add the following ingredients:

As you crumble graham crackers up in the bottom, ask which of your friends can pull the pieces of life together well like we pull these crumbs together to make a sundae?

As you slice bananas on top of the crumbs, ask: Which of your friends help you cut to what's important: helping each other, seeing the good in each other, and other good things?

As you add the smooth vanilla pudding, ask: who are your smooth (find a way to stay calm in crazy times) friends?

Prayer Focus:
Thank you, God that you are my best friend. Thank you for showing me how to find and grow close to good friends. Help me find ways past disabilities to form good friendships no matter what my friends' abilities or disabilities. Amen.

Memory Verse: Proverbs 17:17a ICB
A friend loves you all the time.

Alternate version: (New King James)
A friend loves at all times.

Memory Verse Activity:
Write the words onto papers, one word on each paper. Set the papers on the floor in "hopscotch" order. Let children play hopscotch, chanting "A friend loves at all times" while they hop on the hopscotch course.

Ask: What actions show you are loving at all times? What loving actions do you like from friends?

The Bible says, "Christ accepted you, so you should accept each other" (Rom. 15:7 ICB). That also means, that we need to accept each other no matter what we do because Christ accepts us no matter what we do!

August 25

Life Without Jesus, Midweek
By Mary Rice Hopkins

Scripture:
Proverbs 3:5–6

Lesson Aim:
Jesus is our guide and will help us through our lives.

Bible Skill:
The Bible is like a map that shows us what to do in our lives.

Bible Learning Activity for All Ages: Finding Our Way in Bible Times

Have you ever been lost? What did you do? (Let children discuss.) In Bible times the people didn't have many different ways to travel. They either traveled by walking, by ship, or by riding animals. They had to know the way before they began their journey.

One time, God did something very different. He actually LED the people where he wanted them to go. He did it with a pillar of fire at night and a cloud during the day. God guided the Israelites during their travels through the wilderness after they left Egypt. In the form of cloud by day and fire by night, the pillar was constantly visible to the Israelites. Through this amazing phenomenon, God led the people on their journey from the border of Egypt all the way toward the Promised Land. The pillar of fire gave enough light for the people to travel by night.

The people were very safe on their journey with God watching over them and leading them!

Ask: Why would you like to have been on this journey?

Enrichment for Younger Children: Little Mappers

Needed: Papers with North, South, East, and West written on them (one direction on each paper).

Place the directional papers in the north, south, east, and west of the room.

Guide the children to follow directions with words like: Follow me kids! Let's go North! Now, let's go South! Now, let's go East! Now, let's go West! This is how we follow a map. Have your parents ever followed a map? How does a map help you go the right way?

Let children take turns leading the group one direction or another.

Ask: What else will help you go the right way? The Bible!

Alternate: Imaginary Field Trip

Say: Let's go to the beach! Follow me!

Look, there's the street!

Look there's the parking lot!

Oh, look, there's the beach! What do you see? (Let children respond.)

I see some shells, some sand, some water, lots of waves, people surfing, people swimming, beach towels.

What do you smell? I smell water, suntan lotion, salt water.

What can you touch? I can touch the sand, the water, the shells.

Let children continue reflecting on imaginary experiences and then take an imaginary trip back home! ☺

Memory Verse: Proverbs 3:5–6 ICB

Trust the Lord with all your heart. Don't depend on your own understanding. Remember the Lord in everything you do. And he will give you success.

Alternate version (New King James)
Trust in the LORD with all your heart,
And lean not on your own understanding;
In all your ways acknowledge Him,
And He shall direct your paths.

Enrichment for Older Children: Map Orienteering

Needed: Papers with North, South, East, and West written on them (one on each paper). Any Map.

Place the directional papers in the north, south, east, and west of the room. Have children stand in the center of the room while you ask: What is in the North part of the room? What is in the South? The East and the West? Invite children to list things found in each location.

Explain: When we travel somewhere, we need a map (show map). What does this map show us? *(Samples: How to get where we want to go; the easiest way to get there; what we will see along the way.)*

Did you know that the Bible is sort of like a map, similar to the map you use on your vacation? The Bible tells us the best way to live our lives, it tells us how to get to heaven, and the easiest way to get there.

Ask: How else is the Bible like a map? When do you use a map? When can you use the Bible like a map? ☺

August 29

Life Without Jesus
By Mary Rice Hopkins

Scripture:
Proverbs 3:5–6

Lesson Aim:
Jesus is our guide and will help us through our lives.

Bible Skill:
The Bible is like a map that shows us what to do in our lives.

Bible Lesson: Life Without Jesus Is No Disneyland

Ask: Have you ever been lost and felt very afraid? (Let kids respond.) I remember when I was a child and my family went to Disneyland (substitute for another place if necessary) on a very busy day. There were hundreds and thousands of people and somehow I had wandered away from my mom and dad. I looked up and much to my surprise my mom was nowhere to be found. Well, I was a pretty friendly little kid and fortunately for me a very tall and kind man put me on his shoulders above the crowd to help me see if I could find my family.

Eventually my family was located and we were all relieved. My mom reminded me that I needed to stay right with her and I, of course, said that I would! My mom was just as scared as I was! I was so glad to be back where I was safe.

When people at sea need to know where to go, they might have a compass to lead them to a safe harbor. A compass can also be a valuable tool to have when you're lost in a forest. When you are trying to find your way to a place you've never driven before, you use a map. The map gives you directions and gets you where you need to be.

Song Suggestions:

Get Along Song by Kurt Johnson, a.k.a. MrJ from "Kid Possible" ((Kurt Johnson Music 1995)

Gramma's House by Mary Rice Hopkins from "15 Singable Songs" (Big Steps 4 U 1988)

STOP! Songsheets published by CEF Press P.O. Box 348, Warrenton, Mo. 63383

But sometimes, people don't want to use a compass. They get lost. Sometimes people don't want to use a map—they think they can get there without it so sometimes they get lost.

If we don't have a map or other guide, we just don't know what to do or where to go. You and I will be like that if we are not careful. We all need a guide or someone to show us how to live and find peace and happiness in the world. Without this guide, we are soon led into danger by evil.

God is smart. He has given us this guide. The Bible is like a map. In the Bible, God guides you to know what to do in the good times and in the bad times. It helps you know where to go and what to do. His Spirit is like a living compass that will always tell you when you're going the wrong way. Ask God to lead you on "the path of everlasting life" and He will! (Ps. 138:24).

Even life at Disneyland can be pretty scary if you don't know where to go or if you're lost from those you love!

 Craft for Younger Children: I Spy
Teach children how to play I Spy.

Find something in the room and choose it, but don't tell anyone what it is. You may pick anything you want. Now you say "I spy something that is _____ (what color) or I spy something that is alive, or I spy something that is big." Describe it one description at a time until other children can guess what it is.

Then let a child do the spying and describing. Keep playing until all children have had a turn.

Say: This is a great game to play with your parents while you are in the car. It helps make your journey more fun.

Craft for Older Children: Vacation Games
Prepare items for these games. Teach children the games so they will know them for their next car or plane trip. Encourage children to take the ideas home to their families.

Triangles Cover a sheet with dots, starting with one in first row, two in second row, etc. Each player takes turns connecting two dots horizontally or diagonally. The person who completes a triangle puts his/her initial in that triangle. Person with most triangles wins.

Coin Game Start with ten coins. Person who is "It" conceals several coins in the right hand and places hand on table. Everyone guesses how many coins he/she has. No one can guess the same number as anyone else. The one who guesses correctly gets one point. Let all children have a turn being "It."

Drawing Charades Mom or Dad writes cards of family related jokes, favorite songs, movies, or other items in advance. "It" chooses a card and draws pictures that will help the family guess that phrase. "It" continues to draw clues until someone guesses correctly. That person gets one point, as does the person drawing the clues. The person guessing correctly is the new "It."

String Games String games never go out of style, if you are not familiar with them there are many great books to teach them or sites on the web. Bring a two foot circle of yarn for each family member with which to play the string games.

Snack: Mauka and Makai

Needed: For each child bring one rice cake, chocolate frosting, and blue frosting.

Say: In Hawaii, people use other words to tell directions. Instead of saying "North, South, East, or West, they say Makai and Mauka. Makai (ma kai) means "toward the sea" and Mauka (Mow ka) means "toward the mountains."

Guide the children to make a map of a Hawaiian island. On your rice cake (which will be the island), put a glob of frosting in the center. That is the mountain. Then put blue frosting around the edges. That will be the ocean.

(Point to different locations on rice cake.) If I wanted to go here from here which way would I go, Mauka or Makai? What about here?

Prayer Focus:

Dear God, thank you that you are a light in this world. Thank you for all the healing that you do in our lives. Please help us to become lights in our world by our kindness to others. Help us to be your followers. Amen.

Memory Verse: Proverbs 3:5–6 ICB

Trust the Lord with all your heart. Don't depend on your own understanding. Remember the Lord in everything you do. And he will give you success.

Alternate version (New King James)
Trust in the LORD with all your heart,
And lean not on your own understanding;
In all your ways acknowledge Him,
And He shall direct your paths.

Memory Verse Activity: Heart Verses

Needed: One piece of red construction paper per child, cut into large heart shape.

Write memory verse on white board or poster board.

Say: Let's all say this verse together. What do you think that means?

Who does it say to trust? What will happen when you trust the Lord?

Let's write this verse on our hearts. (Let children write verse on paper heart.)

Now, tell one way that you are going to trust God this week. *(When I'm at school; when I am playing soccer; when I am doing my homework.)* ☺

September 1

Back To School!, Midweek
By Karl Bastian

Scripture:
2 Corinthians 13:5

Lesson Aim:
To remind children of the plan of salvation.

Bible Skill:
Children will understand what salvation means.

Bible Learning Activity Simplification for Younger Children:
Needed: Apple, piece of paper, pencil, ruler, scissors, tape, eraser, glue, markers, towel.

Set all items out on tray. Let children look at them for one minute, then cover with a towel.

Guide the following Bible Learning Activity for Older Children but with this simplification:

Say: What was on the tray? Let children guess the items and uncover them as they are guessed.

Say: These are all items that we use to do our schoolwork. In Sunday's Bible lesson they will mean something else.

Bible Learning Activity for Older Children:
Needed: An apple, piece of paper, pencil, ruler, scissors, tape, eraser, glue, markers, a tray and a towel.

Set all items except the towel on a tray. Let children look at them for one minute, then cover them with a towel. Say: What was on the tray? Let children guess the items and uncover them as they are guessed. When all items have been uncovered, explain to the children what they will stand for in the Bible lesson they will hear on Sunday.

Apple	Fruit in Garden of Eden
Piece of paper	Test with a grade
Pencil	What writes the grade
Ruler	Standard to measure against
Scissors	Sin
Tape	Restore relationship
Eraser	Confessed sins are erased
Glue	God will stick by us
Markers	Permanent relationship with God

Enrichment for Older Children: Make School Great

Needed: Chalkboard and markerboard.

School is starting soon. What do you like about school? What do you NOT like? What would make your school a great school?

(List ideas on the board.)

How can we help our school become a great school? What can you do to help?

(List ideas on the board.)

What worries you about school this year? What are you concerned about?

(List on board.)

What actions does God want you to take to make this school year great? *(listen to my teachers; be kind to every student; help where I can.)*

Let's pray about our new school year and ask God to help us have the best year ever!

Lead children in praying for all that has been listed. ☺

Enrichment for Younger Children: Going to School

Ask: How many of you are starting school this week? What day do you begin? What do you think it will be like? What will you do there? How will you make friends there?

Encourage children: God wants us to be friendly at our schools and make friends. Can you be a friend at school? ☺

Memory Verse: 2 Corinthians 13:5 ICB

Look closely at yourselves. Test yourselves to see if you are living in the faith. You know that Christ Jesus is in you—unless you fail the test.

Alternate version (New King James)

Examine yourselves as to whether you are in the faith. Test yourselves. Do you not know yourselves, that Jesus Christ is in you?—unless indeed you are disqualified.

September 5

Back To School!
By Karl Bastian

Scripture:
2 Corinthians 13:5

Lesson Aim:
To remind children of the plan of salvation.

Bible Skill:
For the child to understand what salvation means.

Bible Lesson: Symbol Talk
Needed: Apple, piece of paper, pencil, ruler, scissors, tape, eraser, glue, markers (optional ending: crayon set with these colors: black; purple; brown; red; white; blue; yellow; green; orange).

Show the apple.

Explain: Apples are often given to teachers as a gift. We give a gift of fruit to show we care about them and appreciate them. God also gave a gift of fruit to the first man and woman—the fruit of the Tree of Life. But there was a tree that God said not to eat from: the Tree of the Knowledge of Good and Evil. But Adam and Eve disobeyed God and ate it anyway. This was the first sin, and people have been sinning ever since.

Show the paper.

Say: When you take a test, the teacher puts a grade on it. If life were a test of how good we are, we have all failed because we all do good and bad things. Write an "F" on the top with a pencil. Next write sins on paper such as selfishness, lying, stealing, cheating, hating, and more. (Ask the kids for suggestions.)

Next, show the ruler.

Say: A ruler is a standard that we measure things against. No one measures up to God's standard of perfection. We have all fallen short of the excellence God expects.

Show the scissors.

Say: Our sin has severed our relationship with God (cut paper in half). But God loved us so much that he sent a Savior to repair our broken relationship with God. Then we are free to live for him, to love him with our good actions.

Show the tape.

Say: Jesus came to repair the break (tape paper back together). Jesus can restore our relationship to God back to what God designed it to be. And what about our sins?

Show the eraser.

Say: When we confess our sins, they are erased if we accept Jesus (erase sins on paper) and then our name is written (show the pencil again) in the Book of Life in heaven. Once you are a child of God your good name can never be changed or taken away.

Show glue.

Say: You can have assurance—God will "stick" by us, through thick and thin (show large and small markers). Your relationship with God is "permanent."

Invite children to take turns telling the same story, each stating what one item stood for.

Optional ending: Show a crayon set and go through the crayons one at a time to talk about God's plan. Here are samples of what the colors could represent.

 Song Suggestions:

I Am the Apple by Cindy Rethmeier from "I Want 2 Be Like Jesus" (Mercy/ Vineyard Publishing 1995)

Watch It Grow by Mary Rice Hopkins from "Good Buddies" (Big Steps 4 U 1994)

Children All Around the World Songsheets published by CEF Press, P.O. Box 348, Warrenton, Mo. 63383

BLACK: (Sin is dark); PURPLE: (Jesus is royal); BROWN: (Jesus came to earth); RED: (Jesus died); WHITE: (Jesus cleansed us and forgave us); BLUE: (We choose baptism to publicly profess our faith in Jesus); YELLOW: (heaven is waiting); GREEN: (In the meantime we grow in Christ); ORANGE: Orange you glad you know Jesus?!

 Craft for Younger Children: Preschool Craft: Apple Necklace

Needed: Bring for each child one large red pompom, cord for necklace, glue and a small amount of green felt or green craft foam.

Say: Apples are a symbol of going back to school. In the early days of our country, students gave apples to their teachers as a way to pay them for teaching. Now students give apples to teachers to show that they appreciate them. Today we are going to make an apple necklace. You can keep it or give it to your teacher to show how much you appreciate him/her!

Help children cut small leaves out of the green felt and glue them to the to top of the apple pompom. Make a loop for the cord. Show the children how to string the pompom onto a cord. Add beads if desired.

 Craft for Older Children: My Art Center

Needed: For each child bring a paint stirring stick or piece of wood 2 inches by 10 inches, 3 clip clothespins, paint, glue, and a magnet strip.

Guide the children to paint the stir stick and the 3 clothespins. When paint is dry, glue the 3 clothespins onto the stir stick evenly spaced with one on each end and one in the middle. With a sharpie, write "My Art Center" across the paint strip. Attach the magnet strip to the back of the stir stick. Put on fridge to display art work!

Snack: Apples, Apples, Apples
Needed: Several different types of apples cut into small pieces.

 Let children sample a variety of apples. Say: What is the difference between these apples? Are some sweeter, different colors, more juicy? Which is your favorite?

It's good that you sampled all of the apples even though you have your favorites. When you get to school, you will want to be with your favorite friends. But it is good to give everyone a chance and see if you can make some new friends. When school starts, try to make two new friends this year!

Prayer Focus:
Dear God, thank you for my school and my teacher. Please help me to do well this year, to pay attention, to learn, to have wisdom, and to be kind. Amen.

Memory Verse: 2 Corinthians 13:5 ICB
Look closely at yourselves. Test yourselves to see if you are living in the faith. You know that Christ Jesus is in you—unless you fail the test.

Alternate version (New King James)
Examine yourselves as to whether you are in the faith. Test yourselves. Do you not know yourselves, that Jesus Christ is in you?—unless indeed you are disqualified.

Memory Verse Activity: Tests! Tests! Tests!
During our lesson we named symbols to help us remember how God plans to save us from sin. If I gave you a quiz on these you might not enjoy it but it would help you remember them. Your teachers will be giving you tests so that you can learn. God encourages you to test yourself too. How do you think you could test yourself? Here are some good questions to ask yourself:

Do you ask God to help you in new situations?

How well do you show the fruits of the Spirit in all situations? (love, joy, peace, patience, kindness, goodness, faithfulness, gentleness, and self-control)

Do you think others see Christ in you?

Do you pray for your teachers?

Do you read your Bible so that you can learn more about God?

You might be able to think of more questions to quiz yourself on the best test of all! ☺

September 8

Who Wants To Be Like Me?, Midweek
By Ivy Beckwith

Scripture:
1 Thessalonians 1:2–10

Lesson Aim:
Kids explore what it means to be an example to others.

Bible Skill:
Kids will learn to lead like Paul led.

Bible Learning Activity for Younger Children: Jesus and Me!
Say: Jesus was a child just like you! We don't know much about his childhood, but we do know some things. Let's compare our lives with his.

Where were you born? Where was Jesus born?

Who came to visit you when you were born? Who came to visit Jesus?

Who are your parents? Who were Jesus' mother and father?

What do your dad and mom do? What did Jesus' earthly dad do?

Even though life in Bible times was very different than it is now, we can still imitate Jesus. How can we do that? (Love people, love God.)

Bible Learning Activity for Older Children: How Are Jesus and I the Same?
Needed: Duplicate an activity sheet as follows and photocopy for each child.

Say: Today we are going to see how similar our lives are to Jesus'. Let's answer these questions. After they fill out sheet say: What did you learn? What other ways can you think of that you are similar to Jesus? What things are different?

How Are Jesus and I the Same?

How Are We Different?

	JESUS	ME
Where were we born?		
Who are our parents?		
What did we do?		
Who were our friends?		
What does my father do?		
What does my mother do?		
What did I wear when I was a baby?		
Why do we obey parents?		

Even though life in Bible times was very different than it is now, we can still live like Jesus. How can we do that? (*Love people, love God.*)

Enrichment for Older Children: Bible Times Locations

Needed: Find a map of Greece and Italy from Paul's time. (There are several good reproducible ones available on the internet.)

Show children where Paul started churches, especially noting Thessalonica.

Say: Paul started many churches. What is a "church?" It is the people who make up the church, not the building in which they meet. The dictionary says that the church is: The whole number of true believers around the world, or all the people who profess to be Christians, or a building made for worship.

Why do you think that Paul started so many churches? Why do new churches start up today? If you started a church, what would it have in it? What would be special about your church? ☺

Memory Verse: 1 Thessalonians 1: 7–8a ICB

So you became an example to all the believers in Macedonia and Southern Greece. The Lord's teaching spread from you in Macedonia and Southern Greece. And your faith in God has become known everywhere.

Alternate version (New King James)

so that you became examples to all in Macedonia and Achaia who believe. For from you the word of the Lord has sounded forth, not only in Macedonia and Achaia, but also in every place. Your faith toward God has gone out, so that we do not need to say anything.

Enrichment for Younger Children: Footprints of Jesus

Needed: Footprints cut from colored sheets of craft foam or from construction paper about the size of an adult foot but close enough together that your children can walk from one to another. Spread them around the room in a path.

Encourage children to walk around the footprints, stepping on them and trying not to step on the ground.

Explain: Walking like Jesus is like what we just did. We find out what Jesus would say or do and do the very same thing. We walk in his footprints. That's another way to say we imitate him.

Ask: What are some things Jesus does that you can do? (*Samples: love people; be kind to younger children; obey parents.*) Guide children to write these on the footprints. Then practice walking on them again. ☺

September 12

Who Wants To Be Like Me?

By Ivy Beckwith

Scripture:
1 Thessalonians 1:2–10

Lesson Aim:
Kids explore what it means to be an example to others.

Bible Skill:
Kids will learn to lead like Paul led.

Bible Lesson: Who Wants to Be Like Me?

Gather children together to tell this story: A long time ago there was a man named Paul who loved God. He wanted other people to know about God so he traveled to countries like Italy and Greece telling people God loved them. Many of these people heard what Paul said and learned to believe in God and love Jesus. When they did this Paul helped them start churches.

Ask: Who can tell me what a church is? Churches are groups of people who come together because they love God. They come together so they can learn more about God and Jesus. They come together so they can help each other. And they come together so they can help people who are not part of the church and tell those people God loves them.

One place Paul went to tell people about Jesus was a town in Greece called Thessalonica. The people Paul met there started a church. Paul couldn't stay with the people in Thessalonica forever because he had to go talk to more people about Jesus. After he left he still wanted to make sure the church was doing well and that the people were taking care of each other and loving each other. So Paul wrote the church letters in order to stay in touch.

Our Bible verse today is from one of the letters Paul wrote to the church in the town of Thessalonica. In this letter Paul told the people of the church many things. In our Bible verse he praised the church for trying hard to live like Jesus did. Paul said that the people in the church at Thessalonica had become an example to people in other churches all over the world.

I think one of the reasons God made sure we were able to read this letter to the church at Thessalonica in the Bible was so we could live like the people of the church in Thessalonica. So let me ask you some questions. What does it mean to be an example to other people? It means that we live in such a way that other people who watch us live, want to live like we do. Because we are kind to other people, the people who watch us live, want to be kind. Because we are willing to give away some of what we have, other people who watch us live, want to give away some of what they have, too.

Now, let me ask you the second question. The way Jesus lived was an example to us. We should want to live like Jesus did. So, tell me some of the ways Jesus lived that we should follow as an example. Include these with children's suggestions:

Jesus loved other people.

Jesus spent time with people whom other people didn't want to be with.

Jesus told the truth. He didn't lie.

Jesus helped people.

So, these are some of the ways we can live like Jesus and be an example to other people.

Ask each child to name one thing they can do this week to be an example of God's love to other people? Let's pray and ask God to help us do this.

 Song Suggestions:

G-Mail! by Dean-o from "Soul Surfin'" (FKO Music, Inc. 1999)

This Is Love by Dean-o from "God City" (BibleBeat Music 2001)

Walk Like Jesus by Mary Rice Hopkins "15 Singable Songs" (Big Steps 4 U 1988)

Children All Around The World Songsheets published by CEF Press, P.O. Box 348, Warrenton, Mo. 63383

Craft for Younger Children: Live Like Jesus Magnets
Needed: For each child bring a magnet strip and a foot shape
cut from colored sheets of craft foam. Bring glue and markers.
Say: Today we are going to make magnets. Give each child a fun foam
footprint. Let children attach magnet to the back of the footprint and decorate the footprint.
Say: Jesus wants us to live like he lived. Jesus loved God. What else did
Jesus do? (*Samples: healed people; loved people; spent time with people
whom other people didn't want to be with; told the truth; helped
people.*) If you live like Jesus did, you are "walking like Jesus!"

Craft for Older Children: Live Like Jesus Magnets
Needed: For each child bring a magnet strip and a foot shape
cut from colored sheets of craft foam. Bring glue and markers.
Say: Today we are going to make magnets. Give each child a fun foam
footprint and direct them to write on it: "Live like Jesus." Attach magnets
to back of footprint.
Say: Jesus wants us to live like he lived. Jesus loved God. What can you
do that lives like Jesus? (*Samples: heal people; love people; spend time with
people whom other people don't want to be with; tell the truth; help people.*)
If you live like Jesus did, you are "walking like Jesus!"
What can you do that WOULD NOT be like Jesus? (*Samples: tell lies;
push; grab all the cookies; cheat.*) It's just as important to not do
bad things as it is to do good things. Walk like Jesus!

Footprints
Needed: "Sole" shaped peanut butter sandwich cookies.

Say: Today we have been learning to be like Jesus and
walk like Jesus. Let's eat these cookies, which will remind us
of footprints.
If you walk on sand, does your foot leave a footprint?
(Yes!) Did you know that your life can also leave a footprint? How can that

be? (*When you are nice to people they remember you; if you are mean, people never forget how mean you were.*)

Living like Jesus and walking like Jesus means that we do things that Jesus would like to see us do, that we don't do what Jesus doesn't want us to do. Say: Let's try to live like Jesus!

Prayer Focus:

Dear God, thank you for Jesus. Thank you for the example that Jesus gave us of how to live our lives. We praise you for all that you have done for us. Help us to live like Jesus; to love others and be kind to everyone. Amen.

Memory Verse: 1 Thessalonians 1:7–8a ICB

So you became an example to all the believers in Macedonia and Southern Greece. The Lord's teaching spread from you in Macedonia and Southern Greece. And your faith in God has become known everywhere.

Alternate version (New King James)
so that you became examples to all in Macedonia and Achaia who believe. For from you the word of the Lord has sounded forth, not only in Macedonia and Achaia, but also in every place. Your faith toward God has gone out, so that we do not need to say anything.

Memory Verse Activity:

Needed: Small foam balls or paper crumpled into balls, index cards, and containers to throw balls into such as a clean trash can. Write the words of the verse onto index cards. Line up words on floor next to trash containers.

Say: We are going to play a game to help us with the memory verse. Show children how to try to throw the ball into the container. If they make it and the ball goes in, they can select a verse card. If they don't make it, they continue to throw the ball until it goes in. When the children have all the cards, help them put the memory verse together. Say the verse several times together.

September 15

It Couldn't Be Worse, Midweek
By Pat Verbal

Scripture:
Exodus 15:22–17:7; Psalm 142:1, 2; Philippians 2:14–15

Lesson Aim:
To help children recognize that complaining does not honor God.

Bible Skill:
I can talk calmly rather than complain.

Bible Learning Activity for Younger Children:
Needed: One bag of candy or something the children would want, one crown.

Say: Today I have a treat for you! I am going to give you some candy, but I need to make a decision. I have 30 pieces of candy and there are 21 of you. What should I do with the rest? I know, I'll choose a king! The king can decide what to do!

Choose the child with the birthday nearest today to be the "King" and put the crown on him. Let the king decide what to do. Whatever he or she decides, some children will not like the decision. Let them discuss it.

Say: It's really hard to make good decisions. In Bible times, the people wanted a king to help them with their decisions, too. God wanted them to just listen to him and not have a king. But they didn't listen to God. They pressed and pressed until he allowed them to have a king.

Was the king able to help with the decision? (yes and no) Sometimes even a king cannot help! That's what the people of Israel found out!

Bible Learning Activity for Older Children: Say No to Pouting

Do you ever pout? Pouting is when you let everyone know in a showy way that you are displeased or dissatisfied with what you have or how people treat you.

Sometimes people pout by being mean, sometimes people pout by being quiet or not doing what their mom or dad ask them to do. How do you pout?

Today, let's just say no to pouting! This is what you can do:

1. Memorize today's Bible verse.

2. Ask a friend and a parent to tell you if you're pouting and pray with you about it.

3. Think of others before you think of yourself, and do kind things as a result.

4. Ask others to forgive you when you are selfish and try harder next time.

Enrichment for Older Children: Mother Teresa

Say to the children:

What are your bad habits?

What are your good habits?

Which is better to have—bad or good habits?

Contentment is a good habit. Let me tell you about someone who didn't have very much but was very content. Her name is Mother Teresa.

Mother Teresa is an outstanding example of a Christian who lived a contented life. As a Catholic nun, she served the poorest people in the world. Her words and actions inspired millions to help the needy.

Mother Teresa never owned a home, a car, pretty clothes, or took a luxury cruise. She never had a computer, a baby grand piano, or a diamond ring. But she had the friendship of caring people.

Her work among suffering and dying people in India was hard, but she never complained. Instead, Mother Teresa had a kind word for everyone. She hugged, smiled, and prayed with people of all races and religions.

Here is what she said about contentment and humility.

If we were humble, nothing would change us—neither praise nor discouragement.

If someone were to criticize us, we would not feel discouraged.

If someone would praise us, we also would not feel proud.

Mother Teresa in My Own Words 1910–1997 (Gramercy Books, New York, 1996)

Enrichment for Younger Children: POUT!

Do you ever pout? Show me how you can pout. (Let children make faces, etc.)

Do you get what you want when you pout?

Let's play "POUT!" Everyone stand up and move around. When I say "POUT!" I want you to freeze and put a "pout" on your face. Okay, Go! (Let children move around until you call out "POUT!" The children freeze. Play several times.)

Say: How do you feel with that pout on your face? Kind of silly, huh?

Let's try not to pout today, okay? Instead let's kindly say what we want or need. What can you do instead of pout? (Let children answer.) ☺

Memory Verse: Philippians 2:14–15 ICB

Do everything without complaining or arguing.
Then you will be innocent and without anything wrong in you.
You will be God's children without fault.
But you are living with crooked and mean people all around you.
Among them you shine like stars in the dark world.

Alternate version (New King James)

Do all things without complaining and disputing, that you may become blameless and harmless, children of God without fault in the midst of a crooked and perverse generation, among whom you shine as lights in the world,

September 19

It Couldn't Be Worse
By Pat Verbal

Scripture:
Exodus 15:22–17:7; Psalm 142:1, 2; Philippians 2:14–15

Lesson Aim:
To help children recognize that complaining does not honor God.

Bible Skill:
I can talk calmly rather than complain.

Bible Lesson: The Complaining Israelites Want a King!

There is an old Yiddish folk tale about a farmer who complained that his house was too noisy. His wife and children were driving him crazy, so he went to see a wise man. The wise man told him to put his chickens in his house and he did. The next week he went back.

"Oh, great wise one, the noise in my house is so bad. It couldn't be worse! What should I do?"

"Do you have a cow?" asked the wise man. The farmer nodded, "yes."

"Put your cow in your house," he said. So the farmer put the cow in his house. The following week he went back.

"Oh, great wise one, the noise in my house is so bad. You should hear it. It couldn't be worse."

This time the farmer was told to put his goats in the house. So, he did.

Each time the farmer went for counsel, the wise man told him to put another animal in his house. Soon the farmer's house was full of yelling, baying, mooing, clucking, barking, and oinking. He was ready to move out, but one last time, he went to see the wise man.

"Oh, great wise one, I'm so miserable in my house. It couldn't be worse!

"Let all the animals out of the house," instructed the clever wise man. "Then come back and see me." The next day the farmer returned smiling.

"Oh, great wise one! Finally, my house is quiet and I have you to thank for it all."

What changed? The farmer's house? Or the farmer?

Since the beginning of time God tried to show his people what he was like. The tranquility of the Garden of Eden revealed God's character, but Adam and Eve messed that up. God sent the prophets to tell the people of his love for mankind, but they killed the prophets. Then he sent judges to solve the people's problems and speak the truth. The Israelites complained that they wanted a king like other nations. So, God gave them a king.

Did having kings make God's chosen people happy? No! Kings created armies and fought over land and power. God's people begged for mercy from bad kings and worshiped good kings instead of worshiping God. Many prayed for a Savior who would set up an earthly kingdom.

When Jesus, their Messiah, came to earth, did they accept him? No! They even complained about God. They complained that Jesus did not use his power to get rid of the evil Romans. Some were jealous of Jesus and complained that he couldn't be God's Son. After Jesus died and rose again, were God's people happy? No! Many did not believe and went right on hoping for some other sign from God.

Complaining is like wearing a blindfold. It hides the big picture. It also makes people very sad. People only see what they want to see instead of seeing God's truth.

Better than complaining is to talk calmly and kindly.

 Song Suggestions:

God's Way Right by Dean-o from "You Got It All" (FKO Music, Inc. 1997)

Let the Lord Have His Way Songsheets published by CEF Press, P.O. Box 348, Warrenton, Mo. 63383

Open the Eyes of My Heart by Norm Hewitt from "Fired Up" (Revelation Generation 2002)

Craft for Younger Children: Crown the King!

Needed: For each child cut a crown from heavy paper and bring jewels to decorate with.

Say: God's people really wanted a king. They complained and asked, and complained and asked and complained and asked until finally God said "OK, I will let you have a king."

God crowned Saul the first king. For a while the people stopped complaining and then they started complaining again. They complained and complained and complained.

Today we are going to make crowns to remind us of the king that God gave the people and that the king did not solve the problem.

God doesn't want us to complain. He wants us to let him help solve the problems instead.

Craft for Older Children: The Grumble Jar

Needed: For each child bring a baby food jar and paint pens.

Say: Today we are going to make a "grumble jar." We will write negative works or thoughts on the outside of the jar with paint pens such as:

no
too hard
bad
why
ugly
sick
yuck
boring
frown faces

On the lid we will write part of the Bible verse: *Do Everything Without Complaining.*

Inside the jar we will place small squares of paper. Each time you complain, make a note and put it in the jar. Use the jar as a reminder that God hears every word. At bedtime, open the jar and take your complaints to God in prayer. Ask God for a solution to that problem. Then praise God for what he has done for you! Your complaints will begin to seem smaller and smaller!

Popcorn Complaints

Needed: Popcorn and popcorn popper.

Say: Did you know that complaints can start out small and get bigger and bigger and bigger? Let's put a little popcorn into the popper and see what happens.

Start with a half cup of popcorn kernels. They look small . . . like some complaints seem small.

Pop the corn and measure the volume. Say: This popcorn is hard when we put it in, sort of like a "hard heart" can be. It is also small like the beginning of a problem. But when there is "heat" or problems, popcorn pops up much larger and grows bigger and bigger!

Ask: What would be better than complaining? (*Samples include: cooperate; talk things out calmly; solve the problem.*)

Prayer Focus:

Dear God, please help me to solve my problems without complaining. Help me to be content. You have been better to me than I could ever imagine. You deserve all my praise. Help me be happy with what I have. Give poor families food and shelter. Amen.

Memory Verse Activity: Shine!

This verse tells us that we can shine! What does that mean? How can we shine?

Have you ever had a flashlight in a dark area? When you turn it on and "shine" it, the dark area becomes light and bright! Everyone feels better because of the shining light.

That's how Christians should be. In a dark world, we should shine! We should shine and light up the darkness! ☺

Memory Verse: Philippians 2:14–15 ICB

Do everything without complaining or arguing.
Then you will be innocent and without anything wrong in you.
You will be God's children without fault.
But you are living with crooked and mean people all around you.
Among them you shine like stars in the dark world.

Alternate version (New King James)

Do all things without complaining and disputing, that you may become blameless and harmless, children of God without fault in the midst of a crooked and perverse generation, among whom you shine as lights in the world.

September 22

Our Generous God, Midweek
By Ivy Beckwith

Scripture:
Matthew 20:1–16

Lesson Aim:
Kids will know our God is a generous, loving God.

Bible Skill:
Kids will rely on God's generosity and love in their lives.

Bible Learning Activity for Younger Children:
Needed: For each child bring grapes in a self-sealing plastic bag and a small glass.

Let's make some grape juice like they did in Bible times. Give each child a self-sealing bag and put in a few grapes. Seal the bag and warn children not to open it. Show children how to squash grapes until the juice comes out. Supervise closely. Pour the juice into small cups to drink.

Say: So many people in Bible times had the job of making the grape juice that Jesus used their jobs in a story. How would you like to have this job of squashing grapes with your feet?

Bible Learning Activity for Older Children:
Act out the Bible parable as follows by assigning students to the following jobs and guiding them to perform the jobs:

Grape Pickers—they begin to pantomime picking grapes at the very beginning of the story. (Have them work really hard so that they begin to get tired.)

• Grape Stompers—Add this group to the story next. They have the job of stomping the juice out of the grapes. (Have them stomp for quite a while so that they are tired also.)

• Juice Strainers—Their job is to make sure that the skins of the grapes are not left in the juice. They bend over at the waist and gently pick little "skins" up and throw them away. Have them act as though this is no effort at all.

• Late Comers—This is the last group of workers. They begin just before the parable ends and stomp a few grapes but not enough to get tired.

Say: Okay, we have all worked very hard to get this juice ready. I'm going to pay you all the exact same salary! Here you go! Is that fair? (NO!) Not usually, is it?

But Jesus told this parable so that we would understand if we love Jesus even at the very end, we will be rewarded with a great gift—the great gift of heaven.

Ask: Why believe in God early then? (*Because you get the benefit of living your whole life happily; because you have more time with Jesus.*)

Enrichment for Younger Children: Money, Money, Money!

Needed: Green paper cut into "dollar bill" shapes or play money.

Say: Do any of you have any money? How did you get it? Did you have to do work for it?

Today we are going to play a game. I will pay you for what you do.

Begin by asking the children to do a series of tasks. After each task, pay all of them the same amount, regardless of who is the best at the task.

Tasks can include:

How many times can you jump on one foot?

How fast can you run from here to there?

How many pieces of trash can you pick up for me?

How quiet can you be?

Soon, the children will observe that they are all getting the same amount of "money" and they will begin to complain. Say: It might not seem fair to us to all get the same amount no matter what you DO, but God loves us all the same no matter what we do! Jesus told this story so that we would understand that. What do you like about being loved equally? ☺

Enrichment for Older Children: Is It Fair?

Needed: An assortment of wrapping paper and ribbon, tape, shoeboxes, treats such as snack cakes or cookies.

Say: Today we are going to wrap some boxes. Divide into groups and in each group we will wrap a box. You may choose how to do it. You will be rewarded for what you do.

Let each group decorate the box they wish.

Say: Wow, these are great! You all did so well.

Then pass out rewards arbitrarily, having nothing to do with how well the boxes are wrapped. You may give a huge piece of cake to one group, a smaller piece to another. Kids will respond, "That's not fair!"

Say: I promised you all a reward and I gave you one. Why isn't it fair?

After children comment, agree that is probably how the people in our Bible story felt, too. Some of them did a better job or worked longer but what they were paid had nothing to do with their work.

Why do you think Jesus told this story?   ☺

Memory Verse: Matthew 20:16 ICB

"So those who have the last place now will have the first place in the future. And those who have the first place now will have the last place in the future."

Alternate version (New King James)

"So the last will be first, and the first last. For many are called, but few chosen."

September 26

Our Generous God
By Ivy Beckwith

Scripture:
Matthew 20:1–16

Lesson Aim:
Kids will know our God is a generous, loving God.

Bible Skill:
Kids will rely on God's generosity and love in their lives.

Bible Lesson: Our Generous God

Gather children together. How many of you like to hear stories? I think we all like to hear stories. Jesus knew that and so sometimes when he taught people about God he would tell a story. These stories helped the people understand more about what God is like. Today we're going to talk about one of the stories Jesus told.

One day a man who owned a lot of land where he grew grapes went out into the town in the morning to find some men to help farm the land. He found some workers and they agreed on a price for the day's work. The workers went out to work in the vineyard. About nine o'clock in the morning the man went back into town and saw some more workers standing around in the center of town waiting for some work to do. The man offered them a job in his vineyard and told the workers he would pay them whatever was right. The men went off to tend to the grapes. The owner of the vineyard went back into town again at noon and at three o'clock in the afternoon and hired more workers agreeing on a wage. Both times he sent men off to work in the vineyard. Then, at about five o'clock in the afternoon, the man went back into town and found more workers standing around waiting for some work to do. The man asked the men, "Why have you been standing here all day doing nothing?" The men said to him, "Because no one has hired us." The vineyard owner told them to go into his fields and work.

Finally, evening came and the man went to the vineyard to pay the workers. He went to the man who managed the workers and told him to pay the workers. "Call the laborers," he said. "Give them their pay, beginning with the last and then going to the first." But, how the man paid the workers surprised the workers. He paid the men he hired at five o'clock in the afternoon the same amount of money he would have paid them if they had worked the whole day.

The news of this spread quickly to the rest of the workers so the ones hired early in the morning expected they would be paid more. But the man paid them the usual wages. When these workers saw this they grumbled about the landowner. They said, "The last workers worked only an hour, and you've paid them equally with those of us who worked all day in the hot sun." The landowner answered their questions. "Friend," he said. "I didn't do anything wrong to you. You agreed with me at the beginning of the day to take the usual daily wage. That's what I gave you. Now, take what belongs to you and go home. I made a choice to give to those hired last the same wages I gave to you. I'm allowed to do what I choose with what belongs to me. Don't be envious because I am generous." And that was the end of the story Jesus told about God. He finished it by turning to the people who were listening and saying, "So the last will be first, and the first will be last."

Now why do you think the man who owned the land paid all the workers the same amount of money? How would you feel if you were one of the

 Song Suggestions:

You Got It All by Dean-o from "You Got It All" (FKO Music, Inc., 1997)

Refiner's Fire from "Change My Heart Oh God for Kids" (Vineyard Music Group 1997)

Little Miracle by Mary Rice Hopkins from "Good Buddies"(Big Steps 4 U 1994)

I Can Know God Songsheets published by CEF Press, P.O. Box 348, Warrenton, Mo. 63383

people who only worked for an hour and still got paid the same amount as those people who worked all day? These men would see the landowner as being a very generous and giving man. He only had to pay them a fraction of what he paid the others. Instead he paid them more because he knew they needed it. The man was very generous with all the riches he'd been given.

Jesus was telling the people that he is a very generous God and gives gladly.

 Craft for Younger Children: Treasure Magnet
    Needed: Bring for each child a milk lid, magnet strip, beads, small "jewels" and glue.

Say: Today we are going to make a special magnet. Show children how to first glue a magnet strip onto the back of the lid and then fill the milk lid with glue and place beads and jewels inside.

Say: You have made a special "treasure" magnet. Use this magnet to remember that you are a treasure to God!

 Craft for Older Children: Generous God Journal
    Needed: Bring for each child six pieces of white paper and one sheet of construction paper. Place all papers together and staple with the construction paper on the outside to form a book.

Say: This is a journal. Does anyone know what a journal is? A journal is a place where you write down the things that happen to you. This is a special journal because we are going to write down everything that God does for us. When you pray for something, write down what you pray for and leave a space to later write down how God answered that prayer. When God does something special for you, write that down too! Find at least three blessings from God to write every day in your journal.

Have children write "Our Generous God" on the cover of the journal and fill in the first page with good things that have happened. Stress: The blessings can be simple like waking up today, getting a hug from your mama, and hearing a bird sing.

Grapes From the Vine

Serve grapes as a snack. Explain to the kids that in the parable, the men were

working in the field picking grapes.

Snack

Alternate idea: Let children make grape juice by putting 10 grapes into a small plastic bag and let children stomp or squish the grapes until the juice comes out.

Prayer Focus:

Dear God, we thank you because you are so generous to us. You give us everything, even when we don't deserve it. Help us to be generous to others in the same way. We love you and we praise you for how wonderful you are. Amen.

Memory Verse: Matthew 20:16 ICB

"So those who have the last place now will have the first place in the future. And those who have the first place now will have the last place in the future."

Alternate version (New King James)
"So the last will be first, and the first last. For many are called, but few chosen."

Memory Verse Activity All Ages: Last Place, First Place

Let children line up on far side of the room. Say: We are going to play first place, last place. We will play this game just like "Red Light, Green Light" only with a twist. Here goes.

Begin playing game calling out "Red Light, Green Light" a few times.

Say: Last will be first! Instruct children to turn around on their spot. Leader goes to the opposite end of the room to begin again.

Say: Does it seem fair to play this way? No, life is not usually like this. But in God's kingdom God wants to give everyone grace. Giving grace means to accept people into his kingdom even at the very last.

September 29

Does God Know Who I Am?, Midweek
By Barbara Platt

Scripture:
Matthew 10:29–31

Lesson Aim:
God cares about the details in your life.

Bible Skill:
I can talk with God about my worries and he will help me find an answer.

Bible Learning Activity for Younger Children: Worry Translation
Needed: a poster or markerboard and marker.

Ask: What are some of the things that you worry about? Go around room and let children tell what worries them. Write these on the poster.

Then invite each child to pick one worry from the poster and say a one sentence prayer to God about that worry. Explain: When we talk with God about our worries, he shows us what to do about them. He cares very much for us.

Bible Learning Activity for Older Children: Birds in the Bible
Needed: For each child bring a grocery-list looking piece of paper and pen.

Give each child a long piece of paper. Say: We make a list when we go to the grocery. Let's make a list of birds to watch for. We will find birds listed in the Bible.

Guide children to look up the following passages and write down the bird from each:

Luke 17:37
Matthew 26:34
Matthew 10:29–31
Psalm 84:3
Proverbs 30:18–19
Ecclesiastes 10:20
Isaiah 38:14
Isaiah 43:20

Enrichment for Younger Children: Clay Birds
Needed: Pictures of birds, play clay.
    Say: Let's look at these pictures of birds. Aren't they pretty?
    How do birds fly? Which is your favorite bird?
    Let's make a bird out of this clay. Let children make their own version of a bird, or copy one from a picture. ☺

Enrichment for Older Children: String Bird Feeders
Needed: Thread, large needles, popcorn, cranberries, raisins, bread cubes, leftover cake.
    Show children how to thread the needle and then string "bird food" items on thread. Make it as long as time allows and wrap it in the tree branches.
    Say: Birds eat so much! This will help birds have a special treat waiting for them! ☺

Memory Verse: Matthew 10:29, 31 ICB
When birds are sold, two small birds cost only a penny. But not even one of the little birds can die without your Father's knowing it. So, don't be afraid. You are worth much more than many birds.

Alternate version (New King James)
Are not two sparrows sold for a copper coin? And not one of them falls to the ground apart from your Father's will. Do not fear therefore; you are of more value than many sparrows.

October 3

Does God Know Who I Am?
By Barbara Platt

Scripture:
Matthew 10:29–31

Lesson Aim:
God cares about the details in your life.

Bible Skill:
I can talk with God about my worries and he will help me find an answer.

Bible Lesson: Sparrows
Needed: Picture of a sparrow.

Have you watched a sparrow in your yard? A sparrow is a bird. You must be very quiet, and very still. A sparrow isn't dressed in flashy feathers. He is really a variety of shades of browns. But the birds are beautiful because of their stripes and sections of brown. Brown coats are really very pretty!

There are many, many sparrows. They could be considered so "common" that we don't think they are special. Some people say that when you've seen one sparrow the other sparrows are just like that one. But are they? No. God knows each one.

And so do the parent birds. Mom and Dad sparrow are very proud of their family—and they take care of each one in a very special way. For days they sit on the eggs to keep them warm. Then . . . one day there is a small noise underneath Mom. It's time! The egg is cracking and there is a tiny bill (that's the new bird's mouth), then a new a new baby bird has hatched from the egg. No, he's not beautiful—except in the eyes of the parents. He's wet, he can't stand on his feet very well, he wobbles around the nest, and squawks. Part of his message is —"I'm hungry!"

Song Suggestions:

Free Inside by Dean-o from "Soul Surfin'" (FKO Music, Inc., 1999)

Little Is Much by Mary Rice Hopkins from "15 Singable Songs" (Big Steps 4 U 1988)

I Can Know God Songsheets published by CEF Press, P.O. Box 348, Warrenton, Mo. 63383

Since Mom and Dad sparrow take very good care of their family one of them goes off to find some good food for the new baby. When they come back they know the certain squawk of that baby and also the wide-open mouth waiting for the food. Yum, the baby swallows the food—and immediately squawks for more. It's a never-ending routine of constantly finding more food for their little ones.

The baby sparrow grows very fast. The feathers dry off, and more feathers grow to make their brown feather coat in its special design just as it was planned. The hard job of learning to fly comes, too. Mom and Dad fly in and out—sure makes it look easy to do. But. it's so far to the ground and can I really depend on my wings to take me to the next tree and beyond?

God planned for the parent birds to help the baby birds learn many lessons, like flying, and how to live with all the other birds. In Matthew 10:29, it tells us that God knows when one sparrow falls to the ground. God knows each sparrow, the ones that you can see and many more that you can't see. He says in Matthew 10:31 that you are more valuable to him than many sparrows. You are very special to God.

 Craft for Younger Children: Birds!
Needed: Bring for each child a paper with the shape of a bird drawn on it, brown craft feathers, and glue.

Show children how to choose feathers and glue them onto the bird shape. As they work explain that Jesus talks about birds. God loves birds. Jesus says that God will take care of you better than he takes care of the birds!

Craft for Older Children: Bird Family
Needed: Variety of sizes and colors of pompoms, small bits of colored foam sheets, glue, google eyes.

Show children how to create "birds" out of materials listed above. Encourage them to make a family of birds.

Ask: In your bird family, who takes care of the babies? What does the mom do? What does the dad do? In your family, what do your parents do for you?

What does GOD do for the birds? What does God do for you? What does God do for your parents? God takes care of us. God knows each bird, God knows each of you!

Snack: Eat Like A Bird!

Needed: Different kinds of edible seeds available in your grocery store such as sunflower seeds and pumpkin seeds.

 Have you ever heard the saying, "You eat like a bird"? People say that when you aren't eating very much, but actually birds eat a lot! They just eat small things. Birds like to eat insects and seeds. Pass around seeds and let the children taste them.

Ask: Would you like to eat these things every day? No! Of course not, because we aren't birds! God gives us food to eat and our food is different from bird food!

Let the children eat more seeds and pretend to be birds.

Prayer Focus:

Dear God, thank you for loving us so much and believing we are so special. Thank you for knowing us personally. We love you and we praise you. Amen.

Memory Verse: Matthew 10:29, 31 ICB

When birds are sold, two small birds cost only a penny. But not even one of the little birds can die without your Father's knowing it. So, don't be afraid. You are worth much more than many birds.

Alternate version (New King James)

Are not two sparrows sold for a copper coin? And not one of them falls to the ground apart from your Father's will. Do not fear therefore; you are of more value than many sparrows.

Memory Verse Activity:
Birds are very special to God, but we are much more special! Write verse on white board. When children have said the verse, erase two words and say it again. Continue until all the words are erased and children know the verse.

October 6

You'll Never Thirst Again, Midweek
By Dean-o

Scripture:
John 4:13–14

Lesson Aim:
God uses everyday items to explain deep spiritual truths.

Bible Skill:
Kids will understand that worshiping Jesus is like drinking good water that never runs out.

Bible Learning Activity for Younger Children: Water Drops
Needed: Blue paper cut into "drop" shapes large enough for children to write their names, medicine dropper, water, wax paper, crayons.

Say: Water was very important in this story. In Bible times, water came out of a well and was very precious. Drop water from dropper onto wax paper so children can examine the drops. Let children make shapes with the droplets on the wax paper.

Pass out blue paper drops. Have children write *Jesus loves (their name)* on the drops. Say: Jesus said if we are thirsty we should come to him. Let's write our names on these drops so we will remember to love Jesus and that Jesus loves us.

Bible Learning Activity for Older Children: Well, Well!
Say: When we want a drink of water, we go to the faucet, turn it on, and get some water! But it was not like that in Bible times. To get water, people usually had to get it out of a pit or hole sunk into the earth. Many different

types of wells are mentioned in the Bible. These include a deep hole dug in the ground, a spring, a fountain, and a pit or hole.

Wells in Palestine were dug through solid limestone rock. Sometimes wells had steps to get the water directly from the pool of water. Other wells had a low wall of stone where you got water by lowering a rope over the side. Jesus sat on a well like this when he talked to the woman of Samaria (John 4:6).

We don't really know how biblical wells were dug. But the process must have been very difficult, because they didn't have tools as good as today. Partly because of this, wells were very valuable. Even as hard as they were to build, ancient wells were very deep. A well called Jacob's well is still 75 feet deep and at one time it may have been twice as deep. Wells had to be deep so that they would not run dry in the summer.

Enrichment for Older Children: Water Race

Needed: Small buckets, one for each team and one large container to hold water and large cups for carrying water.

Guide children to divide into teams according to favorite school subject (*samples: math, reading, science, etc*). Make a starting line near the water container and a finishing line across the room with the bucket at the line.

Say: Getting water out of a well was a hard job but it was even harder to carry the water on your head! Today we are going to have a relay race to see how hard it was! Say: This is a relay race. Fill your cup up and with the cup on your head run to the finishing line. Pour the water into the bucket there. Run back to the water and pass the cup to the next person in line. You are finished when your bucket is full. If you have a child with hearing aids or another reason he cannot use his head, have all children carry the cups on their open palms.

Ready? Go!

Was that hard or easy? Why do you think they carried water on their heads? In Bible times they carried water on their heads because it didn't hurt their backs as much. Since they were carrying a very heavy water jar, they usually carried it this way. How would you like to be a water carrier?

Alternate activity for indoor game: Place small sponges inside the cups so the water won't spill. ☺

Enrichment for Younger Children: Water Race

Needed: Small buckets, one for each team and one large container to hold water, two sponges.

Say: Getting water out of a well was a hard job because if you weren't careful, you could spill most of it. Today we are going to get water out of a pretend well, but we'll use sponges so that we won't spill the water.

Instruct children to divide into teams. Make a starting line near the water container and a finishing line across the room.

Say: This is a relay race. Put your sponge into the water so that it is filled with water. Take it to the other side of the room by the finishing line. Squeeze the water into the bucket there. Run back to your team and give the sponge to the next child. They will do the same thing. You are finished when everyone has a turn.

Ready? Go!

Was that hard or easy? Aren't you glad that we get our water out of a faucet? [NOTE: Be certain to play on a surface covered with carpet so children won't slip on any spilled water.]

Alternate activity for indoor game: Place small sponges inside cups so that the water won't spill. ☺

Memory Verse: John 4:13–14 ICB

Jesus answered, "Every person who drinks this water will be thirsty again. But whoever drinks the water I give will never be thirsty again. The water I give will become a spring of water flowing inside him. It will give him eternal life."

Alternate version (New King James)

Jesus answered and said to her, "Whoever drinks of this water will thirst again, but whoever drinks of the water that I shall give him will never thirst. But the water that I shall give him will become in him a fountain of water springing up into everlasting life."

October 10

You'll Never Thirst Again
By Dean-o

Scripture:
John 4:13–14

Lesson Aim:
God uses everyday items to explain deep spiritual truths.

Bible Skill:
Kids will understand that worshiping Jesus is like drinking good water that never runs out.

Bible Lesson: Water That Keeps On Bubbling
Gather children together and ask: What is Jesus like?

After children tell several illustrations, explain that one of the ways they have learned about Jesus is through experience with him. Jesus knew that personal experience is a good teacher so he often used everyday objects to illustrate big truths. One of these is that a relationship with Jesus is like drinking good water that never runs out.

God gave us a story in the Bible about Jesus meeting a Samaritan woman at a well who was drawing water. After Jesus asked the woman for a drink, she expressed her shock and reminded Jesus that because he was a Jew, he was not supposed to talk to her, a Samaritan. She did not know who Jesus was, or that she was talking to the Son of God! Jesus then told her that she would be asking him for water, for living water, if she knew who he was. He explained that he could give her the gift of living forever.

The Samaritan woman asked Jesus where she could find this magical water. She thought Jesus was talking about real water. Then Jesus made it clear that he was not talking about water that could be found in any well,

Song Suggestions:

Come to the Well by Dean-o from "God City" (BibleBeat Music 2001)

Deep and Wide Traditional

I Believe Songsheets published by CEF Press, P.O. Box 348, Warrenton, Mo. 63383

Little Bit of Love by Mary Rice Hopkins from "Miracle Mud" (Big Steps 4 U, 1995)

but that he was talking about accepting the gift of eternal life, or living water. Isn't that awesome? We cannot get to heaven on our own, and we must go through Jesus, God's only Son. It's a relationship with God himself. He talked personally to the Samaritan woman. He will relate personally to you and to me.

Jesus invites us to drink of his water, so that we will never thirst again. His love will be like a well of gushing water bursting inside of us that fills us with eternal life!

So boys and girls, here's my challenge: Remember that there is only one way to heaven, and it is through Jesus. The heavenly waterway leading to a spring of "cool" salvation is available to all who will believe! Make him your Savior, your Lord, and a day will come when you'll be in heaven with God. Until then you get to live a life of adventure and goodness right here on earth. The bottom line: Accept the gift of Jesus, and you'll never thirst again!

Craft for Younger Children: You Are the Potter
Needed: For each child bring a lump of play clay.
        Say: In Bible times, people made their water jugs out of clay, or pottery. They couldn't buy the jars that they wanted, they had to make them by themselves. Today we are going to make a Bible times water jar. Show children a picture (from book or internet) of a Bible times water jar and encourage them to make one with the clay. Suggest they pretend to carry it on their heads.

Craft for Older Children: Bible Times Water Jug

Needed: For each child bring a 3 ounce plastic bathroom cup, modeling clay.

Say: In Bible times the people made their own jugs to hold water. The jug was lowered into a well or river whenever they needed to get some water. It was usually a clay jar with one or two handles. It was so big that it was usually carried on the head or shoulders. Usually women had the job of carrying water or drawing water from wells (Gen. 24:14).

Today we are going to make a water jar. Using the cup as the center of the jar, mold the clay around the cup. Show children how to do this.

Today we don't have to go to so much trouble to get water, do we? But in Bible times it did take some work to get water, so the fact that Jesus used water in his story shows how special it was to the people.

Snack: Living Water Rocks

Needed: Rock shaped cereal, peanut butter.

 Say: In Bible times the people got their water out of a well. Wells were made out of rocks. Let's make a small well out of our cereal rocks. Show children how to form a well by "gluing" the rocks together with the peanut butter into a well shape.

Prayer Focus:

Dear God, thank you so much for the living water that you have given us. Thank you that we know you have promised that we will never thirst again if we believe in you. Amen.

Memory Verse: John 4:13–14 ICB

Jesus answered, "Every person who drinks this water will be thirsty again. But whoever drinks the water I give will never be thirsty again. The water I give will become a spring of water flowing inside him. It will give him eternal life."

Alternate version (New King James)

Jesus answered and said to her, "Whoever drinks of this water will thirst again, but whoever drinks of the water that I shall give him will never thirst. But the water that I shall give him will become in him a fountain of water springing up into everlasting life."

Memory Verse Activity:

Needed: Paper bags (lunch bag size) crumbled up to look like rocks, bucket filled with clean water, drinking cups. Tape paper rocks around the bucket to look like a well. Divide kids up into two teams according to the color clothes they are wearing.

Say: We are going to learn this verse while we also get a drink of water!

One at a time, go from the starting line to the well. Dip your cup into the water, have a small drink and say, "*Every person who drinks this water will be thirsty again. But whoever drinks the water I give will never be thirsty!*"

Then run back to the starting line.

Continue until everyone has had a turn.

October 13

Who Is Your Hero?, Midweek
By Ivy Beckwith

Scripture:
Leviticus 19:1–2

Lesson Aim:
We can think of God as our hero.

Bible Skill:
Kids will learn what holiness is.

Bible Learning Activity for All Ages: Pass the Beans!

Needed: About 1 pound of pinto beans, cup for each child. Mark lines on the floor about 10 feet apart. Ask children to line up on each side of the line.

Say: We are going to play a game called Pass the Beans. You will have a partner on the other side of the line. Your partner will have lots of beans in their cup; you won't have any in yours. At the signal, your partner can start tossing the beans to you and you must catch them in your cup. You cannot catch them in your hand.

If you need to, you may move closer together. It might help you.

Let children play. Make sure that they try both playing the game far apart for awhile and then closer together.

What was easier? Closer together. Yep, when you are closer together, you can work better together.

Explain: It's the same with God. When you never read the Bible or pray you can't be close to God, even if you love him. But when you talk to God and listen to him by reading his Bible you will find it easier to work with God, to know what he wants you to do in your life.

Enrichment for Older Children: Holy, Holy, Holy

Needed: Tape or CD of the hymn *Holy, Holy, Holy,* words to the hymn.

Teach kids the hymn "Holy, Holy, Holy" (maybe use a CD with an upbeat version). Talk about what the words mean and how it describes the holiness of God. Put these lyrics on an overhead or white board and discuss with the children.

> Holy, holy, holy! Lord God Almighty!
> Early in the morning our song shall rise to thee.
> Holy, holy, holy! Merciful and mighty,
> God in three persons, blessed Trinity!
> Holy, holy, holy! All the saints adore thee,
> casting down their golden crowns around the glassy sea;
> cherubim and seraphim falling down before thee,
> which wert, and art, and evermore shalt be.
> Holy, holy, holy! Though the darkness hide thee,
> though the eye of sinful man thy glory may not see,
> only thou art holy; there is none beside thee,
> perfect in power, in love and purity.
> Holy, holy, holy! Lord God Almighty!
> All thy works shall praise thy name, in earth and sky and sea.
> Holy, holy, holy! Merciful and mighty,
> God in three persons, blessed Trinity.

Say: These words are different from the words we might write today to describe the holiness of God because it uses thee and thy. These words simply mean "you." Discuss, verse by verse what the words mean. ☺

Enrichment for Younger Children: Who's Your Hero?

Did you know that there are superheroes in the Bible? David was a superhero; he killed Goliath. Moses was a superhero; he led God's people to the Promised Land. Joshua was a superhero; he took God's people into the Promised Land. ☺

Alternate Enrichment Activity for Older Children: Write It Down

Needed: Child-friendly Bible dictionary such as the *Student Bible Dictionary*.

Have kids make a list of current heroes (sports figures, movie stars, cartoon characters, fictional characters, etc.) Talk about why these people become heroes. Say: Are these people positive heroes or bad ones? Do they help you or do they teach bad things? Why do people pick bad heroes? Good heroes?

Are any of these heroes HOLY? *(A Christian hero might be.)* God is a superhero who is good and fair and always holy. God is strong and holy and best of all, God loves us! ☺

Memory Verse: Leviticus 19:1–2 ICB

The Lord said to Moses, "Tell all the people of Israel: 'I am the Lord your God. You must be holy because I am holy.'"

Alternate version (New King James)
And the LORD spoke to Moses, saying,
"Speak to all the congregation of the children of Israel, and say to them:
'You shall be holy, for I the LORD your God am holy.'"

October 17

Who Is Your Hero?
By Ivy Beckwith

Scripture:
Leviticus 19:1–2

Lesson Aim:
We can think of God as our hero.

Bible Skill:
Kids will learn what holiness is.

Bible Lesson: Heroes
Gather children together. Ask, "Who can tell me what a hero is?" You are all correct. A hero is someone we look up to and want to be like. Heroes are people we admire because that person has done or stood for something powerful. Even if we don't do so deliberately, we want to be like the hero we admire. We imitate them.

Ask, "Who are some of your heroes? Who do you look up to and why do you want to be like that person? Sometimes we try to look like them by dressing the same way our heroes do. Sometimes we try to do the same things our heroes do or we try to say the same things our heroes say.

"Now it's a good thing to have a hero, especially when our hero is someone who does good actions and who stands for right things. So we need to be careful when we pick our heroes. Someone ought not to be our hero because she sings a song we like or because he can catch a lot of touchdown passes, unless they do good and kind things. We want to pick good people to be our heroes, especially because we want to be like our heroes.

"In the Bible God tells us the story of how God took a group of people, the Israelites, and asked them to make God their hero. God wanted this

Song Suggestions:

He Is Really God! by Dean-o from "You Got it All" (FKO Music, Inc. 1997)

Superman by Mary Rice Hopkins from "15 Singable Songs" (Big Steps 4 U 1988)

My Very Best Friend by Cindy Rethmeier from "I Want 2 Be Like Jesus" (Mercy/Vineyard Publishing 1995)

Holy, Holy, Holy Traditional hymn (words included in activity)

group of people to value the same things God did. God wanted all the other people in the world to understand what God thought was important just by watching how the Israelites lived. So he gave the Israelites a lot of direction on how they should live if they were going to be like God. And God promised them he would love them forever and never, ever leave them.

"Today's Bible verse tells us one of the ways God asked the people to live their lives. God said to the Israelites that because I am holy I want you to be holy, too. I want you to be like me.

"Who can tell me what the word 'holy' means? It's a Bible word we say a lot in church but have you ever really thought about what it means? To be holy means to separate yourself from all that is bad and harmful. It means to be good and to stay away from things that are bad for us and are bad for other people. God can't be anything but holy and good. God won't be bad. But people sometimes choose to be bad. We do things that are bad for us and will hurt other people. God knows this and because he loves us God wants us to be holy and follow him. Then God will be our hero!"

 Craft for Older Children: Elementary Craft: God Wants Us To Be Holy

Needed: For each child bring a heavyweight paper plate, different kinds of beans, and glue.

Show children how to letter the word "HOLY" with glue on the paper plate. Place one kind of beans into the glue spelling the word HOLY. When that is complete, fill in the rest of the plate with a variety of beans forming a "mosaic".

Craft Simplification for Younger Children:
Needed: For each child bring a heavyweight paper plate, different kinds of beans, and glue.

Preparation: For each child: Letter the word *Holy* onto the paper plate for the child.

Show them how to put the beans into the glue to form the word holy.

Superhero Bagels

Needed: Two small bagels per child, cream cheese or other topping. Cut each bagel in half and arrange on plate so that it forms an "S."

Say: Which superhero wears an "S" on his shirt? What does the "S" stand for? If you were a superhero, what letter would be on your shirt? There are many superheroes in our world, but the greatest superheroes defend our faith. They are pastors and teachers and parents and grandparents who teach about God!

Prayer Focus:

Dear God, we thank you for your holiness; we praise you that we can call you Holy. You are a wonderful and pure God. Please help us to have pure hearts. Amen.

Memory Verse: Leviticus 19:1–2 ICB

The Lord said to Moses, "Tell all the people of Israel: 'I am the Lord your God. You must be holy because I am holy.'"

Alternate version (New King James)
And the LORD spoke to Moses, saying,
"Speak to all the congregation of the children of Israel, and say to them:
'You shall be holy, for I the LORD your God am holy.'"

All Ages Memory Verse Activity:

Needed: For each child bring a white crayon, white paper, and markers or water colors.

Direct children to write "HOLY" on a paper with white crayon.

Say: No matter what idols people have, God stands above them because God is holy.

Show children how to paint over the word holy and notice that it stands out from the other colors they paint.

Say: God is holy and God's holiness always stands out!

October 20

The Man Nobody Liked, Midweek
By Terry Platt

Scripture:
Luke 19:1–10

Lesson Aim:
Children will know that Jesus accepts us all.

Bible Skill:
Children will decide to accept others.

Bible Learning Activity for Younger Children: Put Zach in the Tree
Needed: Blindfold, several pictures of a small man, and a picture of a big tree proportional to the man.

Play "Pin the Tail on the Donkey" except put Zach in the tree!

Bible Learning Activity for Older Children: Taxes, Taxes—Not Fair!
Needed: One bag of candy that comes in different colors, three large containers, a table cloth.

Place the containers on the ground on top of a tablecloth.

Say: Today we're going to learn about taxes. Choose the child with the birthday closest to today to be the Tax Collector. Pass out 10 candies to each child (random colors). Have children try to toss the candies into the cups.

Say: The Tax Collector gets to keep all the candy that goes onto the table cloth. You can keep all the candy that goes into the cups.

After children have tossed their candy, say: Was that fair? (No because the tax collector got more than we did.) Yes, you're right, it wasn't fair! But now I need all of you to give the tax collector all your red candies! (You should hear lots of grumbling!) That's how it was in Bible times, the taxes were not fair at all!

Now pass out equal amounts of candy to all kids.

Enrichment for Younger Children: Trees

Needed: Brown paper bags twisted into branch shape, green construction paper cut into leaves.

Explain: The Bible says that Zacchaeus climbed up in a sycamore tree. Sycamores are huge trees that grow 40–50 feet tall. They are great trees to climb. The leaves are heart-shaped. We are going to make a tree that looks like that now.

Show children how to assemble tree by putting the leaves onto the 3-D paper bag tree. ☺

Enrichment for Older Children: Tax Collectors

During Bible times tax collectors were agents or contract workers who collected taxes for the government. The way they got their salaries was to add money onto the taxes they collected. It as a big temptation to add a lot of profit, and many tax collectors did so. The tax collectors became wealthy men through this practice. They worked with the Roman government to collect the taxes of the Roman state. These tax collectors would often be backed by military force.

Tax collectors gathered several different types of taxes. There were land taxes, a poll tax, even a tax for the operation of the temple. The tax collectors were despised by their fellow Jews, probably because they took money and because they took extra money. They were classified generally as "sinners" probably because they were allowed to gather more than the government required and then to keep the extra money.

Jesus, however, taught people not to hate the tax collectors or any other sinners. Jesus accepted and associated with the tax collectors. He ate with them, he gave them his saving grace and he even chose a tax collector (Matthew) as one of his twelve disciples. Jesus wanted people to know that God would welcome the repentant and humble tax collector, but he would not welcome the proud Pharisee. His mission was to bring sinners—people like the tax collectors of his day—into God's presence. ☺

Memory Verse: Luke 19:9–10 ICB

Jesus said, "Salvation has come to this house today. This man truly belongs to the family of Abraham. The Son of Man came to find lost people and save them."

Alternate version (New King James)

And Jesus said to him, "Today salvation has come to this house, because he also is a son of Abraham; for the Son of Man has come to seek and to save that which was lost."

October 24

The Man Nobody Liked
By Terry Platt

Scripture:
Luke 19:1–10

Lesson Aim:
Children will know that Jesus accepts us all.

Bible Skill:
Children will decide to accept others.

Bible Lesson: Zaccheus Was a Little Man

Tell this story: Excitement was everywhere in the city. The teacher who could heal people, make blind eyes to see, and even raise someone from the dead was coming to town. There was a man in the city named Zacchaeus who was curious about the teacher but he didn't know if he should go see him.

No one liked Zacchaeus, and Zacchaeus may not have liked himself. He was a tax collector who cheated. For instance, if a person was to give 3 coins to the government, he would demand 4 or 5 and keep the extras for himself. The people knew he cheated them like this and wanted nothing to do with him.

In the distance, a cloud of dust was becoming visible caused by a large group of people, walking with Jesus on the dry dirt roads. Zacchaeus knew right away that this was the special visitor. He did not want to miss anything and hurried to join the crowd of people. He wanted to hear and see what this teacher, Jesus, was doing.

As he got closer, the people saw him but would not let him join the crowd. Since he was a very short man, it was impossible to see over the group's shoulders. But Zacchaeus was determined. He looked back toward the city and saw a big tree with branches that went over the road. He ran for the tree and climbed up to the branches where he could get the best view. He watched with expenctancy.

As the crowd got right under the tree, Jesus, the Teacher, looked up and with a kind look on his face, called Zacchaeus by name. Jesus looked right up at him! He said, "Zacchaeus, come down, I want to go to your house today!"

Zacchaeus was amazed! So was everyone else! They thought, "Why would Jesus go to his house—we don't even like him!" Zacchaeus left the crowd of people and walked together with Jesus. Onlookers wondered why Jesus would want to be with the most hated man in the city.

Something happened to Zacchaeus that day. Because of Jesus' kindness, Zacchaeus believed that Jesus was the Son of God. He became a follower of Him. To prove his devotion to Jesus he returned the stolen money to the people he had cheated. In fact, he paid them four times the amount he had cheated away from them.

Jesus made the difference in Zacchaeus' life.

Is there someone that you don't like? Is there any way you could be their friend? Your kindness could prompt that mean someone to turn around and begin to do kindness.

 Song Suggestions:

Zacchaeus Was a Wee Little Man Traditional

There Is a Victory for Me Songsheets published by CEF Press, P.O. Box 348, Warrenton, Mo. 63383

Little Is Much by Mary Rice Hopkins from "15 Singable Songs" (Big Steps 4 U 1988)

No Need to Worry by Jana Alayra from "Jump Into the Light" (Montjoy Music 1995)

Craft for Younger Children: Jesus Knows My Name Plaque
Needed: For each child bring a sturdy paper plate, crayons or markers, and scrap lace and ribbons.

Write "Jesus knows MY name" across the top of each plate, and and the child's name across the bottom.

Say: Did you know that Jesus knows your name? Jesus knows all about you, he knows your name, what you like, and who your parents are. He knows what makes you laugh and what makes you cry. He wants you to decorate your life with good actions, good attitudes, and good words.

Say: Pretend these craft materials are good actions, good attitudes, and good words. Decorate your plate with them. Let children decorate the rest of the plate with craft materials or markers.

 Craft for Older Children: God Knows My Name
Needed: Alphabet beads, and cord. Verify that there are enough of the right letters to spell every child's name.

Guide children to search the beads to find the letters in their names and string them on the cord. Tie the ends together to form a bracelet, so the beads don't fall off.

Say: Do you know that Jesus knows your name? Not only does he know your name, he knows all about you! Jesus knows what you like, what you don't like, who your friends are, what school you go to, what your favorite color is—everything about you! Because he knows you, he loves you. He can show you how to do the right thing for the right reason.

Ask: Do you know the names of everyone in the class? Let's play a game to help us learn. Put all bracelets together in a pile and have children choose one bracelet without looking. They then find the child who the bracelet belongs to and put it on his/her wrist. Repeat several times until children have learned the names of all children.

Zach in a Tree

Needed: People-shaped cookies, pretzel rods, small amount of green icing, paper plates.

Give each child a paper plate and show how to create a "tree" with pretzel rods, (break into smaller pieces to make branches). Naming the cookie Zach, place him in the tree.

As children work, repeat that Zacchaeus was very short and because he wanted to see Jesus so much, he climbed up into a tree so that he could see Jesus. That showed great faith in Jesus. Jesus met Zacchaeus that day and changed his life! Zacchaeus was never the same again! He began to be nice to people rather than cheat them.

Prayer Focus:

Dear God, thank you for always loving us and for loving ALL of us. We thank you and we praise you. Please help us to be loving to all people just like you are. Amen.

Memory Verse: Luke 19:9–10 ICB

Jesus said, "Salvation has come to this house today. This man truly belongs to the family of Abraham. The Son of Man came to find lost people and save them."

Alternate version (New King James)

And Jesus said to him, "Today salvation has come to this house, because he also is a son of Abraham; for the Son of Man has come to seek and to save that which was lost."

Memory Verse Activity: Seeking the Lost

Needed: People shapes cut from construction paper. Write a few words of the verse on each shape.

Divide children into teams according to the number of letters in their first names. Let one group hide the people shapes and then let the other group find them. Reverse roles.

Say: Jesus came to find the lost people. What does it mean to be lost? (Let children discuss being lost.) Being "lost" the way that Jesus was talking about is a little different. It means that you don't know God. Jesus wanted everyone to know God and to believe in him. Let's say the verse together.

October 27

Do You Look Like a Jack-o'-Lantern?, Midweek

By Judy Comstock

Scripture:
Matthew 5:14, 16

Lesson Aim:
Learn what a "light" of Christ is.

Bible Skill:
Children will choose to be a witness by letting the light of Christ's love shine through.

Bible Learning Activity and Enrichment for Younger Children: Bible Times Torch
Needed: For each child bring one toilet paper roll, orange and yellow tissue paper.

Explain: Today we are going to make a "Bible Times Light". In Bible times, people had to use torches or oil lamps as lights. They did not have electricity because it wasn't invented yet!

Show children how to put strips of yellow and orange tissue paper into the end of the tube to make it look like fire.

Say: "Let's hold up our torches and pretend we are on a walk at night. Can you see better with these torches? (No, they are pretend.) But if we had a real torch, it would be like a light for us. The light helps us! Jesus says that we are a light. Can you let your light shine?"

Bible Learning Activity for Older Children: Pumpkin Bracelet
Needed: For each child bring a 9" cord or leather lace, and one orange bead, one green bead, one brown bead, one yellow bead, and one clear bead per child.

Pass out cord and beads. Instruct the children to hold the beads until you tell them to string them on the cord.

Say: We are going to hear a story on Sunday. We will tell it now and make a bracelet to remind us of the story so we can tell other people. Remember to bring your bracelet on Sunday.

First, put the white bead on the bracelet. This will stand for the seeds. The farmer planted the pumpkin seeds. He waited a long time and then the pumpkins grew.

One day he came out to his field and he saw the pumpkins! Put the orange bead on your bracelet. This will stand for the pumpkin.

The farmer washed the pumpkins because they were covered with dirt. Let's put a brown bead on our bracelet to stand for the dirt. The brown bead and the dirt also remind us of the bad things (or the sin) in our lives.

Then the farmer cleaned out the yucky stuff on the inside of the pumpkin! Let's put a green bead on to stand for yuck.

To turn a pumpkin into a jack-o'-lantern we need to make "holes" or cuts into the pumpkin. When we clean out the pumpkin and make a place for the light to shine through, we create a jack-o'-lantern! When we put a light inside the jack-o'-lantern, light shines through the holes. Everyone can see the light. When we love God and ask God to forgive our sins, he cleans us up and his light shows through us—just like the jack-o'-lantern! Let's put the clear bead on to show that we have a pure heart, that our sins are forgiven. Then let's put the yellow bead on to remind us that we are a light!

Memory Verse: Matthew 5:14, 16 ICB

You are the light that gives light to the world. A city that is built on a hill cannot be hidden. In the same way, you should be a light for other people. Live so that they will see the good things you do.

Alternate version (New King James)

You are the light of the world. A city that is set on a hill cannot be hidden. Nor do they light a lamp and put it under a basket, but on a lampstand, and it gives light to all who are in the house. Let your light so shine before men, that they may see your good works and glorify your Father in heaven.

Enrichment for Older Children: The Light of the World!

The Bible speaks of light many, many times. Light is not only something that lights up the darkness, but it is also a symbol of God's presence and righteous activity.

Light has been associated with the presence and truth of God since creation. God created light even before human beings were created!

Throughout the Bible, light represents truth, goodness, and God. Darkness, on the other hand, symbolizes evil and the works of Satan.

Several of the miracles recorded in the Bible are related to light and darkness: the "Pillar of Fire" that guided the Israelites in the wilderness (Ex. 3:21), the sun standing still at Gibeon at Joshua's request (Josh. 10:12–13), and the fall of darkness at midday when Jesus was being crucified (Matt. 27:45).

God or God's word, the Bible, are frequently represented as lights or lamps to help us. "Your word is a lamp to my feet and a light to my path" (Ps. 119:105).

Light is also used as a symbol of holiness and purity. Paul counseled the Christians at Rome to "put on the armor of light" (Rom. 13:12).

The New Testament presents Jesus as the best light: "I am the light of the world" (John 8:12). ☺

October 31

Do You Look Like a Jack-o'-Lantern?
By Judy Comstock

Scripture:
Matthew 5:14, 16

Lesson Aim:
Learn what a "light" of Christ is.

Bible Skill:
Children will choose to be a witness by letting the light of Christ's love shine through.

Bible Lesson: Let Jesus Shine Through You

Needed: Pumpkin carved into a smiling jack-o'-lantern, sealed bag of seeds and stringy pulp from the inside of a pumpkin. This can be conveniently stored inside the carved pumpkin until you need to show the contents. Candle, butane candle lighter.

Show the uncut side of the pumpkin. It is most effective if this portion of the pumpkin is stilled marred with dirt from the garden. Ask: Have any of you had a jack-o'-lantern sitting on your front porch or your table? *(Allow time for responses.)* Would any of you want to look like a jack-o'-lantern? *(Most of the children will answer, "No.")* Well, I hope in a few minutes all of you will have decided that is how you want to look.

I have learned a few things about pumpkins and how they become jack-o'-lanterns. First, a farmer places white pumpkin seeds in little mounds of dirt in a field. The plants that grow from these seeds need a lot of room to spread out on top of the ground. Green vines with large leaves soon grow from the seeds. Under these leaves, blossoms grow. Then small pumpkins start peaking out. Over the next few months, the little pumpkins grow larger in the bright summer sun. Then, the farmer cuts the pumpkins from the vines. These pumpkins are dirty because they have grown on top of dirt. All around them is dirt. When the farmer brings the fruit to his barn, he may wash the pumpkins so they will look clean when he tries to sell them.

We are like pumpkins. We have dirt on us. Not dirt from a garden, but dirt from the bad things that we have done. We look like a pumpkin from the field, until we invite Jesus to clean us up. Jesus begins working on the outside and the inside. Yucky stuff that is slimy, stringy, and seedy fills the inside of a pumpkin. *(Show the children your bag of seeds and stringy pulp.)* I cut the top off my pumpkin and scooped all of this from the inside. Some of the yucky stuff in us might be lies we have told, bad attitudes we have shown, and the stubborn "No" we have said. If we let him, God helps us open up and he cleans us through and through.

(Still showing uncut side of pumpkin) I have made some other changes in my pumpkin. Let me show you. *(Turn pumpkin to reveal the smiling face you have previously carved.)* On this side of my pumpkin I have carved a smiling mouth and open eyes. This looks very different than the uncut side. As the Holy Spirit works on us, we begin to change. God loves us so much that he changes us on the outside and the inside. He puts his light inside us so we can shine forth and cause others to praise our Heavenly Father. *(Light the candle after placing it inside the pumpkin.)*

Ask: What are some of the good things you do for others that bring glory to God? *(Allow time for responses. Consider and suggest acts of kindness.)* Doing these kind acts is like letting Jesus shine through you. Are you starting to see why I asked if you want to look like a jack-o'-lantern? *(Allow time for positive responses.)* On your porch the light inside a jack-o'-lantern shines out through the face. Inside a Christian, the light of Christ should shine even brighter than this candle. People see the kind, helpful things you do and those actions can cause others to think about God.

 Song Suggestions:

This Little Light of Mine Traditional

Lighthouse by Mary Rice Hopkins from "Lighthouse" (Big Steps 4 U 1992)

Let's Talk About Jesus songsheets published by CEF Press, P.O. Box 348, Warrenton, Mo. 63383

Less of Me by Mr. Bill from "When I Grow Up" (Mister Bill Music 1997)

Craft for Younger Children: Play Dough Pumpkins
Needed: Heat to boiling: 1 1/2 c water, 1/2 c salt. Remove from heat and add: 2 T vegetable oil, 2 t alum and 2–3 cups flour. Knead until smooth. Add orange food coloring (or package of orange drink mix) until it is the color you want.

Give each child some modeling dough. Let them make their very own pumpkins to take home.

 Craft for Older Children: Pumpkin, Pumpkins!
Needed: For each child bring 18 inches of plastic white dryer vent, green and orange pipe cleaners and green felt. Spray paint the dryer vents ahead of time with orange spray paint and make into a circle by attaching the two ends with chenille wire "ties". This will form the pumpkin. Bring tacky glue.

Say: This time of year, we think of pumpkins when we think of Fall. Today we are going to make a table decoration to remind you that it is Fall, a time of Thanksgiving.

Curl the green pipe cleaner around your finger. Put a little glue on the pipe cleaner and place on top in center hole of pumpkin. Cut out two green leaves and place on top of pumpkin.

Alternate Craft for All Ages: Pumpkin Necklace
Needed: Orange fun foam, cord, and beads.

Cut pumpkin shapes out of orange fun foam. Poke a hole in the top of each pumpkin and let children string on cord for necklace. Add beads, if desired.

Seed Feast!
Needed: Roasted pumpkin seeds, popcorn kernels, and popcorn popper.

 Say: Today we are going to eat seeds! These kernels of corn grow into corn on the cob and these pumpkin seeds grow into …what? Right! A pumpkin!

Pop the corn and pass out popcorn and pumpkin seeds to eat.

Alternative snack: Pumpkin Pie or Pumpkin Bread

Prayer Focus:

Thank you, God, for making pumpkins. Thank you for your son, Jesus, who came as a light into a dark world. We ask you to help us also be a light in a dark world as we grow and learn to serve you. Amen.

Memory Verse: Matthew 5:14, 16 ICB

You are the light that gives light to the world. A city that is built on a hill cannot be hidden. In the same way, you should be a light for other people.
Live so that they will see the good things you do.

Alternate version (New King James)

You are the light of the world. A city that is set on a hill cannot be hidden. Nor do they light a lamp and put it under a basket, but on a lampstand, and it gives light to all who are in the house. Let your light so shine before men, that they may see your good works and glorify your Father in heaven.

Memory Verse Activity: Match Game!

Needed: Orange circles of a variety of sizes. Write the words of the verse on the circles—one word on each circle. Make two sets.

Place the circles on a table with the words down. Play a matching game with the circles. To play, let one child select a circle. Turn it over and read a word on it. The child then tries to "match" it with the circle with the same word by turning another circle over. If they are a match, the child gets another turn. If they are not a match, it is someone else's turn. Continue until all circles are matched. Say the verse together.

November 3

Is Freedom Really Free?, Midweek
By Dan Chun

Scripture:
2 Corinthians 3:17

Lesson Aim:
Children will learn what true freedom is.

Bible Skill:
Children will understand and appreciate the freedom that we have in our country and in Christ.

Bible Learning Activity for Younger Children: Hide and Seek
Teach children how to play "Hide and Seek" with a place designated as "Free."

After playing for several minutes ask: How did you like it when you were tagged? Did you like it better when you were free? Was it nice to have a place that you could tag and instantly become free?

Jesus is like that. When we know Jesus and do what he says, we have freedom. No matter what is going on outside us, there is a place where we are free.

Elementary Bible Learning Activity: Kite Bulletin Board!
Give the children a piece of construction paper with an outline of a kite (a diamond shape). Have the children cut out the kite shape and decorate their kites.

Write "Freedom Comes from God's Spirit" on the kites and hang on the bulletin board or from the ceiling of the classroom.

Enrichment for Older Children: Veterans Day

Ask: Do you know what a VETERAN is? A veteran is somebody who has served in the military, especially during a war. Veterans Day was first established to honor the veterans of World War Two. But people soon decided that Veterans Day would be a time to honor ALL American veterans of ALL wars.

Celebrating Veterans Day helps us to set aside a time to remember the important purpose of Veterans Day: to honor America's veterans for their patriotism, love of country, and willingness to serve and sacrifice for the common good.

Ask your parents and grandparents if they are veterans. If they are, let them tell you what they did while they were in the military.

Ask: What does honor mean?

In a Christian dictionary, it says that honor means "An expression of great respect."

Ask: Have you ever had an "honor?" What did you receive it for?

Today we are "honoring" our Veterans. They are the people who served our country in the military. We are going to do things to show great respect. It might not seem like a lot to do, but one of the best things that we can do to honor someone is to say, "thank you." Veterans served our country and maybe even went to war so that we could have freedom.

Jesus also gave us freedom that is even more important than military freedom. In John 8:31 verse today, Jesus says that the *truth* will make us free. He says, "Then you will know the truth, and the truth will make you free."

What do you think that means? Jesus is the truth, everything he says is true, and Jesus makes us free! Free from sin and free to enjoy eternal life with God! ☺

Enrichment for Younger Children: Being Free!

Have children cross their arms around themselves and hold as tightly as they can. Stress that this be more than a hug but very tight instead. Ask: How do you feel right now, kind of uncomfortable? Yes, you do because you aren't free!

Now let go of yourself—how do you feel now?

Jesus is like that, too. If you don't know Jesus you might feel tight and uncomfortable because you have no true freedom. When you know Jesus, Jesus sets you free and you feel great! ☺

Memory Verse: 2 Corinthians 3:17 ICB

The Lord is the Spirit. And where the Spirit of the Lord is, there is freedom.

Alternate version (New King James)
Now the Lord is the Spirit; and where the Spirit of the Lord is, there is liberty.

November 7

Is Freedom Really Free? (Veterans Day)
By Dan Chun

Scripture:
2 Corinthians 3:17

Lesson Aim:
Children will learn what true freedom is.

Bible Skill:
Children will understand and appreciate the freedom that we have in our country and in Christ.

Bible Lesson: Free to Fly
Needed: Kite with tail and string attached to kite.

Tell this story: I bet many of you have flown a kite. Katie, could you hold this ball of string that is attached to the kite, and Bobby, could you hold up the kite for me?

There are many ways we can get a kite to fly. We can run with it and then let out more string as the wind grabs it and it flies higher and higher. Or if it is a windy day, we just stand with the kite and then let it fly up into the sky giving it more and more string as it tugs.

Once a kite is up in the sky, we can let out more and more string and it gets higher and higher. We can see it dance around up in the air. It seems so FREE and FRISKY, and it can go anywhere the wind takes it. It can fly up, down, to the side, right or left.

As long as we hold on to that string and as long as the wind blows, that kite will remain way up high in the sky.

But you know what? If you ever let go of that string . . . the kite will fall to the ground. The kite is only free to fly up in the sky if it is tied to something or someone.

Song Suggestions:

One Way Songsheets published by CEF Press, P.O. Box 348, Warrenton, Mo. 63383

Faith of Our Fathers Traditional

I Will Fight This Fight by Jana Alayra from "Jump Into the Light" (Montjoy Music 1995)

This Is How We Overcome by Norm Hewitt from "Fired Up" (Revelation Generation 2002)

As we think about our country on this Veterans Day weekend, we need to remember that we have a lot of freedom and liberty, but the reason we have that is because we are tied to the principles of the Bible and of one nation under God, with liberty, and justice for all.

Today each of us has the right to life, liberty, and the pursuit of happiness because men and women who served in the military, whom we call Veterans, served and protected their country so that we might have freedom today.

Our kites fly high and free only when we are tied to the principles of freedom that God gave us. They are the same principles that the Veterans protected. We have much to be thankful for. Let's pray.

 Craft for Younger Children: Flag Paintings
Needed: Powdered soft drink mix (red and blue) and white glue, white construction paper.

Mix powdered drink mix with white glue to form "paint." Show children a picture of our flag and let them try to paint a flag. Point out the number of stripes and the number of stars. Say: Our flag reminds us that we are free, that we have freedom. We are so blessed that we live in a place where we have freedom. Explain that we are painting with glue to show that freedom tends to glue people together in all the right ways.

Ask: Do you know anyone that has been in the Army, Navy, Marines, or Air Force? If you do, today would be a good time to thank them for what they have done to keep our country free. One good way to say thank you is to give them the picture that you just painted!

Craft for Older Children: Thank You Card
Needed: Blue, white and red construction paper, gold star stickers.

Say: Today we are going to make a Thank You Card for the veterans that go to our church. Show children how to make a flag with the materials provided. Write "Thank You" on the cards and pass out to veterans following church. Or arrange for the children to deliver these to the veterans during the worship hour.

Prayer Focus:

Dear God, thank you for giving us freedom, to be as free as a kite . . . but may we always remember that our freedom is only strong if it is tied to your strength and love. May we remember well the memory of the men and women who have served to protect our country and to assure that we will all have life, liberty, and the pursuit of happiness. Amen.

Memory Verse: 2 Corinthians 3:17 ICB

The Lord is the Spirit. And where the Spirit of the Lord is, there is freedom.

Alternate version (New King James)
Now the Lord is the Spirit; and where the Spirit of the Lord is, there is liberty.

Memory Verse Activity: Flag of Freedom
Needed: Red, white and blue construction paper. Let children make pictures of the flag or something similar. Write 2 Corinthians 3:17 on the paper.

Say: "What does this verse say about freedom? Where can we find freedom?"

God gives us true freedom, freedom that no one can ever take away.

November 10

What Is the Right Thing to Do?, Midweek
By Barbara Platt

Scripture: Acts 3:1–10

Lesson Aim:
To help children know that God can heal.

ible Skill:
Your caring action can bring God's good gifts to someone you know.

Bible Learning Activity for Younger Children: Miracle! Get Up and Walk!
Preview the story from next Sunday's Bible lesson about the crippled man
that Jesus healed. Let children then act out the story with actions like these:

    Say: Pretend to lie still because you cannot walk.

           But Jesus says, "Get up and Walk!

           Now you can JUMP, WALK, RUN!

Bible Learning Activity for Older Children: Miracles!
Jesus performed many miracles in the Bible. The apostles performed some
miracles, too, and this story is about one of the miracles that the apostles
did. Peter saw that this man needed money but he decided to give him
something better—he made him well. Did Peter do this by himself? No! He
said, "In the name of Jesus Christ!" before he told him to get up and walk.

Using a white board or large piece of paper, let children write some great
things that have happened to their families, such as: dad getting a new job,
grandma getting well, making a new friend, or solving an argument.

Then encourage them to list smaller things that happen to help us such
as: doing well on an assignment, doing well in a game, holding back when
temper strikes, etc.

When your list is complete, ask: Which of these things was a miracle? Which can we do by ourselves? Stress that miracles happen whenever Jesus is involved and a new friendship is just as miraculous as a physical healing. In our story today, there was an absolute miracle, but sometimes it isn't so clear. God helps us with everything we do.

God is always available to help you. When you ask God for help, ask in Jesus' name, just like Paul did in our story.

Enrichment for Younger Children: Care in Ways that Help

The man in the Bible story was lame. Sometimes that is also called crippled or paralyzed. What do these mean? It means that the man could not walk.

What can you do to help someone in a wheel chair? What can you do to help someone with a cane? What about someone with a walker? Stress that the most important thing to do is to talk to them, to treat them like a friend. Then after that we can ask for ways to help. Third, go back to simply being a friend. Don't let the wheelchair get in the way. ☺

Enrichment for Older Children: Poor People

There are poor people in many many places. It was the same during Bible times. Even though there will always be poor people, the Bible tells us to be concerned about them.

God cares about the poor. The Psalms repeatedly emphasize that God helps the poor. He often does this through human hands.

Jesus had great compassion for the poor (Luke 6:20). Luke, who especially emphasizes concern for the poor, relates Christ's mission statement from Isaiah, "He has anointed Me to preach the gospel to the poor" (Is. 61:1; Luke 4:18). The rich young man was instructed by Jesus to sell his possessions and "to distribute to the poor" (Luke 18:22). Jesus' followers cannot remain unconcerned about the poor of the world.

Instructions about considerate treatment of the poor are found in the Old Testament and the New Testament. The law, as well as the prophets, warned against oppressing the poor and crushing the needy (Deut. 24:14; Prov. 14:31; Amos 2:6; 4:1).

So what should you do when you see a poor person? What should you do when you see someone who needs help? Listen to what God is telling you to do and do it! ☺

Memory Verse: Acts 3:6 ICB

But Peter said, "I don't have any silver or gold, but I do have something else I can give you: By the power of Jesus Christ from Nazareth—stand up and walk!"

Alternate version (New King James)
Then Peter said, "Silver and gold I do not have, but what I do have I give you: In the name of Jesus Christ of Nazareth, rise up and walk."

November 14

What Is the Right Thing to Do?
By Barbara Platt

Scripture:
Acts 3:1–10

Lesson Aim:
To help children know that God can heal.

Bible Skill:
Your caring action can bring God's good gifts to someone you know.

Bible Lesson: A Better Gift

Tell this story: Have you ever seen someone begging? Has anyone that you don't know come up to you and asked for money? Have you seen someone along the side of a road with a sign asking for money? (Let children comment.)

There is a story in the Bible about this: One day, Peter and John, were going to the temple to pray. While they were walking along the road they passed some men that were carrying their friend. They were carrying him because he was lame which means he couldn't walk. Everyday they carried him to a place called Beautiful Gate.

The beggars sat by the Beautiful Gate and asked people for money. When they asked Peter, he said to the man, "Look here." The lame man turned and looked at them hoping for money. Peter said, "We don't have any money for you! But I'll give you something else! *In the name of Jesus Christ of Nazareth, walk!*"

Peter took the man by the hand and pulled him to his feet. When he stood on his feet, an amazing thing happened. His feet and anklebones were healed and strengthened so that he came up with a leap, stood a moment, and began walking, leaping, and praising God. The same man who had to be carried everywhere was jumping up and down, and walking!

Everyone was watching. People were pushing and shoving to get a better look. The crowd grew bigger and bigger. Everyone began moving, but no one wanted to leave. What was going to happen next?

The man who had been carried to the gate now WALKED into the temple with them. The people were totally surprised to see this man who had been begging at the temple door every day. Now he was walking. This was impossible! They all rushed out to part of the temple called Solomon's Porch where the man was holding tightly to Peter and John. Everyone was awed by the wonderful thing that had happened. But how could this be?

Peter saw how eager the people were to see the miracle. He felt this was a great opportunity to talk to the crowd. Surely they would listen to the Good News about Jesus. He began by asking, "What is so surprising about this? And why look at us as though we, by our own goodness and power, made this man well?" It is by the power of Jesus that this happened, they explained. "Even though you killed Jesus, God brought him back to life. Now change your mind and attitude to God and turn from your sin. Jesus' death and resurrection has made the way for your sins to be forgiven. We know this is hard to understand. It must be your decision."

Do you think the people were surprised? This man who has been carried by others to the temple begging at the door for so many years is now jumping and walking. How can this be? But even though this was a great miracle, Peter told them that there was a more important miracle happening. He let the man's healing become a way to show God's power to forgive sins.

God can work great miracles for people. But the most important thing that God does is to forgive. God loves you and wants to save you from your sins. God will forgive you any time you ask.

 Song Suggestions:

Walking and Singing by Mary Rice Hopkins from "Miracle Mud" (Big Steps 4 U 2000)

Faith Will Do by Dean-o from "You Got It All" (FKO Music, Inc. 1997)

Walking and Leaping Traditional

Jump Into the Light by Jana Alayra from "Jump Into the Light" (Montjoy Music 1997)

Craft for Older and Younger Children: Make a Bank
Needed: For each child bring one container with lid such as coffee can, wipes box, oatmeal container, and items to decorate with.

Say: Today we are going to make a bank. We will then try to earn money to put into the bank and use it for a service project. Show children how to decorate their container. Brainstorm ideas for earning money for your service project.

Say: Jesus asked us to help each other. How can you help someone in your neighborhood by using or not using our banks? Let children brainstorm. Some great ideas are:

• Collect money in the banks that you made and find a good way to donate the money.

• Arrange for a clothing donation among the families in your church. Donate the children's clothes to a mom's shelter.

• Join Samaritan's Purse, Habitat for Humanity, or Love Loaf to participate in their projects.

Snack: "Poor Boy" Sandwiches

Needed: An assortment of sandwich meats and cheeses, bread, and condiments.

 Show children how to make the sandwich of their choice. Say: We call these sandwiches "Submarine" sandwiches now, but a long time ago they were called "Poor Boy Sandwiches." How do you think they got that name? They got the name because the poorer people just used whatever they had left when they made their sandwiches, just like our sandwiches today had lots of different things on them.

Some people do not have enough to eat. What can you do about this? What would it be like if you didn't have enough to eat? How would you feel if you were hungry? How can you help in a way that won't embarrass them.

Prayer Focus:

Dear God, thank you so much for what you do for us and what you give to us. We thank you that you meet all of our needs. We praise you for being a God who knows everything about us and knows just what we need. Amen.

Memory Verse: Acts 3:6 ICB

But Peter said, "I don't have any silver or gold, but I do have something else I can give you: By the power of Jesus Christ from Nazareth—stand up and walk!"

Alternate version (New King James)
Then Peter said, "Silver and gold I do not have, but what I do have I give you: In the name of Jesus Christ of Nazareth, rise up and walk."

Memory Verse Activity:
Needed: Verse written on white board, assortment of toy coins.

Have toy coins in the center of the room on the floor. Say: We are going to play a game that is like "Fruit Basket Upset." Divide the class into two teams according to the day of the month they were born (all born the 1–15 on one team, 16–31 on another). Seat the teams opposite each other.

Divide the verse into segments of two or three words. Assign one person on each team to each group of words.

Peter said, I don't have any, silver or gold, but I do have something else, I can give you. By the power, of Jesus Christ, stand up and walk.

Call out a part of the verse. Children who have those words will jump up and try to get some of the toy coins. Children can either grab coins or gain coins by tagging the other person after they get coins.

Continue playing until verse is memorized!

November 17

Thanks, but No Thanks, Midweek
By Johanna Townsend

Scripture:
Philippians 4:12–13

Lesson Aim:
Saying "thank you" shows love and expresses God's power.

Bible Skill:
Children will express thankfulness.

Bible Learning Activity for Younger Children: Thank You!

In the Bible, we learn to say "thank you." What do you say "thank you" for? Let children answer.

Then ask: What words do you use to say "thank you" for:

Your food?	Your toys?
Your clothes?	Your house?
Your friends?	Your parents?
Your little brother?	

When you love someone and they do something nice for you, you say "thank you." Saying thank you shows you love them! Be sure to thank both people and God for these things. When you thank a person, God is happy. When you thank God, he is happy, too.

Bible Learning Activity for Older Children: Say "Thank You"

Say: Let's make a list of what we can say "thank you" for. On the white board write a column for "Parents," "God," "Teacher," "Friends," "Brothers, and Sisters."

Under each category, let children brainstorm ways that they can say "Thank you" to each of these groups of people.

Enrichment for Younger Children: Thank You Game

Play London Bridge with the children saying:

We say Thank you when we're kind, when we're kind, when we're kind

We say Thank you when we're kind,

Just say "Thank You!" (Child caught will say thank you to everyone) ☺

Enrichment for Older Children: Thanksgiving

The Pilgrims who sailed to this country aboard the *Mayflower* were originally members of the English Separatist Church (a Puritan sect).

The Pilgrims set ground at Plymouth Rock on December 11, 1620. Their first winter was terrible and many people died. But the fall harvest of 1621 was a bountiful one, so they decided to celebrate with a feast! They invited 91 Indians who had helped the Pilgrims survive their first year. They were so thankful to the Indians and believed that they would not have made it through the year without their help. ☺

Memory Verse: Philippians 4:12–13

I have learned the secret of being happy at any time in everything that happens. I can do all things through Christ because he gives me strength.

Alternate version (New King James)

I know how to be abased, and I know how to abound. Everywhere and in all things I have learned both to be full and to be hungry, both to abound and to suffer need. I can do all things through Christ who strengthens me.

November 21

Thanks, but No Thanks
By Johanna Townsend

Scripture:
Philippians 4:12–13

Lesson Aim:
Saying "thank you" shows love and expresses God's power.

Bible Skill:
Children will express thankfulness.

Bible Lesson: The Secret to Happiness

Needed: Bible, a small carton of buttermilk or a package of tofu, and small plastic cups. Have enough samples of buttermilk or tofu for all children to taste. Be prepared for strong reactions from some children who like or don't like the taste.

Ask: How many of you have tasted buttermilk / tofu before? (Have some samples prepared for those who would like to taste buttermilk/tofu.) Do you like it? It may or may not taste good to you. What other foods does your family serve that you don't like? That you do like? Food is necessary for life. Are you thankful for the food you have to eat, even when you don't like it? (Wait for response.) Do you know the other two substances we need for life? (Wait for children to answer air and water.) Have you ever thanked God for the air you breathe and the water you drink? (Wait for response.) I know I forget to thank God for these substances.

How thankful are you? Do you thank God wholeheartedly and gratefully for everything you have daily or do you just give him a "Ho Hum", "I've got better things to do!" and "By the way when can I have a new bike?" type of thankfulness? (Read Phil. 4:12 in your Bible.) Paul had been beaten, stoned,

Song Suggestions:

Lord I Give My Heart by Mark Thompson from "Yes Yes Yes"! (Markarts 2000)

Say Thank You by Mary Rice Hopkins from "Miracle Mud" (Big Steps 4 U 1995)

Outta Sight by Dean-o from "Soul Surfin'" "(FKO Music, Inc. 1997)

God's Power Songsheets published by CEF Press, P.O. Box 348, Warrenton, Mo. 63383

thrown in jail, and suffered many hardships because he told people about Jesus Christ, yet still he thanked God. Though he lived through good times and bad, Paul had learned to be thankful for God's blessings no matter what happened.

Today we celebrate the Thanksgiving season. Let's focus on thanking God for what we have and begin looking for ways to bless those who have less than we do. (Invite the children to thank God for one physical blessing such as food and one non-physical blessing such as a mom or dad.)

Stress: Every gift comes from God, and God trusts us to share what we have with others.

 Craft for Older Children: We Give Thanks

Needed: Bring for each child an orange pumpkin shape, three small hearts, one green chenille wire, and leaves, all cut from craft foam.

Show children how to punch a small hole in the top of the pumpkin shape with a green chenille wire, and then twist it to make a stem. Add the leaves to the top and curl the ends of the stem around a pencil. On the three hearts write (one word per heart) We Give Thanks.

Say: At Thanksgiving time, we think about giving thanks and being thankful. We are thankful for all that God has done for us. Let's glue these hearts onto the top of our pumpkin to remember to give thanks to God.

Craft for Younger Children: Pine Cone Turkey

Needed: For each child bring a plump pine cone (spherical shaped about 1 1/2"–2" diameter) 1 red and 1 orange bumpy chenille stem, 5 other colors of bumpy chenille stems, Glue, wire cutters.

Preparation: Cut the bumps apart in each chenille wire. Using wire cutters, cut in the center of the thin place, leaving the "bump" intact. Shape the red bump into an "S" and glue it onto to rounded end of cone for the head of the turkey. Shape the orange bump into a "V" for the goggle. Bend the other bumps and glue into the pine cone for feathers. Let dry.

Snack: Candy Turkeys!

Needed: Bring for each child a caramel, three pieces of candy corn, two Dove chocolates, a striped chocolate cookie, and a Thanksgiving cupcake liner.

Guide children to assemble the turkeys using caramel candy squares for the body, candy corn for the beak and eyes, Dove chocolates for the base and feet, striped chocolate cookies for the tail and feathers. Set the turkey in a Thanksgiving cupcake liner.

Say: "Thanksgiving is a special time of year, a time when we eat lots of food. One of the special things that we like to eat is turkey. Do you eat turkey or something else at your house on Thanksgiving? What tradition would you like to start for Thanksgiving in your family?

Prayer Focus:

Dear God, thank you for all that we have. We know everything that we have comes from you. Make us aware of the needs around us. Give us concern for them. Show us how to reach out and help. May this holiday season be filled with thankfulness for your great love and care for each of us you have created. Amen.

Memory Verse: Philippians 4:12–13

I have learned the secret of being happy at any time in everything that happens. I can do all things through Christ because he gives me strength.

Alternate version (New King James)
I know how to be abased, and I know how to abound. Everywhere and in all things I have learned both to be full and to be hungry, both to abound and to suffer need. I can do all things through Christ who strengthens me.

Memory Verse Activity:

Have you ever been told a secret? What was it? Did you tell anyone?

A secret can also be something that is very special, something that you CAN tell someone. Paul learned a secret like this and he told everyone by writing it in the Bible.

What was Paul's secret?

Can you be happy all the time?

Who can your strength come from?

What do you think "all things" are?

Memorize the verse together by saying it several times.

November 24

Beware of Bullies, Midweek
By Pat Verbal

Scripture:
2 Samuel 21:15–17; Psalm 27:1

Lesson Aim:
To help children see that God is just.

Bible Skill:
To work hand-in-hand with God to promote fairness.

Bible Learning Activity for Younger Children: No More Meanness
Have you ever met a mean person? What did they do that was mean? Mean people are not nice! Sometimes we call mean people "bullies." Have you ever met a bully? Have you ever been a bully? What happened?

There were mean people in the Bible, but God does not want us to be mean. God wants to help us to be kind.

Can you be nice when someone is mean to you? How can you do that? Let children discuss ways to be kind.

It's hard to be kind when someone is being mean, but that is how God wants us to act.

God is never mean; God is always fair.

Bible Learning Activity for Older Children: Bullies in the Bible
Cain who killed his brother Abel
Joseph's brothers who SOLD him
Pharoah who would not let the Hebrews leave Egypt
King Saul who was a bully to David
Goliath who was a bully to all Hebrews

King Herod who wanted to kill Jesus and killed lots of babies

Saul, who was a bully to all Christians until God changed his life and his name! When he was no longer a bully, his name was Paul!

What should you do when someone acts like a bully?

Enrichment for Older Children: God is Just

Say: While most people try hard to be good examples, bullies give lessons on how NOT to act. Since you can't get away from them, you might as well learn from them. Watch trouble makers closely. Then, remember to do the opposite and you'll make good friends.

Troublemakers have been around since Bible times. Unlike Bible heroes who did mighty deeds for God, these bad guys always wanted their own way. Their greed often led to lies, hatred, and even murder. Do you think God loved these rascals as much as he loves his obedient followers?

The answer is YES, but he was very disappointed in them. He showed obedient people what to do about the bullies. ☺

Enrichment for Younger Children: Why Fight Giants?

(For your understanding: Young children are full of good questions. As they move through the concrete stage of development, they begin to understand that life is not always fair. They notice that bad things can happen to good people. During this time, children discover new fears. They meet a "Goliath" in their own lives and ask: Why would anyone fight a giant?)

Ask children to think of their favorite fairy tale. Help them identify the villain in such tales as Hansel and Gretel, Snow White, Sleeping Beauty, and Peter Pan. Ask: "What did the villains teach the heroes and heroines in these stories?" (Good wins over evil. Be brave. You can do it.) What strategies did each hero use and how will you do the same?

Explain that David fought the giant because he didn't like him making fun of Israel's God and because he trusted God to help him. He also learned a lot about himself. The battle tested his courage, and he must have felt very good when it was all over.

Ask children to draw a picture of their biggest fear or challenge. Direct them to talk with God about what he wants them to do about the challenge and to add that to the picture. ☺

Memory Verse: Psalm 27:1 ICB

The Lord is my light and the one who saves me. I fear no one. The Lord protects my life. I am afraid of no one.

Alternate version (New King James)

The LORD is my light and my salvation; whom shall I fear? The LORD is the strength of my life; of whom shall I be afraid?

November 28

Beware of Bullies
By Pat Verbal

Scripture:
2 Samuel 21:15–17; Psalm 27:1

Lesson Aim:
To help children see that God is just.

Bible Skill:
To work hand-in-hand with God to promote fairness.

Bible Lesson: Beware of Bullies

Ask: Have you ever met a troublemaker? You can find troublemakers every-where.

They tease, name call, and push others around. They demand their way, refuse to say please or thank you, and assume the world revolves around them. Sometimes we call them bullies. Maybe one lives in your neighbor-hood or goes to your school or comes to your family gatherings.

Here's a story about a bully: After school one day, Robby and Carrie's sit-ter read the rules for the coloring contest sponsored by a local grocery store: At the opening of the new store, five pictures will be chosen to win a big Easter basket. The other pictures will be hung in the store's front window. So, kids, do your best!"

The children immediately went to work on their pictures. Carrie looked at some of her mom's magazines to get an idea of the colors she would use. In her art box she found some pastel glitter and colored glue.

Robby quickly grabbed the markers and started coloring as fast as he could. Because Robby wanted to go outside to play, he finished first.

"Stop trying to be so perfect," Robby yelled at his younger sister. "You know I'm the best at art."

Carrie just smiled at him and kept outlining the beautiful, spring tulips in her picture. "I'm not trying to be perfect," Carrie said. "I'm taking my time."

"Take all the time you want," said Robby sticking out his tongue. "I'm still going to win that basket of candy. You don't have a chance!"

Later, when Carrie went outside to swing, Robby slipped into the house and hid her picture behind the refrigerator. He put his picture on the kitchen counter for his parents to see after work.

Ask: Why was Robby being such a bully? How should Carrie have acted toward her brother?

As you discuss this with the children, bring out points such as: Robby decided that his winning was more important than anybody or anything else; Robby chose not to care about doing wrong; Robby had likely gotten away with doing wrong before.

Here's another story, this one from Bible times: David's hands shook as he wiped the sweat from his brow and replaced his helmet. The afternoon sun beat down on Israel's troops engaged in another fierce battle with their enemies, the Philistines. These were no ordinary soldiers. One, a distant cousin of Goliath, carried a bronze spear with a tip that weighted 300 shekels (about 20 pounds). He bragged he'd kill David this time with his new sword.

Will these ugly, godless bullies ever give up and go home? David teased, trying to draw his first officer's attention away from his own weakened condition.

"Please, Sir, let me escort you to the top of the hill where you can oversee the battle," begged his first officer. "You're much too tired to fight anymore today."

David grabbed the horn of his saddle and straightened his aching back. I've faced a few giants in my day, and with God's help, I will kill one more! His horse charged forward into the thick of the battle. His head throbbed as he tried to recall the faith he had as the young boy who challenged a giant with a simple slingshot.

Suddenly, David was blinded by the glare of a silver blade. Thundering hooves raced faster and faster toward him. Clutching his shield, he prayed, *I call to the Lord, who is worthy of praise, and I am saved from my enemies* (2 Samuel 22:4). Those words were the last thing he remembered.

Song Suggestions:

Play From Your Heart by Jana Alayra from "Jump Into the Light" (Montjoy Music 1995)

Good Buddies by Mary Rice Hopkins from "Good Buddies" (Big Steps 4 U 1994)

Four Letter Word L-O-V-E Songsheets published by CEF Press, P.O. Box 348, Warrenton, Mo. 63383

Change My Heart Oh God by Eddie Espinosa from "Change My Heart Oh God for Kids" (Mercy/Vineyard Publishing 1982)

David's nephew, Abishai (a-BISH-eye), had been watching David's back all day. When Abishai saw David fall from his horse, Abishai rode in to rescue him. Quickly Abishai struck down the boastful Philistine and killed him. David's army won a victory that day.

What two things protected David from harm? (prayer and friends) How can you watch the back of someone at your school?

 Craft for Younger Children: What Scares You?

Needed: Aluminum foil, paper plate, glue, ribbon.

Say: Are you ever scared? When do you get scared?

Directions: Glue piece of aluminum foil in center of paper plate. Then have children write words, "I will look to God when I get scared" on the plate.

Now look in the plate and tell me who can talk to God when fearful. Yep, you!

Craft for Older Children: God is Just to YOU!

Needed: Aluminum foil, paper plate, glue, ribbon.

Say: Who is the fairest person you know? What fair things does this person do that you want to imitate? Someone who is always fair is called "just." That means that they always do the right thing. God is just.

Directions: Glue piece of aluminum foil in center of paper plate. Then have children write words, "God is just . . . I can be, too" on the plate.

Action Words

Needed: Alphabet cereal.

Pour a box of alphabet cereal in the center of the table. Let children work in teams of 2–3 to create words that represent what they might do if a bully was bothering them. (*run, tell, stop, hide, listen, talk, pray, go home.*)

Have plenty of cereal to snack on during the discussion.

Prayer Focus:

Dear God, I thank you that you are such an awesome God. I thank you and praise you that you are such a strong and powerful God that never hurts the weak. Please help me to call on you if I encounter a bully and know that the only true strength comes from you. Amen.

Memory Verse: Psalm 27:1 ICB

The Lord is my light and the one who saves me. I fear no one. The Lord protects my life. I am afraid of no one.

Alternate version (New King James)
The LORD is my light and my salvation; Whom shall I fear? The LORD is the strength of my life; Of whom shall I be afraid?

Memory Verse Activity: The Lord is My Light Switch Cover
Needed: For each child bring one light switch cover, art foam or cardboard, glue, yarn.

Guide children to cut a light switch cover from art foam by using an actual light switch cover as a pattern. Write the Bible memory verse, "The Lord is my light," on the foam. Outline it with glue and attach bright colored yarn.

Attach the art foam to the light switch cover with double stick tape.

Each time the child turns the light off and on, he will remember God is with him and that God will be just.

December 1

But, It's Mine!, Midweek
By Ivy Beckwith

Scripture:
Philippians 2:1–2

Lesson Aim:
We should be generous with others and not think we are better than other people.

Bible Skills:
Kids discover actions that show a spirit of generosity.

Bible Learning Activity for Younger Children: First Aid Kits
Needed: Items for First Aid Kit including bandages, first aid cream, and more.)

Say: The Bible tells us to help each other. How do you think you can do this? What are some of the things that you can do even though you are a child?

One of the ways that you can help is to have a first aid kit to help children when they are hurt. What should go into the kit? Let children create first aid kits for their school classrooms.

Bible Learning Activity for Older Children: Helping Hands
The Bible tells us that we should help each other. How can we do that? Guide children to think about ways to earn money to buy school supplies and clothes for children who need them. Perhaps they have possessions and clothes that are in excellent condition.

Ask: How could we give these without making the recipient feel "poor" or different?

Alternate Bible Learning Idea for All Ages: Glove Gifts

Needed: Two sets of off-white gardening gloves (one in child size and one in adult size), markers.

Pass out inexpensive, off-white gardening gloves to the children, one per child. Have them decorate the gloves and give them to a neighbor or friend who does gardening.

Prepare a second set with the words, "I will be generous." Challenge children to wear the gloves to do a chore for someone.

Enrichment for Younger Children:

Needed: Squirt bottles with water in them, paper towels.

Say: Today we are going to clean the room and I need your help! Who can help me?

Show children how to dust and clean the tables with the squirt bottles and towels.

Say: Thank you so much! You are all great helpers! ☺

Enrichment for Older Children: Who Are Those Bell Ringers?

Every Christmas we see them outside stores, ringing their bells. But who are they and what do they believe? They are the Salvation Army and they are Christians just like you and me.

William Booth began The Salvation Army in July 1865. Preaching to a small congregation in the slums of London, his spirit was as militant as that of a professional soldier while battling an almost overwhelming army. Thieves, gamblers, and drunks were among Booth's first converts to Christianity. His congregation was desperately poor. He preached hope and salvation. His aim was to lead them to Christ and link them to a church for continued spiritual guidance.

In 1867, Booth had only 10 full-time workers. By 1874, the numbers had grown to 1,000 volunteers and 42 evangelists. They served under the name "The Christian Mission" and Booth assumed the title of General Superintendent, although his followers called him "General." Known as the "Hallelujah Army," the converts spread out to the east end of London into neighboring areas and then to other cities.

In 1878, people called his congregation a volunteer army. He crossed out the words "volunteer army" and wrote in "Salvation Army." The Salvation Army is still active and growing today. ☺

Memory Verse: Philippians 2:1–2 ICB

Does your life in Christ give you strength? Does his love comfort you? Do we share together in the Spirit? Do you have mercy and kindness? If so, make me very happy by having the same thoughts, sharing the same love, and having one mind and purpose.

Alternate version (New King James)
Therefore if there is any consolation in Christ, if any comfort of love, if any fellowship of the Spirit, if any affection and mercy, fulfill my joy by being like-minded, having the same love, being of one accord, of one mind.

December 5

But, It's Mine!
By Ivy Beckwith

Scripture:
Philippians 2:1–2

Lesson Aim:
We should be generous with others and not think we are better than other people.

Bible Skills:
Kids discover actions that show a spirit of generosity.

Bible Lesson: Hurray for the Salvation Army!
Needed: Small bell.

Gather children together. Ring bell and ask children: "At Christmas time, how many of you have seen the men and women who stand outside of stores ringing bells?" (Allow time for children to respond.) Why are those people standing outside those stores ringing the bells? They are collecting money to give to people who don't have enough money to buy food or pay the heating bill in the winter. Have you ever seen people put money in the buckets? Have you ever put money in the buckets?

Our Bible verse for today tells us why it's a good thing to put some of our money in those buckets and why we should be generous with the things we have. A man named Paul who wrote letters to churches a long time ago today wrote our Bible verse. He had a message from God to these churches and the message we're talking about today is that people who love God and Jesus should not be selfish.

People who love God and Jesus should not think they are better than other people and people who love God and Jesus should be more concerned about the needs of other people in the same way they care about their own needs. So in a small way we are pleasing God when we give money to the bell ringers at Christmas time. We could do other things with the money we drop in the bucket. Maybe we could buy a candy bar with it. That would taste good. Or maybe we could buy a toy with it. That would be fun to play with. Or maybe we could put the money in the bank and save it up to buy something really special. When we take that money and give it to someone else we're saying to that person he is important. Doing this makes God happy and shows that we love God.

There are other ways we can act generously instead of selfishly. There are other ways we can show people they are important to us. Can you think of some things you can do this week with your family and your friends to help them instead of helping yourself first? We've talked about giving money to people who don't have as much as you do, but there are other things you can do. Let's talk about what some of those are. [Give kids a chance to talk about ways they can be generous and show love to others such as help a sibling with a chore, take turns telling stories rather than dominate, value each person, talk nice about people who are being gossiped about.]

By not thinking we are better than other people, we show humility. By not being selfish, we please God and show other people we love them. Everybody wins!

 Song Suggestions:

Say Thank You by Mary Rice Hopkins "Miracle Mud" (Big Steps 4 U 1995)

I'm Not Too Little Songsheets published by CEF Press, P.O. Box 348, Warrenton, Mo. 63383

Pure Heart by Norm Hewitt from "Fired Up! "(Generation Ministries 2002)

You're In My Heart to Stay by Jana Alayra from "Dig Down Deep" (Montjoy Music 1997)

Craft for Younger Children: I Can Help!
Needed: For each child bring a paper plate, construction paper, glue, markers or crayons.

Trace around children's hands onto the construction paper and cut out. Write on paper plate—My hands can help! Show children how to glue their hand prints onto the plate so the writing shows.

Say: How can you help at home? How can you help at church? Let each child contribute an idea for one place or another. Even though you are a child, you can help!

 Craft for Older Children: I Will Be Generous Banner
Needed: One banner sized paper or butcher paper, markers.

Guide children to cooperate on drawing a banner for the classroom. Write, "I WILL BE GENEROUS" in large letters across the banner. Trace around hands below writing.

Let children decorate the handprints on the banner.

Snack: Smile!

Needed: Small containers of applesauce, plastic spoons and hot cinnamon candies. Let children make a smile in their applesauce with candies.

How do you feel when you smile? Everyone feels better when they smile. You can make someone happy just with your smile!

Prayer Focus:

Dear God, thank you for all that you give me. You are a wonderful God. Please help me to help others, use my hands to work for you. Amen.

Memory Verse: Philippians 2:1–2 ICB

Does your life in Christ give you strength? Does his love comfort you? Do we share together in the Spirit? Do you have mercy and kindness? If so, make me very happy by having the same thoughts, sharing the same love, and having one mind and purpose.

Alternate version (New King James)

Therefore if there is any consolation in Christ, if any comfort of love, if any fellowship of the Spirit, if any affection and mercy, fulfill my joy by being likeminded, having the same love, being of one accord, of one mind.

Memory Verse Activity:

Needed: 6 sheets of construction paper with the following words written on them: Strength, Love, Mercy and Kindness, Happy, Sharing Love, Having one Mind.

Give one sheet of paper with words to 6 different children. Have them stand in order, holding words up for all to see. Say the verse, emphasizing what is on the papers. Keep saying the verse until all children have learned it.

December 8

What Makes a Gift a Gift?, Midweek
By Karl Bastian

Scripture:
Romans 6:23

Lesson Aim:
Jesus is both a gift, and a guide for gift-giving.

Bible Skill:
I can celebrate Jesus by giving good gifts.

Bible Learning Activity for Younger Children:
Needed: Jingle bells—3 per child, chenille wire.

Show children how to thread jingle bells onto chenille wire and then form bracelet. Put bracelet on and let children "jingle" them.

Say: Let's get in line and have a jingle parade. Line kids up and walk around jingling the bracelets. Say: What do you plan to give your family members for Christmas? What can you make even if you have no money? Let children discuss including such ideas as writing a poem or drawing a picture.

Say: Christmas is such a fun way to celebrate Jesus! Jesus is our very special gift. Let's praise him with our jingles. Lift up your hand and shake and say, "Jesus loves you! Merry Christmas!"

Bible Learning Activity for Older Children: "The Price Is Right"
Needed: Bring in about 5 items in gift boxes that vary in price range.

Have the children write on a piece of paper a list of the items in order of how much they cost starting with the least expensive gift first. When they have all finished, put the gifts in order and see who came the closest to getting them all in order.

Enrichment for Younger Children:

Needed: 3 wrapped presents, one in beautiful paper (the largest one), one in newsprint (the smallest one), and one in between. Put small presents inside—a meal toy inside the beautifully wrapped one, a slightly better present inside the middle one, and a bag of treats for all kids inside the newsprint wrapped one).

Say: Wow, look at these presents! Which one do you think is the best? (Let them guess; they should guess the largest one.) Well, let's see. Let one child open each present. Which one is really the best? Yes! You're right! The one that didn't look as good. Sometimes we think that some gifts are really valuable when they aren't.

God gave us a very special gift that is free. It is wonderful! Some people may not want or take the gift, but we will! When we love Jesus and accept him in our life we can have the gift! The gift is eternal life with Jesus! How will you celebrate that this Christmas? ☺

Enrichment for Older Children: Eternal Life Gift

On a piece of paper write the following questions:

1. What is the best gift you ever received?
2. What is the worst gift you ever received?
3. What was the most expensive gift you ever received?
4. What was the best gift you ever gave? Have the children answer the questions and discuss them.

We all get gifts and we all give gifts all the time. Jesus is the best guide for showing us how to give and receive gifts. He has already given us the first gift—himself. ☺

Memory Verse: Romans 6:23 ICB

When someone sins, he earns what sin pays—death. But God gives us a free gift—life forever in Christ Jesus our Lord.

Alternate version (New King James)
For the wages of sin is death, but the gift of God is eternal life in Christ Jesus our Lord.

December 12

What Makes a Gift a Gift?

By Karl Bastian

Scripture:
Romans 6:23

Lesson Aim:
Jesus is both a gift, and a guide for gift-giving.

Bible Skill:
I can celebrate Jesus by giving good gifts.

Bible Lesson: What Makes a Gift a Gift

Needed: a wrapped present, a receipt. Be ready to incorporate the three short "skits" in this lesson.

Explain: There are three requirements for a gift to be a GIFT!

What makes a gift a gift? Listen for responses and let kids discuss this. Well, first of all, a gift is a gift when it is offered to you. You can't go to the store and BUY a gift for yourself; it wouldn't be a gift! Nor can you ask for it. Someone has to offer it to you, someone else has to buy it or make it. Then it can be a gift.

Here's how NOT to do it: (Hold out gift like you are going to give it to someone, but have someone else come along and just TAKE it and say, "Thanks!")

What else makes a gift a gift?

It must be free! It costs the giver something, but not you.

Here's how NOT to do it: (After kids open presents and hug and thank Dad, he gets out a receipt and names off the amount each kid owes! He demands they pay from their allowance!)

Ask: What would you do if this happened to you? What would you do if you opened all your presents on Christmas and then you got a bill for them? Would it still feel like you have received a gift?

What is #3 for a gift to be a GIFT? The gift must be accepted!

Here's how NOT to do it: (Someone gives a gift to another. They respond with exuberant thanks and excitement, but then leave without the gift!)

Explain: When someone gives you a gift but you do not take it, it's not a gift anymore. Can you imagine doing that?

If even ONE of these requirements is not met, IT IS NOT A GIFT!

Boys and girls, even though you can't imagine not accepting a gift that is offered to you, many people do just that. You see, God has OFFERED salvation through Jesus, His Son! People try a lot of ways to get to God, but the only way to get into a relationship with God is through the gift he is offering —all other ways do not work!

Second, salvation is a gift because salvation is FREE! People try a lot of ways to "buy" salvation—good works, giving money, prayer, etc. These are good things to do, but they don't get you salvation; it is a free gift. Those are things you do as a RESULT of the gift to say "thanks" to God!

Third, salvation must be received (or accepted). Lots of people think heaven sounds like a great place, they believe Jesus died on the cross, and want to know God—but they never bother to receive the gift!

 Song Suggestions:

The Best Gift by Mary Rice Hopkins from "Merry Christmas" (Big Steps 4 U 1990)

Silent Night Traditional

Treasure of My Heart by Jana Alayra from "Jump Into the Light" (Montjoy Music 1995)

It's Jesus Love by Dean-o from "Game Face" (Biblebeat Music 2003)

Craft for All Ages: Salvation Message for Kids
Needed: Paper strips for each child in the following colors: gold, black, red, green, and white.

Say: We are going to make a paper chain to decorate our Christmas tree. But this paper chain will be special—it will also tell you about the best gift! There is a wonderful story in the Bible. It is all about Jesus and how he saves us from our sins.

Pass out gold strip. This gold strip stands for heaven. We want to go to heaven one day when we die, don't we? Heaven is a wonderful place to be! We will live with God there. Make a circle with the strip and staple.

But one thing keeps us from going to heaven—it is sin. Pass out black strip.

No one can be in heaven if they have sin in their life. This black strip will stand for sin. Add the black strip to the gold strip, beginning a chain.

Since God knew you would sin, but God still wanted you to be in heaven, he sent his Son Jesus to die on the cross. Jesus was perfect; he had no sin at all. Because he died, you have a chance to have your sins taken away from you. Pass out red strip. Ask: What do you think this red strip stands for? Yes, you're right, the blood of Jesus. That is your gift. Add it to the chain.

God is offering that gift to you; that he will take away your sins. If you accept Jesus, if you tell Jesus you will love him and serve him and believe in him, a wonderful thing happens! When God looks at you he doesn't see sin, he just sees Jesus! Pass out the white strip. This white strip will stand for the pure heart that God will see when he looks at you! Add it to the chain.

This gift is being offered and it is free. But it must be accepted. Are you ready to accept this gift? If you are you can pray this prayer:

Dear Jesus, I know that I am a sinner and that I need a Savior. Thank you for dying on the cross for me, thank you for your life. I believe in you and I accept you as my Savior. Please forgive me for the sins I have done. Please help me to grow in you now. Amen.

Pass out green strip. This green strip stands for new life, for growing. This will remind us to grow in our Christian life. How do you grow? You read the Bible, pray, and do the right thing. You show kindness to people, you consider others' needs as you would your own, and so on. As you see God's ways working, you want to obey more. Add this strip to your chain.

The Best Gift

Needed: For each child bring a paper baking cup (used for cupcakes),

 chocolate pudding, a shredded wheat biscuit, one 1 inch pretzel nugget, one mini marshmallow and spoon.

Dip each baking cup 1/2 full with pudding. Give to children. Show them how to make a manger scene by spreading the wheat biscuit (straw) into pudding, using the pretzel as the baby and marshmallow as the head.

Say: This will remind us of the very best gift that we can ever get or give; Jesus, the Son of God!

Prayer Focus:

Dear God, thank you for the very best gift of all, your Son, Jesus Christ. We thank you for this wonderful gift. During this Christmas season, help us to remember that we already have the best gift. Amen.

Memory Verse: Romans 6:23 ICB

When someone sins, he earns what sin pays—death. But God gives us a free gift—life forever in Christ Jesus our Lord.

Alternate version (New King James)
For the wages of sin is death, but the gift of God is eternal life in Christ Jesus our Lord.

Memory Verse Activity:

Needed: Play money.

How much should it cost to get eternal everlasting life with God?

We don't have an answer for any of these questions, do we? But we do think that sin should cost something and eternal life should cost something, too.

But with God, any sin costs so much that the punishment is death. But since God loves us so much, God gave us a great gift instead of death. If you accept Jesus, you will get a great gift—Jesus Christ and life forever with God! ☺

December 15

Better Than Santa Claus, Midweek
By Johanna Townsend

Scripture:
Mark 10:13–16

Lesson Aim:
For children to understand that Christmas is all about Jesus who loves them.

Bible Skill:
The Christmas season orbits around Jesus Christ.

Bible Learning Activity for All Ages: Ornaments
Needed: For each child bring a blue Christmas ball, and star stickers (the office supply kind that come in a package with silver, red, green, blue and gold in the pack).

Give each child a ball. Say: We are going to remember the story of Christmas today by making an ornament about the story.

Guide this process: Long ago, in Bible times there were shepherds watching their sheep in a field. Let's put a green star on the ball to remind us of the shepherds in the green field. While children lick the star and put it on, explain that the shepherds were having an ordinary evening when suddenly they saw angel.

Let's put a silver star on to represent the angel. While children lick the star and put it on, explain that the angel told the shepherds that there was good news! A baby was born that would be the Savior! Suddenly there were many angels singing "Glory to God in heaven!" Let's put a few more silver stars on to stand for the angels.

The angel told the shepherds to find Jesus in a manger. They left to find him. They found Mary and Joseph who had put the Baby Jesus in a manger. They put him there because there were no nice places to stay, they were all full that night. Let's put the red star on to stand for "Stop!" there is no more room! While children lick the star and put it on, explain that since there was no more room, they found a quiet place to stay while the Baby Jesus was born.

Later, some wise men followed a special star to look for Jesus. Let's put a blue star on to stand for the night sky where they saw the star.

They found him and worshiped him and brought him special gifts. Let's put a gold star on to represent the gifts.

Today Jesus is still the best gift we could ever receive. Let's use this ornament to remember the story of his birth.

Enrichment for Older Children: Make an Advent Wreath

Needed: For each child bring 4 cardboard toilet paper rolls, 1 cardboard paper towel roll (cut 3 inches off to make it a little larger than the other rolls), glue and tape, yellow tissue paper, purple, pink, white and green construction paper and a 9 inch paper plate.

Say: Today we will make an Advent wreath. The Advent wreath is a wonderful tradition that will help us remember the story of Jesus' birth throughout the Christmas season.

Cover the paper towel tubes with construction paper making one pink and three purple "candles." Cover the towel roll with white paper, making it the "Christ candle."

Glue yellow tissue paper "flames" onto the candles and glue or tape the candles onto the paper plate. Let dry. While it is drying, carefully add green construction paper leaves to create a wreath effect.

Say: Let's look at this wreath and talk about what it means. The green wreath stands for life, the three candles that are purple stand for hope, peace, and love. The pink candle stands for joy. The flames on the candles stand for Jesus is the light, which lights up the darkness and the white candle, the Christ Candle, stands for Jesus!

Enrichment for Younger Children: Clay Ornaments

Needed: Prepare craft dough as follows: 1 cup flour, 1/2 cup salt, one cup water, 3 T oil, 1 package green drink mix (for green clay) and one package red drink mix (for red clay).

Mix all ingredients together except drink mixes. Divide clay in half and add one drink mix to each half.

Say: Waiting for Christmas is hard, isn't it? Today we will make some ornaments to decorate your house. Give each child a lump of both colors of dough. Let children create ornaments.

Let them dry until Sunday when children can take them home, or send them home to dry there. Stress: Christmas is fun because it is when we celebrate Jesus! ☺

Memory Verse: Mark 10:15–16 ICB

"I tell you the truth. You must accept the kingdom of God as a little child accepts things, or you will never enter it." Then Jesus took the children in his arms. He put his hands on them and blessed them.

Alternate version (New King James)

"Assuredly, I say to you, whoever does not receive the kingdom of God as a little child will by no means enter it." And He took them up in His arms, put His hands on them, and blessed them.

December 19

Better Than Santa Claus
By Johanna Townsend

Scripture:
Mark 10:13–16

Lesson Aim:
For children to understand that Christmas is all about Jesus who loves them.

Bible Skill:
The Christmas season orbits around Jesus Christ.

Bible Lesson: Better than Santa Claus
Show the picture of a child in the lap of Santa Claus. Ask: How many of you have had your picture taken sitting in the lap of Santa Claus, or seen someone getting a picture made with Santa Claus during the Christmas season? (Ask for a show of hands.) What was it like? (Encourage responses.) Did he say anything to you? (Ask for show of hands.) What did he say? (Ask two or three to share what Santa talked to them about.) Wow! I am impressed! You still remember what he said to you and for some of you it has been more than a year since this happened. Let me ask you one last question. How important did you feel when you had that special time with him? (Ask for a response from several of the children.)

Special events happen to each of us. Some we never forget. I am sure this type of event happened to a group of children long ago when Jesus lived on the earth. On that day Jesus was traveling somewhere in Judea with his disciples. A number of parents with their children approached them and asked the disciples if Jesus would pause to pray with their children giving them a blessing. The disciples, who were Jesus' good friends and traveling companions, impatiently told the children not to bother Jesus with such nonsense

Song Suggestions:

Wrap It All Up by Mary Rice Hopkins from "Mary Christmas" (Big Steps 4 U 1993)

Glory by Mary Rice Hopkins from "Mary Christmas" (Big Steps 4 U 1993)

Oh, Come Let Us Adore Him Traditional

Silent Night Traditional

and asked the parents to move on out of the way. Jesus saw what was happening and became disturbed by the disciple's behavior. He beckoned the children to come to him and spent time holding them, talking to them, and blessing them before resuming his journey.

Wouldn't it have been great to be one of those children Jesus blessed? (Let children collectively react.) Do you think that a conversation held with Jesus on that day is greater to remember than one we could have with Santa Claus? (Collective response.) Why do you suppose Jesus stopped and spent time with the children? (Let a few children respond.) How does this story make you feel about Jesus? (Let two children give a response.)

Explain: The good news is that we can have special moments with Jesus any time we open our Bible and read his words.

 Craft for Older Children: JOY BANNER!
Needed: For each child bring colored craft foam about 6" x 10", template of letters J-O-Y and additional craft foam or felt in contrasting color to cut letters from.

Let children cut the letters JOY out of foam or felt and glue them onto another piece of the same material. Let them decorate as desired, creating a "Joy Banner."

Say: "Why do you think we talk about JOY during the Christmas season? We sing *Joy to the World*. What does that mean? Jesus gives us joy which is a kind of deep-down happiness that no one can take away. When Jesus was born, he brought true joy to the world.

Joy is not the same as just being happy; joy is a deep feeling that only Jesus can give. It stays even when you're sad on the outside.

Craft for Younger Children: Christmas Photo Frame Ornament

Needed: Small photo of each child and cardstock, glitter, ribbon, sequins.

Cut shapes out of cardstock and let children glue their photos onto the shape they pick. Let children decorate their frame however they choose. Let them take it home to give as a special ornament gift.

Christmas Candles

Needed: Candle shaped snack cakes, yellow candies.

Show children how to make a "candle" from snack cake by sticking the yellow candy into the end, making it look like a flame.

Say: "Candles are very important at Christmas time. We like to light them to celebrate Jesus, for Jesus is the light of the whole world. As you eat, discuss the following questions:

What is the darkness?

How does light help the darkness?

What does "Jesus is the light of the world" mean?

How can we also be a light?

Prayer Focus:

Dear God, thank you so much for your wonderful gift—the best gift ever which is your Son, Jesus. Help us to remember that the Christmas season is all about Jesus. Amen.

Memory Verse: Mark 10:15–16 ICB

"I tell you the truth. You must accept the kingdom of God as a little child accepts things, or you will never enter it." Then Jesus took the children in his arms. He put his hands on them and blessed them.

Alternate version (New King James)

"Assuredly, I say to you, whoever does not receive the kingdom of God as a little child will by no means enter it." And He took them up in His arms, laid His hands on them, and blessed them.

Memory Verse Activity:
Needed: A sign that says "Heaven". Put on one side of the room.

Say Pretend that heaven is over there. How can we get to heaven?

(Let one child walk over) Can we walk in like this? (No!)

(Let one child run over) Can we run in like this? (No!)

(Let one child "fly" over) Can we fly in like this? (No!)

(Let one child "swim" over) Can we swim in like this? (No!)

(Let one child crawl over) Can we crawl in like this? (No!)

(Let one child walk backward over) Can we walk backward like this? (No!)

So, how do we get into heaven according to our verse? Receive it! Yes, what does that mean to "have faith" or "receive it?" It means believing in Jesus who you cannot see. It means knowing that Jesus will save you and accepting Jesus as your Savior and Lord. It means always trusting in Jesus and doing what he says to do!

Teacher should chant the following words, let children echo:

"I assure you,

anyone who doesn't have

their kind of faith

will never get into

the kingdom of God."

Then he took the children

into his arms and

placed his hands on their heads

and blessed them.

December 22

The Epiphany (Wise Men), Midweek
By Vicki Wiley

Scripture:
Matthew 2:2, 10

Lesson Aim:
For children to learn about the Magi and Church Year.

Bible Skill:
To embrace God's great plan for his people.

Bible Learning Activity for All Ages: Christmas Is Coming in a Few Days!
The Magi or kings were men from the East who were led by a star to worship the infant Christ. These men were actually "astrologers" or people who studied the stars all the time. They really knew this was a new and special star that they were seeing. It was so special that their response was very joyful. They rejoiced, worshiped and brought gifts to the baby Jesus. They followed the star to the King of their heart.

Bible Learning Activity for Younger Children:
Needed: Stars, perhaps those made in the craft activity.
The wise men followed the star to get to the baby Jesus. Choose the child with the birthday closest to today to be the first leader. This child holds the star up and the other children follow them. Change leaders until everyone gets a chance to be the "star". Let children complete game by kneeling down and singing, "O Come Let Us Adore Him."

The wise men followed a star to get to the baby Jesus. When they got there, they worshiped and adored him.

Bible Learning Activity for Older Children: The Magi

Ask: Who were the Magi?

Explain that they were special people who came to see Jesus when he was very young. Who were these people?

• They were called the "Magi" which means that they had some special wisdom.

• They studied the stars all the time and knew this star that they now saw was very special.

• The Bible calls them Magi, but some songs call them kings.

• They probably were not kings because kings would have so many other things to do that they would not be able to study the stars.

• After the Magi had seen the Christ child they were warned about Herod's bad intentions toward baby Jesus. This must have been a warning from God.

Joseph took his family immediately to Egypt after the Magi left. The gold that the Magi gave them probably helped with this move.

Enrichment for All Ages: How the Church Tells Time

Needed: For each child bring a pencil, silver or gold cord and chenille wires in these colors; purple (2), white (2), green (2), red.

Do you know how to tell time? How do you tell time? (Give kids plenty of opportunity to share their answers.) Do you know what season it is now? How do you know when it is winter, summer, spring, or fall? What is different in each one?

The church tells time a little differently. The church doesn't use a clock, but it does have seasons. These church seasons are different though. They are built around events in our faith history. The church has seasons called Advent, Christmas, Epiphany and Lent, Easter, Pentecost, and Ordinary Time. These seasons tells us about the life of Jesus.

The seasons all have colors to go with them. Some churches use these colors in their worship rooms. Some pastors wear the colors and some churches also have banners to show the colors. Does anyone know what these colors are? The colors are purple, green, white, and red.

Today we are going to learn how we can remember Jesus' life with the colors of the church. As I tell you about each season, I will give you a chenille wire that will remind you of that season. You will curl the wire around the pencil and then put the chenille wire "bead" on the cord. When we are finished, you will have a necklace to remind you of the church year.

Advent

The first season of the church is Advent and the color of Advent is purple (Pass out purple chenille wires and pencils.)

Does anyone know what happens during Advent? (the days before Christmas!)

Purple stands for kings and royalty. Since Jesus is the King of all, when we are preparing for Christmas, we use purple to show how special Jesus is. This is the season we celebrate Jesus' birth!

Show children how to wrap the purple chenille wire and then put it onto the cord.

Christmas

Pass out the white wire. Guide children to wrap it around the pencil while you explain: The next season is Christmas. What happens at Christmas? Christmas is when we celebrate how special Christ is to us. We celebrate that Christ loves us and knows each of us. For this season we use the color white. White stands for purity, joy, and hope.

Show children how to put the white chenille wire on the cord.

Epiphany

Pass out the green wire. Guide children to wrap it around the pencil while you explain: The next season is Epiphany. Epiphany is when we celebrate the Magi and how they worshiped Jesus. We celebrate baptism and what it means to us. This season begins after Christmas and the color is green. We use green because green stands for life and growing and we celebrate growing in Christ!

Show children how to put the green chenille wire on the cord.

Lent

Pass out the purple wire. Guide children to wrap it around the pencil while you explain: The next season is Lent. Lent is when we begin to think about Jesus and the sorrow and sadness that he was about to go through. We think about our faith and we know that God is always with us no matter what we are going through. This season begins after Epiphany and the color is purple again. This time purple stands for sorrow and prayer.

Show children how to put the purple chenille wire on the cord.

Easter

Pass out the white wire. Guide children to wrap it around the pencil while you explain: Jesus came back to life! This is a very important day for Christians! We use white to show that we are joyful and we feel great!

Show children how to put the white chenille wire on the cord.

Pentecost

Pass out the red wire. Guide children to wrap it around the pencil while you explain: The next season is Pentecost. Do you remember what happened at Pentecost? Yes, you're right, Pentecost is when Peter was preaching and the Holy Spirit came down to the people. Pentecost is very special because the Holy Spirit still lives in us today, when we believe in Jesus Christ. The color for Pentecost is red. Red stands for the power and "fire" of the Holy Spirit.

Show children how to put the red chenille wire on the cord.

Ordinary Time

Pass out the green wire. Guide children to wrap it around the pencil while you explain: The last season is ordinary time. Some churches call this "Season after Pentecost." What does that mean? Yes, this means that we learn about the other stories about Jesus during this time and we grow in Christ. This season lasts until Christ the King Sunday, the week before Advent begins.

Show children how to put the green chenille wire on the cord.

Now look at the necklace and you can see each color. Each one can remind you of the different parts of the life of Jesus. You can even teach someone else about the church year by showing them what you made. When we are Christians and we love Christ, every single bit of his life is important to us.

Memory Verse: Matthew 2:2, 10 ICB

They asked, "Where is the baby who was born to be the king of the Jews? We saw his star in the east. We came to worship him." When the wise men saw the star, they were filled with joy.

Alternate version (New King James)
"Where is He who has been born King of the Jews? For we have seen His star in the East and have come to worship Him." When they saw the star, they rejoiced with exceedingly great joy.

December 26

The Epiphany (Wise Men)
By Vicki Wiley

Scripture:
Matthew 2:2, 10

Lesson Aim:
For children to learn about the Magi and Church Year.

Bible Skill:
To embrace God's great plan for his people.

Bible Lesson: Epiphany

Yesterday was Christmas! Did everyone have a great day? Are you looking forward to the New Year? In just a few days everyone will be celebrating the end of one year and the beginning of the next. We will all be buying new calendars to use. But in the church, our year is a little different.

We have one more Christmas Season holiday coming—it is called Epiphany. Does anyone have any idea what "Epiphany" means? Let's look at the dictionary and see what it says:

epiphany (UNDERSTANDING)

the experience of suddenly understanding or becoming aware of something that is very important to you or a powerful religious experience.

This was exactly what happened when the wise men saw the star. They had never seen a star like that before; that star was new. At the same time, they became aware of something very important and had a powerful religious experience; the best religious experience that someone could possible have—they met Jesus Christ.

We celebrate Epiphany on the last day of the twelve days of Christmas, so it is on January 6. In some countries, The Nativity scene is left in every home until the Epiphany when the "Magi", or the three kings, bring presents for the baby Jesus.

Song Suggestions:

We Three Kings Traditional

Follow that Star by Mary Rice Hopkins from "Mary Christmas" (Big Steps 4 U 1993)

I Open My Heart by Mark Thompson from "Yes Yes Yes!" (Markarts 2000)

Day by Day by Jana Alayra from "Jump Into the Light" (Montjoy Music 1995)

This week we will begin a new year. The Christmas holiday will soon be over and you will have new decisions to make. What star will you follow? Will you be like the wise men, and follow the one that leads you to Jesus? Will you make this a year where your faith really grows, where you learn more about Jesus than you ever have?

The year 2005 can be very special for you—you can have an *epiphany* and understand more than you ever have before about Jesus!

King's Cake

Needed: One Bundt type cake with almond hidden inside, icing, crown.

 Explain: In Germany children celebrate Epiphany with a "King's Cake." A King's Cake is a cake with an almond hidden in it. The children decorate the cake, and then they cut it and eat each piece. Whoever gets the almond is the King and gets to wear a crown for the day.

 Craft for Younger Children: Star Wand

Needed: For each child bring a star cut from yellow sheets of craft foam (2–3 inches), a 12 inch dowel rod, a length of gold curling ribbon already cut into 12 inch pieces and curled.

Say: The wise men followed a star that led them right to Jesus. Today we are going to make a "Star Wand" to help us remember that story.

Guide children to tie the ribbon to the top of dowel. Glue a star on the other end of the ribbon last and let it dry. Show children how to hold "wand" up in the air and "follow the star."

Craft for Older Children: Follow that Star!

Needed: For each child bring a star cut from yellow sheets of craft foam (2–3 inches), an 8 inch x 1/4 inch dowel rod, several pieces of gold curling ribbon, glitter, glue, a raisin box wrapped in brown construction paper.

Say: The wise men followed a star that led them right to Jesus. Today we are going to make a craft to help us remember that story.

Show children how to spread a thin coating of glue onto the star and then glitter the star. Shake off excess and let it dry while you do the rest of the craft.

Guide children to make a house out of the raisin box by having the children draw a door and a window on the box.

Draw Mary, Joseph, and baby Jesus figures standing against the outside wall.

Cut several pieces of curling ribbon and curl. Tie these to the top of dowel. Glue the glittered star on and attach to "house" with tape or glue.

Prayer Focus:

Dear God, thank you for this holiday season. We thank you for the focus on the wise men and how we can also be wise by searching for you. Thank you for our new year. Please help us to serve you more. Amen.

Memory Verse: Matthew 2:2, 10 ICB

They asked, "Where is the baby who was born to be the king of the Jews? We saw his star in the east. We came to worship him." When the wise men saw the star, they were filled with joy.

Alternate version (New King James)

"Where is He who has been born King of the Jews? For we have seen His star in the East and have come to worship Him." When they saw the star, they rejoiced with exceedingly great joy.

Bonus Lesson

Showdown at Mt. Carmel
By Rick Wesselhoff

Scripture:
1 Kings 18:17–40

Lesson Aim:
That sometimes God wants us to be in a place where, if we don't pray to him, we will fail. His glory is revealed to our unbelieving friends when they see the answer to our prayer.

Life Skill:
That kids will develop a stronger understanding of the power of prayer.

Bible Lesson: God Shows His Power

For three long years it did not rain.
People waited. It never came.
But Israel would not repent even still.
They still worshiped Baal upon a hill.
So the time did come when the Lord did say,
"Go back, Elijah, to the Israelites today.
And teach them who rules the earth and the sky.
It is NOT Baal . . . It is I!"

The stage was set. The battle will soon begin.
Who is really Lord: Who will win?
From near and from far the people came
To witness the battle between the name
Of Baal, a god made of stone and lies,
And the Omnipotent One, Yahweh, Lord most high!

The prophets of Baal and Asherah were there
Dancing and shouting so all could hear.
But the crowd did stop and the crowd did hush
When the prophet Elijah stepped out from the brush.
One man of God, Elijah, that was all,
The only one brave enough to stand up tall
And take on 450 men.
He looked in to the crowd and said to them then,
"It is time, people, for you to decide.
If the Lord is God, then stand on His side.
But if Baal is God, then choose whom you'll serve.
Choose one God and do not swerve."

The prophets of Baal prepared an ox
And laid it on their altar of rocks.
Elijah once again addressed the crowd
And read the rules, clear and loud:
"Let the prophets of Baal kneel down and pray
And ask their god to send fire today.
Then I will pray to the Lord for fire.
We'll see who is God and who is a liar."

The prophets did dance. And the prophets did shout,
"Answer us, Baal," they all cried out.
Elijah just laughed and laughed with delight
To see the men pray, but no fire in sight.
He taunted, "Maybe your god is busy today.
Maybe he's sleeping or he's gone away."

The prophets of Baal did pray and pray.
But finally they gave up at the end of the day.
Elijah laughed again. What a joke!
Then he rebuilt the Lord's altar, which had broke.
And he prepared the ox and laid it there
And all the people gaped and stared
As Elijah dug a ditch all the way around
And without so much as even a sound

Filled the ditch with water and then
Poured more water on the altar again.
Now it was Elijah's turn.
But everyone knows that fire won't burn
On the altar when the altar is wet.
The people couldn't wait to see what happened next.
Elijah prayed a prayer that day
That only a man of God could pray.
"God, bring your fire right here, right now.
Show the people your mighty power.
May the people see and then
Turn their hearts to you again."
God always answers when a man of God prays:
And FIRE poured down from the sky in a blaze.
The fire burned up the big, gray ox.
It burned up the soil and even the rocks.
It licked up the wet wood and the water, too.
It did things that fire is not supposed to do.
Every single person who was in that crowd
Fell to the ground and shouted loud,
"The Lord is God! We know now it's true!
We've seen today what the Lord can do." [*]
The prophets of Baal tried to run away.
Only Elijah was left that day.
God had done what God set out to do.
The people again believed God's Word is true!
No Baal, No Asherah, no false god of stone
Can ever match the Lord, for the Lord alone
Is Almighty, All-Powerful, All Knowing, All True.
No one can do what the Lord can do!

---

* Speaker notes: make one craft as explained below and use three or four trick candles placed into "altar". Pour water into the bowl, wetting the candles, sponges and the twelve "rocks". Then light the trick candles. Only adults should be allowed access to matches. Follow instructions on the trick candles to safely extinguish the flame.

Song Suggestions:

All Things Are Possible "Shout to the Lord Kids", Integrity Music

Outta Sight by Dean-o 1999 from "Soul Surfin'" (1999 FKO Music, Inc.)

God's Power CEF Press, P.O. Box 348, Warrenton, Mo. 63383

Pray, Pray, Pray by Mary Rice Hopkins © Big Steps 4 U "Good Buddies"

For discussion:

Why did the prophets of Baal pray for so long and not get an answer?

But why did God answer Elijah right away when Elijah prayed?

What is something you need God's help with? Can you pray for God's help right now?

Elijah would have failed without God's help. He didn't have a backup plan. He didn't have any other way out. Either God was going to answer Elijah's prayer, or Elijah would fail and fail big. Sometimes God wants us to pray risky prayers. Sometimes God wants us to be in a place where if God does not answer prayer, we will fail. When we need anything God wants us to pray and trust him that he will take care of it for us. If we think, "Maybe God will help and maybe he won't," chances are great that God will decide not to help. He waits until we say, "I believe that God will answer my prayer. And now I will live like it."

Twelve Stones of Israel

Needed: Graham crackers, softened cream cheese (or peanut butter), raisins.

Spread graham crackers with cream cheese. Allow children to count out 12 raisins. They arrange the 12 raisins as they please.

Elementary Craft: "Hear Me, O Lord That the People May Know You Are Lord."

Needed:

1. Disposable cereal-sized bowls.
2. Play dough either purchased at a store or made with this recipe:

1 c. flour

1/2 c. salt

2 t Cream of tartar

Saucepan

1 c. water

1 T Oil

1 t Food coloring

Small bowl

Mix dry ingredients into saucepan. Combine liquid ingredients into small bowl and mix until smooth. Add this mixture to the dry ingredients and mix well.

Cook over medium heat until mixture forms ball, stirring constantly.

Knead ball until mixture is cool and smooth before using. Store in an airtight container.

3. Inexpensive kitchen sponges.

Instruct children to roll small pieces of dough into "stones." Each bowl should contain the twelve stones of the twelve tribes of Israel. The instructor is to cut up the kitchen sponges representing the ox.

4. Lastly, add approx. 1/4 cup of birdseed around the bottom of the bowl. Now they have the altar of Elijah.

Prayer Focus:

Pray a "risky" prayer. Tell God what you need:

"Dear God, I know you can meet my needs. One thing I really need is:_____.

I trust you to help me. I trust you to do something big for me and answer my prayer like you answered Elijah's prayer. In Jesus' name." Amen.

Craft for Younger Children: Hear Me, O Lord.

Needed: Small cut up pieces of blue, blue-green, violet, orange, and yellow colored tissue paper. Wax paper trimmed 8" x 8" squares. Yarn. Hole punch. A clothes iron and some kind of ironing surface (or use ironing board if space allows). Give the children the tissue paper and instruct them to place the blue ones on the outside edge of the square of wax paper. Tell them to put the warm colors of tissue paper in the middle. Carefully lay the square down on surface without disturbing their placement of tissue squares. Place another sheet of wax paper on top. Iron the sheets together, sandwiching the color tissue. Note how the wax will create a seal between the two sheets and the colored paper. Thread a small piece of yarn through a hole that is punched at the top. They now have a mobile of how God's fire came down into the water and answered Elijah's prayer.

Memory Verse: 1 Kings 18:37a ICB

Lord, answer my prayer. Show these people that you, Lord, are God.

Alternate version (New King James)
Hear me, O LORD; hear me, that this people may know that You are the LORD God.

Memory Verse Activity:

To make this a "risky" prayer, you now have to do something. As you say this verse in your prayer, act like you already know that God will answer your prayer. God's power and glory was revealed to the unbelieving Israelites when God answered Elijah's prayer.

     Write down: I believe that God will answer my prayer, so what I will do is _____. I believe God's power will be shown to my unbelieving friends when he answers my prayer.

The Calling

By Roger Fields

I am a minister.

I minister to the largest mission field in the world. My calling is sure; my challenge is big; my vision is clear; my desire is strong; my influence is eternal; my impact is critical; my values are solid; my faith is tough; my mission is urgent; my purpose is unmistakable; my direction is forward; my heart is genuine; my strength is supernatural; my reward is promised; and my God is real.

In a world of cynicism, I offer hope. In a world of confusion, I offer truth. In a world of immorality, I offer values. In a world of neglect, I offer attention. In a world of abuse, I offer safety. In a world of ridicule, I offer affirmation. In a world of division, I offer reconciliation. In a world of bitterness, I offer forgiveness. In a world of sin, I offer salvation. In a world of hate, I offer God's love.

I refuse to be dismayed, disengaged, disgruntled, discouraged, or distracted. Neither will I look back, stand back, fall back, go back, or sit back. I do not need applause, flattery, adulation, prestige, stature, or veneration. I do not have time for business as usual, mediocre standards, small thinking, outdated methods, normal expectations, average results, ordinary ideas, petty disputes, or low vision. I will not give up, give in, bail out, lie down, turn over, quit, or surrender.

I will pray when things look bad. I will pray when things look good. I will move forward when others stand still. I will trust God when obstacles arise. I will work when the task is overwhelming. I will get up when I fall down.

My calling is to reach boys and girls for God. It is too serious to be taken lightly, too urgent to be postponed, too vital to be ignored, too relevant to be overlooked, too significant to be trivialized, too eternal to be fleeting, and too passionate to be quenched.

I know my mission. I know my challenge. I also know my limitations, my weaknesses, my fears, and my problems. And I know my God. Let others get the praise. Let the church get the blessing. Let God get the glory.

I am a minister. I minister to children. This is who I am. This is what I do.

Greater Reward

By Roger Fields

According to Jesus, people who serve in children's ministry will receive greater reward than those who serve in other departments within the church. That's right! We can expect children's workers to be more blessed than ushers, greeters, choir members, parking lot attendants, and the rest of the church. All those departments are important, and God will reward those who serve in them, but the fact remains that children's workers possess a promise from Jesus that others simply don't have.

Jesus said it like this in Matthew 10:42: "And whoever gives one of these little ones only a cup of cold water in the name of a disciple, assuredly, I say to you, he shall by no means lose his reward." Jesus does not here tell us what the reward is. We do know, however, from this explicit statement that if you can simply transport the snacks from the kitchen to the kid, you have a reward that cannot be erased or lost. Jesus puts His word on the line for children's workers.

Jesus expounds on this in Matthew 18:5 when He says, "Whoever receives one little child like this in My name receives Me." Here's the secret. For every child you receive into your children's ministry, you receive Jesus that many times over. If you only have five children in your Sunday school or children's church, you are receiving the presence of the Lord fives times over. With the presence of the Lord multiplied you can expect great reward. Jesus never went anyplace where He didn't do something good. Expect good things to happen to you if you receive children in the name of Jesus. Don't be timid about believing what Jesus was bold enough to say. Expect reward and expect His presence.

God told Moses that the success of the nation of Israel was determined by their commitment to teach their children (Deut. 6:1–7). Reward follows our commitment to children's ministry.

Children's workers have mistakenly waited for the pastor and congregation to express appreciation for their labor of love. Oftentimes, pastors and congregations don't understand all that it takes to minister to children each week. They don't know the challenge. They struggle to comprehend what you do to prepare to teach kids. Don't let what you perceive as a lack of appreciation bother you. Jesus can reward you better than the pastor or the congregation.

Put your faith in what Jesus said. There is a reward. And if you receive children, you can't ever lose it.

The Seven Greatest Questions Facing Children's Ministry

By Roger Fields

The primary issue facing children's ministry is defining what it is and is not, then shaping it accordingly. Perceptions of adult ministry are predictable. People expect preaching, teaching, counseling, weddings, funerals, music, fellowship, and an annual picnic. In contrast, children's ministry prompts a variety of expectations. Other than take-home papers and a summertime VBS, most people, even church boards, don't know what children's ministry should do or be. To help further the discussion, I submit my outlook on these fundamental questions.

1. Need or Vision?

Are you driven by what you need or by what you see? Every children's ministry has needs. Many of them have critical needs. But people will rarely follow a need. They follow a vision. It is easier to recruit a team of people who have caught your vision than it is to beg people to help you out. Nobody ever volunteered for Jesus. He recruited the people He wanted based on His vision. "I will make you fishers of men" is a vision statement. "Please volunteer to be a teacher because the fifth grade boys killed two last week" is a need statement. Do you think in terms of what you need or do you plan based on your vision of what could be? Never stop clarifying your vision. Let your vision lead the way. Give people the opportunity to join a team that's going somewhere. Talk about your vision more than you talk about your needs.

2. Images or Substance?

Are you willing to allow images to define your children's ministry? Left unattended, children's ministry will always be reduced to its lowest common denominator: cute pictures. David facing down the giant with a raggedy slingshot, Daniel sitting in the corner petting a cuddly lion, and Noah leading cutesy animals two by two up the plank—all make great bulletin board décor. But left without explanation, they become religious images void of power. Children need to understand the substance of a Bible story. Noah trusted God when the whole world laughed at God. David believed the promises of God covered even big, loud giants. Daniel prayed openly to God in front of lots of mean people. In each case, God proved to be reliable. Boys and girls need a God they can believe in. Pictures don't always rise to the task. After decorating the room, let the images fade into the background while you communicate the meaning of the Bible story.

3. Circumstances or Choice?

Are we impacted more by events that happen to us or by the choices we make? The Bible is full of stories about real people who overcame real problems by making right choices. Making good choices will defeat bad circumstances. Help kids understand that lots of bad things will happen in this world, but their response will determine what quality of life they experience. Their choices of right and wrong will make the difference, even when circumstances rise up against them. Let kids know they don't have to live under the dictatorship of circumstances. There is power in making right choices.

4. Process or Decision?

Is salvation a process or a decision? While none of us knew very much when we accepted the Lord, people aren't absorbed into the kingdom of God little by little; they are born into the kingdom of God all at once. And it happens because we made a decision. At some point, we decided to trust Jesus as our Lord and Savior. Salvation is not a process; it is a decision. Don't let fear stop you from giving children the opportunity to make that decision. Jesus was the one who said, "Do not forbid the little ones from coming to Me." Peter closed his sermon on the day of Pentecost by saying, "This promise is for you and your children." Jesus never told children to act more like adults to come into the kingdom. He said it the other way around. He told adults to be more like kids to come into the kingdom. There is power in making a decision. There is exceptional power in making a decision to put your life and faith in Jesus. Ask this question: Could a child grow up connected to my church and never receive God's gift of salvation? You don't have to offer a traditional altar call, and high-pressured invitations are never appropriate for anyone, especially children. But some way, somehow, give kids the opportunity to make a decision to receive Christ.

5. Teach or Reach?

Are you focused on what you teach or what kids learn? There is a difference. You can teach Old Testament history, the life of Christ, your church doctrine, and even a bag full of Greek words, but if the kids aren't learning, none of it matters. What you teach means nothing. What kids learn means everything. Your scope and sequence needs to do more than impress the church board; it needs to connect with kids. Check your teaching methods. Do they meet your need to feel like a "real" teacher or the kids' needs to learn? Traditional classroom methods might meet the expectations of your parents and church board, but they will never reach today's kids. Find out what communicates to the boys and girls God brings to you. Use interaction. Sing to music that relates to kids. Use drama. Don't be afraid to try a new teaching method. It might work.

6. Passive or Active?

Are children the church of tomorrow or are they part of the church of today? While kids are still learning and growing, that doesn't mean they are in a spiritual holding tank until they grow up. Children are part of the church today. People who haven't yet received the Lord are the church of tomorrow. You don't have to grow up to serve God. Many kids in the Bible accomplished feats for God before they grew up. Samuel served God in the temple. A Jewish servant girl sent a military commander to a prophet to get healed of leprosy. David dropped Goliath. Josiah turned a nation back to God. A boy donated fish and bread so Jesus could feed a crowd. The only thing we know about Jesus between His birth and His baptism is that He had to be "about His Father's business." All were kids. And all served God before they grew up. Could it be that one reason why adults today act as though sitting in church is their service to God is because we trained them that way? "Sit up straight with your hands to yourself" is the only challenge many of them received in church as kids. We trained them well. Encourage kids to pray for others, share their faith, lead praise and worship, and serve in the church. Let them be about their Father's business.

7. Values or Relationship?

Is our highest objective to provide good values or to lead kids to an authentic relationship with God? Life skills are vital and should be taught. But knowing God is better than having values. When a storm hits, a solid relationship with the living Lord is stabilizing while values get shaken. It is our knowledge of God that provides what we need for life and godliness (2 Pet. 1:2–4). Help kids to know God. They will be drawn to whatever you focus on. Focus on God. It is the knowledge of God that will impact lives. If all you teach about are the evils of drugs, alcohol, and sex, you will draw kids to drugs, alcohol, and sex. Teach them about God, His character, His promises, His plans. Let Bible stories illustrate what God is like. If you teach boys and girls about God, they will get to know Him. And that will last them for a lifetime.

Revealed to Babes

By Roger Fields

In Luke 10, seventy followers of Jesus return from their first ministry trip. They are a little excited as they explain to Jesus (as if He didn't know), "Even the demons are subject to us in Your name." They were surprised to discover that there is more power in ministry than they expected. Jesus used the opportunity to define their spiritual authority while making it clear that having their names written in heaven provides the real reason for celebration. Then Jesus got happy.

With joy He thanked God for something. It is that "something" that should make all of us in children's ministry take notice. Here is what Jesus said.

I thank You, Father, Lord of heaven and earth, that You have hidden these things from the wise and prudent and revealed them to babes. Even so, Father, for it seemed good in Your sight. All things have been delivered to Me by My Father, and no one knows who the Son is except the Father, and who the Father is except the Son, and the one to whom the Son wills to reveal Him (Luke 10:21, 22 NKJV).

Before wading too deep into Christian education, we should remember that divine understanding from God the Father will take us farther than mere Bible knowledge. Revelation trumps wisdom and prudence. Bible knowledge is important, and we must commit ourselves to teaching it to our children. However, Bible knowledge alone will not help Johnny at school on Monday if all he has in his heart are the books of the Old Testament in order. Johnny needs divine understanding of who Jesus is to him. That's our primary objective in children's ministry, to position children so that God the Father can reveal His Son in their hearts.

This objective changes the scope of children's ministry. If intellectual comprehension takes second place to Godly revelation, and if Jesus taught that God reveals truth about Himself to "babes," then children need not be thought of as lagging spiritually behind adults. Though adults outweigh children in intellectual ability, children may have the advantage when it comes to divine understanding.

If I were to stand before a congregation holding a shoebox containing an unknown object, intellectual capacity would not be enough to reveal to even the smartest what was in the box. If I brought a five-year-old girl up front and allowed her to peek inside the box revealing a feather, she would have understanding that not one adult would possess. She, and no one else, knows that my shoebox contains a feather. I revealed to her what no one could know without my lifting the lid.

Luke 10:21, 22 teaches that our Father in heaven loves to "lift the lid" for "babes." He loves to reveal His Son Jesus to the simple. Adults who rely on their own wisdom run at a disadvantage when trying to comprehend God. Children, and adults with humility, get a better look into the box. That is why children's ministry is vital. The eight-year-old girl in your children's church probably has the edge on the college professor sitting in the adult service. With Father God taking such an active role, maybe kids are getting more from your children's ministry than you thought.

The Importance of Purpose, Mission, and Vision in Your Children's Ministry

By Karl Bastian

We've all heard the quotation, "Without vision the people perish." But what *is* vision when it comes to your children's ministry? In the 90s it became very "hip" to have statements of purpose, mission, vision, and goals. But what do these words mean, and how do they relate to each other? I often see these terms misused or used interchangeably as though they all mean the same thing. The reality is that each of these words has a specific and significant role in providing your ministry with focus, direction, and a way of evaluating your progress.

It is essential for any thriving ministry to know its purpose, mission, and vision in order to succeed. Look closely at any vibrant ministry and you will find them. Even if they are nowhere recognized in print, if the ministry is alive and growing, one interview with its leader will reveal them. Without them, the ministry *will* perish! So what do these words mean and what is the difference between them? Here is a basic description of each with a sample statement. Keep in mind these are *samples*. There is no magic in copying them. You need statements that are *yours* and tailored to your ministry's needs.

PURPOSE: Why do you exist?

Your purpose states *why* you even have a children's ministry in the first place. Do you exist merely to provide child care during adult programs? If not, make your purpose known! A purpose will be true of almost every children's ministry because it is more general in focus, but still has the power of enabling you to say "no" to good things that do not fit your purpose.

Sample: We exist to supplement the family in their efforts to lay a spiritual foundation that, in God's timing, will lead a child into a relationship with God through Jesus Christ and then to provide for them a place where they can grow in their knowledge and love for God.

MISSION: What are you going to do?

Your mission takes the purpose a step further in explaining, "O.K., what is *your* children's ministry going to *do* in order to act on that purpose? A mission will be more unique to your ministry.

Sample: Our mission is to equip parents and volunteers to impact the world through reaching and teaching children.

VISION: What will it look like when you are done?

Purpose is important, but can go unstated, since most people know what it is. Mission is more critical as it gives your ministry focus and direction. *Vision is essential* because without a vision you will never know if you accomplished anything! Throwing a dart at a wall and then drawing a target around it may make you look good, but most likely both the dart and the target will be in the wrong place, and you will end up with targets all over the wall! *A vision is a description of what your ministry will look like when you are "done."* It gives you something to aim for. As the saying goes, if you aim at nothing, you are sure to hit it! Vision says, "Hey, folks, this is where we are going!" It provides a horizon to set your hearts on and a task to set your hands to. It enables you to say "no" to good things that won't bring the vision into reality.

If your vision statement describes what already exists, it is time to either move on, or it's time to get a new vision! Your vision needs to be created by your leadership team and/or key leaders. Your vision must be bought into and agreed to by everyone who will be a part of making it happen. There are even times to remove a good worker if they have a different vision than the team. We can disagree on some of the how-to's, but everyone's got to be working on the same vision! Different areas of ministry may work on different aspects of the vision, or get there in different ways, but in the end the whole group needs to arrive at the same place.

A vision statement need not be as short as a purpose or mission statement. Some ministries have a vision statement that is a page long! Paint a verbal picture of what you want your ministry to look like. Be bold, and don't limit it to present staff and resources—trust God and watch what He will do! If the vision comes from Him, He will be faithful to bring it to pass!

Sample: We want an ever-growing number of children to visit our church, find a place where they feel loved, come to know Christ, and continue to grow through fun and life-changing experiences. We want parents to find a place where their lives are impacted by what they see happening in the lives of their children. We want their experience from the moment they arrive until they leave to be one of surprise and delight. We want to see every child in our ministry discipled one-on-one by a parent or loving adult before they leave the children's ministry so that they will know basic doctrine, be practicing the spiritual disciplines, and have acquired the biblical skills needed to survive the turbulent teenage years and prepare them for a life of loving, obeying, and serving God.

HOMEWORK ASSIGNMENT FOR LEADERS:

If you do not currently have a written purpose, mission and/or vision:

1. Write out what *you* think is your ministry's purpose, mission, and vision.

2. Ask your leadership team / key leader to do the same (without showing yours!)

3. Compare them—and share them. Talk about what you discover.

4. As a team, develop a purpose, mission, and vision statement, and then communicate with the volunteers in your ministry.

5. Spend some time praying about your vision and asking God to open your eyes to what He wants to do in your ministry.

If you do already have them in writing:

1. Get out a blank sheet of paper, and write them out. Do you have them memorized?

2. "Pop Quiz" your team at your next meeting and give a yummy prize to those who know them the best, and challenge everyone to learn them by memory.

3. Do an evaluation with your team: where are we? Is there anything we are doing that doesn't fit the mission? How close are we to making our vision a reality? Are any adjustments needed?

4. Is your mission posted somewhere so that parents and visitors know what you are about?

5. Spend some time praying about your vision and asking God to open your eyes to what He wants to do in your ministry.

Give Your Children's Ministry a Name

By Roger Fields

As I travel I am amazed at how many children's ministries don't have a name. Their meetings have names: Sunday School, Junior Church, Awana, Royal Rangers, etc. But they have no name that refers to the children's ministry as a whole. Hence, their children's ministry has no identity.

Here are some guidelines for choosing a children's ministry name that encompasses all of the meetings and activities involving children between the nursery ages and the teenage youth group.

1. Does the name sound intriguing? The name should leave something to the imagination. For example, "Kidz Zone" sounds more interesting than "Third Grade Class."

2. Does the name convey the idea of motion or activity? "Kids Alive" or "Kids on the Move" (Willie George's children's ministry) sounds like something in motion rather than an institution mired in tradition. If you want to convey that your children's ministry is routine and ordinary, then the "Children's Ministry of *Your-Church-Name*" will work fine.

3. Pray about it. Ask God to give you something that captures His heart for your children's ministry. Ask Him to reveal to you a name that communicates to children and parents what you believe God wants your children's ministry to become. Don't be stuck on what others have done before. Carve out something unique.

After you create your new name, use it. Make it into a logo. Either use a graphic program to develop it yourself or pay a graphic artist. Most will do it for about $200. Get a full color version and a black and white version.

Put the logo on the walls. Put it in your newsletter. Put it everywhere you can. Brand your children's ministry with your new name. Saturate the church with it so that it becomes the name people use when they speak of your children's ministry.

The name alone won't make your children's ministry effective or exciting. But it will help to communicate where you want to go. Who knows? It might even inspire your workers to begin thinking of ways to make your ministry have more of a positive impact on children.

God's Word Is for Kids

By Roger Fields

The power of the Word of God will work for kids. We often quote Paul from 2 Timothy 3 about the power of God's Word. Rightfully so. We forget, however, the context of Paul's statement is in reference to Timothy having learned the word as a child. Let's see the whole text from 2 Timothy 3:15–17:

And that from childhood you have known the Holy Scriptures, which are able to make you wise for salvation through faith in Christ Jesus. All scripture is given by inspiration of God, and is profitable for doctrine, for reproof, for correction, for instruction in righteousness, that the man of God may be complete, thoroughly equipped for every good work.

Encourage children to trust the Word of God. Build faith in your kids. Tell them about a God who will come through for them. When you tell a Bible story, emphasize the faithfulness of God.

Don't major on minors.

David picking up five rocks is not the point of the story of his victory over Goliath. Walking in the power of God's covenant is the message from that story. David believed he had a covenant with God while the adults weren't so sure.

The lions' den is not the message of the story about Daniel. It wouldn't have mattered if the king had chosen to throw Daniel into a rattlesnake pit. The point is that Daniel stood up every day and declared his trust in the Lord by praying with his window open. God blessed him by prospering all that he did. Daniel is a story about the supernatural protection of God for people that serve Him in a pagan environment.

Kids need to know that God is just as alive and trustworthy as He ever was.

Never forget that "Faith comes by hearing and hearing by the Word of God" (Rom. 10:17). If you don't teach your kids the Word, they won't have faith unless they get it from somewhere else.

When I was the children's pastor in a local church, my objective every week was to send those kids home talking about what they learned in children's church to the extent that every parent was saying to themselves, "Dear Lord, I wish I was in children's church. My kids are learning more than I am!" This will happen when God's Word overflows in your own life to the point where you teach it with an anointing that touches the lives of children.

The Church of Today

By Roger Fields

Kids are not the church of tomorrow; they are part of the church of today. You do not have to grow up to serve the Lord. Kids in the Bible didn't grow up first. Many served the Lord effectively *before* they ever grew up.

Josiah became king at eight years of age. Shortly after, he began to go through Israel smashing idols and leading a return to God. The nation turned around because one kid knew he didn't have to grow up first. Josiah was not interested in becoming a future servant of God; he served God as a kid. The Bible calls him the best king Israel ever had.

A young servant girl walked up to the rich, powerful Syrian commander, Naaman, and suggested that he travel to Israel where Elisha would minister healing to his leprosy on behalf of God. Naaman agreed, and the rest is biblical history. When Jesus launched His ministry in Luke 4 He referred to two Old Testament stories, and one of them was the healing of Naaman. All of that happened because a little girl didn't wait until she grew up to serve God.

Samuel, a young boy brought to the temple by his mother, heard God's voice reveal the fate of Israel while Eli, the high priest, seemed oblivious to the danger Israel faced. A kid, not the high priest, heard God's voice.

Could there have been anyone else in the crowd of over 5,000 that brought lunch the day Jesus taught the vast crowd? A boy stepped up and offered his lunch in faith, enabling Jesus to multiply it to the mass of people. If the boy had waited to grow up first, there would have been a lot of hungry people that day.

David slaying Goliath is the classic example. A shepherd boy takes on Goliath in front of the adults. When David was through, Goliath never bothered anyone again. Even though David stood on God's covenant, faced a giant, and won, he was still a kid.

Mary and Joseph found Jesus at twelve years of age in the temple "about His Father's business." That's the objective: to bring kids to a place where they are "about their Father's business" *before* they grow up.

Interaction: The Key to Children's Ministry

By Roger Fields

Inside the heart of most children is a battery waiting for the opportunity to propel the child into some sort of action. The battery is made for action, not observation. Children have an internal urge to do something, not watch something. You can offer the most compelling puppet skit on earth, but if the option exists to participate in something that looks like fun rather than watch something that looks like fun, children will opt to participate every time. That's why children would rather ride the attractions at a theme part as opposed to watching the shows.

If you're still unconvinced, a simple experiment will persuade you. Walk to the front of a group of elementary-aged children, raise your hand, and proclaim, "I need a volunteer!" Hands will fly upward. Most will volunteer before they have any concept of what it is they are volunteering to do. They will take a risk rather than chance missing out on something fun to do. Try this with adults and you'll be standing there looking pretty silly.

Studies have shown that children retain only about 10 percent of the information they hear, but up to 90 percent of what they hear, see, and *do*. That's the good news. What children enjoy most is also your best teaching tool: interaction.

Effective teaching asks this question, "How can I involve the kids in learning this truth?" Or put another way, "What can I give them to do that will help them learn this lesson?" Answer either of those questions creatively and you are a world-class teacher.

Here are some of the best methods of incorporating interaction into your teaching style.

1. Use games that illustrate a point. The game will involve some or all of the children, while the friendly competition will compel their attention.

2. Use games to review material already covered. Review games are fun, they reinforce what was taught earlier, and they provide motivation for learning. The motivation arises from the kids as they anticipate using the lesson information for competitive results later. It is simply hard to overstate the value of effective review games.

3. Involve kids in handling anything you use for object lessons. Don't wave a broom around and preach about how the Holy Spirit sweeps the dirt

out of our lives. Select a kid to come up and sweep while you are describing how the Holy Spirit sweeps the mess out of God's people. Let the kid hold up the broom.

4. Select kids to help serve. If your only challenge to children is to "sit up straight and be still," then don't be shocked when they grow up to resist serving in church. We have multitudes of adults who just sit there in church. They don't do anything, and part of the blame is ours. We trained them that way. We told them for years to sit up straight and be still and that's what they do. Let kids take up the offering, pray out loud, or read scripture. Encourage them to serve the Lord during the week. Let them share how they prayed for mom and dad, shared their faith, or cleaned their room.

Help kids define their faith in terms that transcend passive belief. Help them to think in terms of action. They won't mind at all.

50 Ways to Discover New Workers

Compiled by Kidologist, Pastor Karl Bastian

1. Pray much for the Lord's choice and guidance in positions to be filled. Ask the Lord to give you insight as to the interest and ability of the individual being considered, and the type of position for which he/she may be best suited.
2. Make use of a talent survey or an interest finder to discover possible personnel.
3. Have personal conferences with individuals. "Talk over" the spiritual opportunities available, the individual's interests, and his/her abilities; discover where the person would like to work.
4. Check membership applications for areas of interest, abilities, past training, and experiences of those applying for membership.
5. Be a good listener. Watch for "key" ideas or "clues" to help in discovering workers.
6. Keep a notebook on items of interest which would be significant in discovering and placing individuals in positions in the children's ministry.
7. Observe carefully and continually. Think of individuals and positions you have open. Consider the individual's personality, training, and possibilities.
8. Know individuals: their capacities, interests, abilities, and challenges.
9. Present spiritual opportunities for service interestingly and challengingly.
10. Keep a card file of who *is* and who *will be* available. This card file should have: personal data, qualifications, training and experience, type of service for which best suited, age group, interests, record of interviews.
11. Try to see the potential of people "in the rough." Do not expect perfection. Be willing to prepare and train them for the job.
12. Encourage the pastor to challenge individuals for service through his sermons.
13. Be friendly and interested in people personally.
14. Conduct your search for individuals in a business-like manner. Do not make a person feel like he/she is a "last resort" or "the only thing left."

15. Keep an up-to-date list of the potential workers needed. When visiting with people, talk about the spiritual opportunities which are open.

16. Work through other staff members to discover potential workers.

17. Find out why the person is not doing something at the present time. You may get some insights that will prevent losing other workers. Perhaps there is something you need to change.

18. Give specific qualifications and duties required for each position so that the person knows exactly what is expected of him/her.

19. Set standards high. Make people feel that the job is important and that not just "anyone can do it."

20. Provide a continuous training program of leadership development so that people may be given the help they need. Award certificates and diplomas for work completed.

21. Have a committee who will visit and appoint staff members. Explain details of qualifications and duties. Be sure the individual has a good understanding of the position offered.

22. Educate the church membership on the importance and need for workers. Do this through church bulletins, newsletters, sermons, etc.

23. Be persistent but tactful in contacting people. Do not give up the first time a person is contacted for a job.

24. Fit a person for the position to be filled. Individual interests and capacities will provide more specific motivation for service.

25. Stress "opportunity" rather than "obligation."

26. Use a letter of invitation to serve. Follow up with a personal interview.

27. Enlist in more minor positions first. Advance the person when they are ready. (Give them time to prove themselves.)

28. Make use of a casual invitation. Observe how a person responds.

29. Provide adequate materials for the job. Do not expect people to buy their own materials and supplies.

30. Expect accountability with responsibility. Let people know this as they take a position.

31. Show appreciation for what is done! This is good publicity. *Never* fail to say "thank you." A recognition banquet or dinner may be appropriate for your workers to show your appreciation.

32. Have impressive installation services for workers as they take their places of responsibility.

33. Set the precedent that you let workers do their job and that you have confidence in them.

34. Approach or make the appeal on a spiritual level—a motivation for Christian service. Prepare worthy motivation.

35. Pay special attention to the new leader. Encourage them in every way you can!

36. Keep a list of personnel needs. Fill your personnel needs first. Then plan a waiting list.

37. Interview newcomers to the church. Find out their interests and abilities.

38. Check senior high, young people, and adult classes for personnel.

39. Encourage prospects to attend conferences, leadership camps, and other Christian education events.

40. Be interested in the total life of your workers. Commend when possible.

41. Show workers their contribution in service in relation to the overall children's ministry.

42. Stress loyalty to God and to the local church.

43. Provide spiritual growth opportunities for your workers. Do everything you can to help meet their spiritual needs.

44. Conduct an enlistment or service day program in the church.

45. Investigate possibilities from VBS and camp staff or other areas for responsibilities of the children's ministry.

46. Magnify the place of the teacher or leader in the life of the church.

47. Have a standard form which your personnel must sign as they join the church staff.

48. Present needs in an interesting and challenging manner. Have a Sunday school night, a training hour night, a weekday club night, etc. Give a brief survey of the positions available, the qualifications needed, and the types of training provided.

49. Encourage people to work as apprentices until they are able to handle a position by themselves.

50. Avoid censoring workers in public or criticizing them in front of prospective workers. Other workers may wonder (if this type of thing is done) if at some later date they may come before the same firing squad.

How to Recruit a F.A.T. Ministry Team

By Roger Fields

Imagine this. Jesus concludes the Sermon on the Mount saying, "This ministry needs your help. I still need seven more disciples to complete our goal of twelve. If God is leading you to serve in this important ministry, please see Peter. He'll be the one standing in the back with a clipboard. Thank you for your help!"

That kind of begging would have demeaned the office of the disciple. Instead of using the beg-and-plead method, thus giving the impression that He was desperate enough to take anyone who signed up, Jesus actively recruited the ones He wanted. Being a disciple of Jesus was an honor.

Our desire to enlist new children's workers often results in making our ministry look weak and desperate. We write bulletin spots that beg people to enlist as children's workers. We plead from the pulpit. We even instruct Madge (she's the children's director) to stand up at the end of a service as the contact person for those who feel the Holy Spirit's conviction to sign up. And none of this ever works! People don't step forward to volunteer for children's ministry. They don't sign the clipboard in the foyer. And nobody ever talks to Madge after the service.

Why? Why don't typical churchgoers respond to the needs in children's ministry? Why has the children's ministry in most churches been seen as the black hole of the church, sucking people in, never to be seen again?

The reason people seldom respond to our pleas for help is because we have reduced children's ministry in the eyes of the church to a desperate entity that grasps and holds its victims until we have extracted their last ounce of energy. They see our children's ministry as a sticky web that grabs and holds its victims until the bitter end.

We eagerly accept any warm body who will volunteer. And we can't understand why our bulletin announcements don't send droves of workers into our children's department. But no one ever volunteered for Jesus. He recruited the ones He wanted to build a strong team.

Here are some recruiting steps that work better than any bulletin announcements.

1. Refuse to beg for workers. Whatever you do, don't make your children's ministry look weak and desperate.

2. Put out the word that working in the children's ministry is by invitation only; no volunteers will be accepted. You can use the bulletin for this announcement. Make it known that from now on working in the children's ministry is an honor. People who truly are called to this ministry will let you know.

3. Use various means to discover who would make a good worker. Recommendations from current workers and membership applications will help.

4. Look for F.A.T. people: faithful, available, and teachable. Faithful people are hardworking, responsible, and on time. Available people have schedules that adapt to the ministry instead of insisting that the ministry accommodate their schedule. Teachable people flow with the vision and methods of your ministry instead of continually telling you how they did it back home.

5. Approach the people you want in private and present your vision for children's ministry. It honors them that you would single them out and ask them to help you, especially if they know that working in your children's ministry is by invitation only. Let them catch your excitement.

6. Give them a point of entry that will not intimidate them. Explain that they will not be asked to teach the lesson. Give them a responsibility that will not scare them off. Then train them on the job by watching and helping them.

7. Ask for a specific time commitment. Six months works well. Stay true to your word. Don't rewrite the job description by recruiting some for three months, some every other week, and some for a year. Be consistent.

8. Give them a couple of days to pray about it. Don't let them give you a "yes" answer at that moment. It makes the commitment seem trivial.

9. Pray for them. Children's ministry is the most challenging ministry in the church. Ushers never go home in tears because people won't scoot over. It's children's workers who sometimes get frazzled because things didn't go as planned.

10. Honor your workers. Treat them as an elite group. Make them feel like a team. Many of them will stay long past their six-month agreement.

11. Repeat the process with others. Keep new people coming in. Don't forget, no one ever volunteered for Jesus. Recruit quality people. Go after the best. Let the church know that it is an honor to minister to children. Instead of begging, build a F.A.T. team.

10 Top Reasons that Children's Pastors Fail

By Roger Fields

1. **Unclear vision.** If you don't know where you are going, you can't be the leader it takes to run an effective children's ministry.
2. **Unable to get along with others.** People won't *go along* with you if they can't *get along* with you.
3. **Unbelief in God's Word.** If you can't walk by faith, children's ministry is a tough place to be.
4. **Under-funded children's ministry.** It takes money to do things right.
5. **Untrained workers.** You have to be able to work through other people. You can't do everything yourself.
6. **Unteachable spirit.** I don't know everything. You don't either. When you stop learning, you stop growing. And that's deadly.
7. **Unable to resolve conflict.** There will be conflict. Absence of conflict is a fantasy. But true leaders know how to resolve conflict.
8. **Uncooperative workers.** No matter whose fault it is, if your workers aren't with you, you won't go very far.
9. **Unwilling to take time off.** That's right. Workaholics eventually hit the wall. Spend time with your family.
10. **Unrealistic expectations.** Have a clear vision, but don't set your sights so high that you are guaranteed to fail.

Create an Environment that Captures the Imagination

By Roger Fields

Time and money that you spend creating an exciting environment will pay for itself many times over. The kids will respond by offering their attention, while adults will respond by placing their children in your care. Some will even consider becoming a part of the ministry structure. While children may not be wowed by the colorful set three months down the road, parents will continue poking their heads into the room imagining what it would be like to work in such an inviting environment. Beige walls, an overhead projector, and rows of metal chairs will not work the same magic. Here are some suggestions.

1. Decide whether or not you are willing to develop your children's ministry into something beyond the ordinary. If you are content to simply have a place for the kids to go to keep them out of the adult service, then you will find these suggestions too much work.

2. Develop a name for your children's ministry that sounds fun. Names such as Sunday school, children's church, or primary church hardly arouse curiosity or provoke interest. If it sounds dull, it probably is dull. So come up with something with pizzazz. Make the name of your children's ministry compelling. Two word names normally work best such as: kids' place, power house, nitro kidz, etc.

3. Pick a theme for every children's department. Theme possibilities include western, outer space, tropical, safari, circus, etc. Choose one that seems to connect with the age group that you are trying to reach.

4. Design a logo for each department. A graphic artist will probably design one for about $200. Make sure you get it in .tif format (300 dpi) on a disk. The artist should provide a full color image and a black and white image. Decide on the name before you talk to the artist, and show him anything you have seen that you like. He can't copy it, but it provides some idea of what you are looking for.

5. Close off the room while you are working on it. If it takes more than one week, choose an alternate place for your children's church until you are done. Lock the room.

6. Take down all bulletin boards. Let me repeat that. Take down the bulletin boards. Only a few people read them, and they make your room look cluttered. Would a theme park allow some sorry-looking bulletin board to exist alongside its main attraction? No! Take down anything that is not first class. The general rule of thumb is that if you wouldn't put it in your living room, then don't put it in the church.

7. Never use visible space for storage. Never leave old tables, chairs, paint cans, ladders, or wooden shelving in any place that's openly visible. Rent a storage unit if you don't have adequate space for storage in the church. Would you leave a ladder in the middle of your living room? Then why use a lower standard for the ministry God has given you?

8. Strip the walls and paint them. Use good paint, and pretend that you are decorating the lobby in a Disney hotel. Use colors that coordinate with your theme. If you have a good painter in the church then beg for his help. Don't have a work night and turn loose every teenager who can swing a paint brush.

9. Construct a platform that coincides with your theme. If your theme is western, then construct a wooden wall and sidewalk that look like the front of a general store or sheriff's office. If your theme is tropical, then construct a dock and bait shop. Find an airbrush artist who can reproduce your logo in the middle of the back wall of the platform.

10. Purchase props that enhance your theme. Mount the props to the walls and platform of your room. If your theme is outer space, then you will want stars and comets on the walls. Anything that looks futuristic will probably work. You can put the word out in your church that you are looking for stuff to go with your theme, but be prepared to get some pretty sorry stuff. If you don't have the courage to turn some of it down, then don't ask.

11. Make sure the lighting is good. Purchase some floodlights to brighten up the platform area. Make sure there is adequate lighting to keep the room from appearing dingy. Let in sunlight if you can, but make sure you have good blinds to make the room dark when you need to.

12. Select a Sunday morning for the grand opening.

Use Quick Drama to Energize Your Ministry

By Roger Fields

Children are born with two fundamental, internal drives. They have a craving to do something and a fear of missing something. Interaction fulfills the first one, and quick drama capitalizes on the second.

Anyone with kids (I have four girls!) constantly has the experience of seeing your child exhausted an hour after bedtime and fighting to stay awake so as not to have to go to bed. On the verge of total exhaustion after a fast-paced day, children seldom ever stand up in the middle of the living room and announce, "You know, I've had a busy day. I think I'll turn in if that's okay with you folks." Why? Why do children fight to stay up even after they're worn out from the day's activity? There is only one reason: they are afraid they will miss something! They think that if they go to bed at 8:30 Michael Jordan might drop by at 8:35 and they'll miss the whole thing. Kids are new to life and they are programmed to want to take it all in.

You can use this to enhance your effectiveness as a children's educator. If you want to add a little pizzaz to your children's ministry while communicating your lesson with greater impact, you should consider using quick drama. Here's how it works, and it's easier than you might think.

At the designated time, without warning, your character(s) barge through the door interrupting your children's church. Of course, they're not really interrupting; you knew they were coming all along. But to the kids it seems unplanned and eventful. The character(s) look a bit odd, they are loud and overbearing, and they seem oblivious to the fact that you are trying to conduct children's ministry. Within two minutes they are gone, leaving most of your kids looking somewhat bewildered, but in that flurry of activity they managed to reinforce the point you are trying to communicate with the children. Chances are your kids will remember what happened.

Here are some simple principles that make quick drama effective.

1. Use unfamiliar people to play the parts. They don't have to have the acting ability of Tom Cruise; they just can't look like Miss Betty in a wig.

2. Never introduce the characters. They should peek in, to make sure you're not in prayer, and then barge in fast and loud.

3. Do not rehearse the lines. They will sound contrived. Just go over the two or three main points and then go for it. The kids won't know if you leave something out.

4. Allow the actors to grow into their parts. As they continue to make appearances in the coming weeks they will get better and better.

5. Do not let an actor/actress play more than one role.

6. Give them a costume that fits the part. If a custodian barges in, he/she should have coveralls, painting hat, boots, etc.

7. If possible, give the character an object to hold that fits the part. A farmer should have a rake. A mailman should have a mailbag. A policeman should have a stick. A maintenance man should have a toolbox.

8. Use adults. Adults, rather than teenagers, seem to more effectively command the kids' attention. You'll be surprised at how easy it is to recruit adults to do this as long as they can re-enter the adult service after they play their part.

9. Make it quick. The character should leave before the kids are ready to stop listening. Leave them wanting more.

10. Vary the frequency, if you use several different characters. One character may come in every week. Another might come in two or three times per month. Another may only come in once every four or five weeks.

11. Do not barge into the room using quick drama with preschoolers. They will not appreciate your creativity. They like things warm and predictable. Quick drama is neither.

12. Don't be afraid of making a mistake. Some skits will flop. Some will *really* flop. The successes, though, will outnumber the failures.

Adventure Bay uses Shriver the Diver to introduce object lessons and Percy the Pirate to illustrate what happens when you don't live by God's Word. Barnacle Bill is the hard-of-hearing maintenance man being developed for year two. Whether you use ours or make up your own, you'll have a lot of fun, and you'll see the kids retaining more of the lesson material. And by the way, don't be surprised if some of those adults you recruit to play a character ask how they can become regular children's workers.

Children's Ministries List

National and International Conferences and Conventions

APCE Conference
Sponsored by: Association of Presbyterian Church Educators
Contact:
    Pat Murphy, Registrar
    100 Witherspoon St.
    Louisville, KY 40202–1396
    1–888–728–7228, ext. 5460
    www.apcenet.org
    Email: pmurphy@ctr.pcusa.org

Bilingual Children's Ministries University
Sponsored By: One Way Street, Inc.
Contact:
    Susan Schmidt
    One Way Street, Inc.
    P. O. Box 5077
    Englewood, CO 80155–5077
    303–799–2159
    www.onewaystreet.com
    Email: events@onewaystreet.com

BTI Children's Ministry Conference
Sponsored By: Bring Them In
Contact:
    Larry Hipps
    11323 Hughes Rd.
    Houston, TX 77089
    281–481–8770
    www.bringthemin.com
    Email: lhipps@sagemontchurch.org

Children's Pastors' Conference
Sponsored By: International Network of Children's Ministry
Contact:
    International Network of Children's Ministry
    P. O. Box 190
    Castle Rock, CO 80104

The Fellowship of Christian Magicians International Convention
Sponsored By: The Fellowship of Christian Magicians
Contact:
    Jim and Kris Austin
    435 Oak St.
    Des Plains, IL 60016
    847–296–7573
    www.fcm.org
    Email: jim@jimages.org

The International Festival of Christian Puppetry and Ventriloquism
Sponsored By: One Way Street, Inc.
Contact:
Susan Schmidt
    One Way Street, Inc.
    P. O. Box 5077
    Englewood, CO 80155–5077
    303–799–2159
    www.onewaystreet.com
    Email: events@onewaystreet.com

MOPS International Leadership Convention
MOPS stands for M.others O.f P.reschoolerS.
Contact:
    Marcy Decker, Events Manager
    MOPS International
    P. O. Box 102200
    Denver, CO 80250
    303–733–5353
    Fax: 303–733–5770
    www.mops.org
    Email: info@mops.org

Promiseland Conference
Sponsored By: The Willow Creek Association
Contact:

    Nancy Gruben
    The Willow Creek Association
    67 E. Algonquin Rd.
    South Barrington, IL 60011
    847–765–0070
    Fax: 847–765–5046
    www.promiselandonline.com

Online Networks

Childrensministry.com
    www.childrensministry.com

Children's Ministry Magazine
    www.cmmag.com

Children's Ministry Today
    8469 Seton Ct.
    Jacksonville, FL 32244
    909–777–3339
    www.childrensministry.org
    Email: info@childrensministry.org

Children's Pastors' Network
    8469 Seton Ct.
    Jacksonville, FL 32244
    909–777–3339
    www.childrensministry.org/the_network/index.htm
    Email: info@childrensministry.org

Kidology, Inc.
    535 Andrew Lane
    Lake Zurich, IL 60047
    847–726–9860
    www.kidology.org
    Email: tim@kidology.org

Sunday School Teachers' Network
   www.christiancrafters.com

National Organizations and Associations

Association of Christian Schools International (ACSI)
   P. O. Box 35097
   Colorado Springs, CO 80935
   1–800–367–0798, ext. 115
   Fax: 719–531–0716
   www.acsi.org
   Email: david_smitherman@acsi.org

Child Evangelism Fellowship
   P. O. Box 348
   Warrenton, MO 63383–0348
   1–800–300–4033
   www.gospelcom.net/cef

Children's Ministries of America
   P. O. Box 4974
   Oak Brook, IL 60522
   1–888–922–0702
   Fax: 630–916–1140
   www.childrensministries.org

Christian Educators Association International
   P. O. Box 41300
   Pasadena, CA 91114
   626–798–1124
   fax: 626–798–2346
   Email: info@ceai.org
   www.ceai.org

Christian Jugglers Association
   1709 West Seminary Dr.
   Fort Worth, TX 76115

Contact: Nathan Dorrell
1–800– 363–4410
Fax: 980–754–2750
www.juggling.org
Email: cja@juggling.org

The Fellowship of Christian Magicians
7739 Everest Ct. N.
Maple Grove, MN 55311
763–494–5655
www.fcm.org

The Fellowship of Christian Puppeteers
FCP Mail Center
107 Moore Allen St.
Dudley, NC 28333
919–731–2261
www.fcpfellowship.org

For Kids Only, Inc.
P. O. Box 10237
Newport Beach, CA 92658
1–888–646–9584
www.fko.org

International Network of Children's Ministry
P. O. Box 190
Castle Rock, CO 80104
1–800–324–4543
www.incm.org

Performance Artists

Astounding Bruce Carroll
32695 Cypress Dr.
Springfield, LA 70462
www.astoundingbruce.com
Email: astoundingbruce@yahoo.com

Dean-o and the Dynamos
  BibleBeat Music
  P. O. Box 7407
  Laguna Nigel, CA 92607
  1–866–656–2328
  www.biblebeatmusic.com
  Email: deano@biblebeatmusic.com

The Donut Man and Duncan
  Rob Evans
  P. O. Box 1625
  Beach Haven, NJ 08008
  609–492–2363
  www.donutman.com
  Email: rob@donutman.com

Dr. Kaos
  311 S. Fourth Street
  St. Charles, IL 60174
  405–314–3484
  www.drkaos.com
  Email: booking@drkaos.com

Evelyn James, Storyteller
  P. O. Box 133233
  Tyler, TX 75713
  903–939–9039
  www.itellstories.com
  Email: espjames@tyler.net

For HIS Kidz
  P. O. Box 292
  Zelienople, PA 16063
  1–866–774–7469
  www.forhiskidz.com
  Email: info@forhiskidz.com

Geddy the Gecko
    John Mallory
    412 S.E. Fourth Ter.
    Dania Beach, FL 33004
    954–924–0218
    www.geddythegecko.com
    Email: geddy@geddythegecko.com

Mark Thompson, Ventriloquist
    Mark Arts, Inc.
    P. O. Box 2321
    Redmond, WA 98073
    1–800–867–6579
    www.markthompson.org
    www.markarts.com
    Email: mark@markthompson.org

Mary Rice Hopkins and Co.
    P. O. Box 362
    Montrose, CA 91021
    818–790–5805
    www.maryricehopkins.com
    Email: booking@maryricehopkins.com

Miss Pattycake
    Integrity Music Just for Kids
    www.integrity music.com

Mister Bill
    P. O. Box 3677
    Redondo Beach, CA 90277
    310–727–9877
    www.mrbillsworld.org
    Email: info@misterbill.org

Ned and Joan Way
    P. O. Box 19229
    Louisville, KY 40259
    509–361–4267
    www.NoWay.org
    Email: way@aye.net

Jeff Smith
    "God Rods"
    Salt and Light Ministries
    5105 Timbercreek Court
    Richmond, VA 23237
    www.saltandlightmin.org

Wendy and the James Gang
    P. O. Box 431
    Granville, OH 43023
    1–888–548–7625
    www.wendyandthejamesgang.com
    Email: david.james@livingrock.com

Products and Services Directory

Bible Games

Bible Games Company
    P. O. Box 237
    Fredericktown, OH 43019
    1–800–845–7415
    www.biblegamescompany.com

Susan Harper "The Game Trunk"
    www.chministries.com
    940–367–4755

Child Abuse Prevention Resources

    Strang Communication
    The Guardian System
    600 Rinehart Rd.
    Lake Mary, FL 32746
    1–800–451–4598
    www.charismalife.com

Children's Books

Augsburg Fortress Publishers
    100 S. Fifth St., Suite 700
    Minneapolis, MN 55402
    1–800–328–4648
    www.augsburgfortress.org

Barbour Publishing, Inc.
    1810 Barbour Sr.
    Uhrichsville, OH 44683
    1–800–852–8010
    www.barbourpublishing.com

Christianbook.com
    P. O. Box 8000
    140 Summit St.
    Peabody, MA 01961–8000
    978–977–5060
    www.christianbook.com

Cokesbury
    201 Eighth Ave. S.
    Nashville, TN 37203
    1–800–672–1789

Eerdmans Books for Young Readers
    255 Jefferson Ave., S.E.
    Grand Rapids, MI 49503
    1–800–253–7521

Standard Publishing
    8121 Hamilton Ave.
    Cincinnati, OH 45231
    1–800–543–1353
    www.standardpub.com
    Email: customerservice@standardpub.com

Tommy Nelson
    P. O. Box 141000
    Nashville, TN 37214
    615–902–1485

Tyndale House Publishers
    351 Executive Drive
    Carol Stream, IL 60188
    1–800–323–9400
    www.tyndale.com

Warner Press, Inc.
    Church Sales Department
    P. O. Box 2499
    Anderson, IN 46018

Waterbrook Press, Inc.
    c/o Random House, Inc.
    280 Park Avenue (11–3)
    New York, NY 10017
    Fax: 212–940–7381
    www.randomhouse.com

Children's Bulletins

Children's Worship Bulletins
    Communication Resources
    4150 Belden Village St.
    Fourth Floor
    Canton, OH 44718
    1–800–992–2144
    www.ChildrensBulletins.com

Children's Church Supplies/Resources

Axtell Expressions, Inc.
    Dept. CM, 230 Glencrest Cir.
    Ventura, CA 93003
    805–642–7282
    www.axtell.com

Betty Lukens, Inc.
    711 Portal Street
    Cotati, CA 94931
    1–800–541–9279
    www.bettylukens.com

Bible Candy
    www.biblecandy.com
    877–643–8922

Bring Them In
    11323 Hughes Rd.
    Houston, TX 77089
    281–481–8770
    www.bringthemin.com

Children's Bible Activities Online

Communication Resources
    4150 Belden Village St.
    Fourth Floor
    Canton, OH 44718
    1–800–992–2144

Children's Ministry Today
    8469 Seton Ct.
    Jacksonville, FL 32244
    904–777–3339
    www.childrensministry.com

Group Publishing Company
    P. O. Box 485
    Loveland, CO 80539
    1–800–747–6060
    www.grouppublishing.com

KidMo!
    1113 Murfreesboro Road
    Suite 106–145
    Franklin, TN 37064
    www.Kidmo.com
    Email: Bill@Kidmo.com

LifeWay Church Resources
   One Lifeway Plaza
   Nashville, TN 37234
   1–800–458–2772
   www.lifeway.com

One Way Street, Inc.
   P. O. Box 5077
   Englewood, CO 80155–5077
   303–799–1188
   www.onewaystreet.com

Picture This!
   Dan Peters, President
   236 Castilian Ave
   Thousand Oaks, CA 91320
   www.bibledraw.com

The Train Depot
   3244 Commerce Center Pl.
   Louisville, KY 40211
   1–800–229–KIDS
   www.TrainDepot.org

Warner Press, Inc.
   Church Sales Department
   P. O. Box 2499
   Anderson, IN 46018

Children's Music

Christianbook.com
   P. O. Box 8000
   140 Summit St.
   Peabody, MA 01961–8000
   978–977–5060
   www.christianbook.com

Integrity Music
   1000 Cody Rd.
   Mobile, AL 36695
   251–633–9000
   www.integritymusic.com

Mary Rice Hopkins
   P. O. Box 362
   Montrose, CA 91021
   818–790–5805
   www.maryricehopkins.com

Dean-o
   Biblebeatmusic.com

Tommy Nelson
   P.O. Box 141000
   Nashville, TN 37214
   615–902–1485

Word Music
   3319 W. End Ave. Ste. 201
   Nashville, TN 37203
   1–888–324–9673
   Email: questions@wordmusic.com

Children's Themed Environments
Wacky World Studios
   148 E. Douglas Rd.
   Oldsmar, FL 34677–2939
   813–818–8277

Children's Videos/DVDs

Mary Rice Hopkins
    P. O. Box 362
    Montrose, CA 91021
    818–790–5805
    www.maryricehopkins.com

Dean-o
    Biblebeatmusic.com

Integrity Music
    1000 Cody Rd.
    Mobile, AL 36695
    251–633–9000
    www.integritymusic.com

Standard Publishing
    8121 Hamilton Ave.
    Cincinnati, OH 45231
    1–800–543–1353
    www.standardpub.com
    Email: customerservice@standardpub.com

Tommy Nelson
    P.O. Box 141000
    Nashville, TN 37214
    615–902–1485
    www.thomasnelson.com

Tyndale House Publishers
    351 Executive Drive
    Carol Stream, IL 60188
    1–800–323–9400
    www.tyndale.com

Choir/Choral Resources

Brentwood Benson Music
 741 Cool Springs Blvd.
 Franklin, TN 37067
 1–800–846–7664
 www.brentwoodbenson.com

LifeWay Church Resources
 One Lifeway Plaza
 Nashville, TN 37234
 1–800–458–2772
 www.lifeway.com

Lillenas Publishing Company
 2923 Troost Ave.
 Kansas City, MO 64109
 1–800–877–0700
 www.lillenaskids.com
 Email: music@lillenas.com &
 Email: drama@lillenas.com

Christian Education Resources and Curriculum

Augsburg Fortress Publishers
 100 S. Fifth St., Suite 700
 Minneapolis, MN 55402
 1–800–328–4648
 www.augsburgfortress.org

Bible Visuals International
 P. O. Box 153
 Akron, PA 17501
 717–859–1131

Caring Hands Ministries
 309 Hollyhill Ln.
 Denton, TX 76205
 940–367–4755
 www.chministries.com

Children's Bible Activities Online
    Communication Resources
    4150 Belden Village St.
    Fourth Floor
    Canton, OH 44718
    1–800–992–2144

Christian Ed Publishers
    9230 Trade Pl.
    San Diego, CA 92126
    1–800–854–1531
    www.ChristianEdWarehouse.com

Cokesbury
    201 Eighth Ave. S.
    Nashville, TN 37203
    1–800–672–1789
    www.cokesbury.com

Cook Communications Ministries
    4050 Lee Vance View
    Colorado Springs, CO 80918
    1–800–323–7543
    www.cookministries.com

Creative Teaching Associates
    5629 E. Westower Ave.
    Fresno, CA 93727
    559–291–6626
    www.mastercta.com

Gospel Light
    2300 Knoll Dr.
    Ventura, CA 93003
    805–644–9721
    www.gospellight.com

Great Communications Publications
  3640 Windsor Park Dr.
  Suwanee, GA 30024–3897
  1–800–695–3387
  www.gcp.org

Group Publishing Company
  P. O. Box 485
  Loveland, CO 80539
  1–800–747–6060
  www.grouppublishing.com

Marketplace 29 A.D.
  P. O. Box 29
  Stevensville, MI 49127
  1–800–345–12AD
  www.marketplace29ad.com
  Email: bjgoetz@marketplace29ad.com

Microframe Corporation
  P. O. Box 1700
  Broken Arrow, OK 74013
  1–800–635–3811
  www.nurserycall.com

Regular Baptist Press
  1300 N. Meacham Rd.
  Schaumburg, IL 60173
  1–800–727–4400

Standard Publishing
  8121 Hamilton Ave.
  Cincinnati, OH 45231
  1–800–543–1353
  www.standardpub.com
  Email: customerservice@standardpub.com

Strang Communications
  Kids Church
  600 Rinehart Rd.
  Lake Mary, FL 32746
  1–800–451–4598
  www.charismalife.com

Upper Room Ministries
  1908 Grand Ave.
  Nashville, TN 37212
  1–800–972–0433
  www.pockets.org

Christian School/Daycare Programs

Betty Lukens, Inc.
  711 Portal Street
  Cotati, CA 94931
  1–800–541–9279
  www.bettylukens.com

Cokesbury
  201 Eighth Ave. S.
  Nashville, TN 37203
  1–800–672–1789
  www.cokesbury.com

Jtech Communications, Inc.
  6413 Congress Ave., Ate. 150
  Boca Raton, FL 33487
  1–800–321–6221
  www.jtech.com

Christian School Resources

Augsburg Fortress Publishers
     100 S. Fifth St., Suite 700
     Minneapolis, MN 55402
     1–800–328–4648
     www.augsburgfortress.org

Classroom Supplies

Church Ministries Distribution
     Free Shipping! All Publishers!
     Email: john@churchministriesdistribution.com

Christian Ed Publishers
     9230 Trade Pl.
     San Diego, CA 92126
     1–800–854–1531
     www.ChristianEdWarehouse.com

Regular Baptist Press
     1300 N. Meacham Rd.
     Schaumburg, IL 60173
     1–800–727–4440

Communication Systems

Jtech Communications, Inc.
     6413 Congress Ave., Ate. 150
     Boca Raton, FL 33487
     1–800–321–6221
     www.jtech.com

Long Range Systems, Inc.
     9855 Chartwell Dr.
     Dallas, TX 75243
     1–877–416–4050
     www.pager.net

Microframe Corporation
P. O. Box 1700
Broken Arrow, OK 74013
1–800–635–3811
www.nurserycall.com

Seeker Nursery Paging Systems
3860 Canterbury Walk Dr.
Duluth, GA 30097
1–866–575–3713
www.seekercommunication.com

Craft Resources
Guildcraft Arts & Crafts
100 Fire Tower Dr.
Tonawanda, NY 14150
1–800–345–5563
www.vbscrafts.com

Curriculum
Big Idea Productions
206 Yorktown Center
Lombard, IL 60148
630–652–6000
www.bigidea.com

Bring Them In
11323 Hughes Rd.
Houston, TX 77089
281–481–8770
www.bringthemin.com

Caring Hands Ministries
309 Hollyhill Ln.
Denton, TX 76205
940–367–4755
www.chministries.com

CharismaLife
    600 Rinehart Rd.
    Lake Mary, FL 32746
    1–800–451–4598
    www.charismalife.com

Christian Ed Publishers
    9230 Trade Pl.
    San Diego, CA 92126
    1–800–854–1531
    www.ChristianEdWarehouse.com

Cokesbury
    201 Eighth Ave. S.
    Nashville, TN 37203
    1–800–672–1789
    www.cokesbury.com

Cook Communications Ministries
    4050 Lee Vance View
    Colorado Springs, CO 80918
    1–800–323–7543
    www.cookministries.com

Gospel Light
    2300 Knoll Dr.
    Ventura, CA 93003
    805–644–9721
    www.gospellight.com

Great Commission Publications
    3640 Windsor Park Dr.
    Suwanee, GA 30024
    1–800–695–3387
    www.gcp.org

Group Publishing Company
P. O. Box 485
Loveland, CO 80539
1–800–747–6060
www.grouppublishing.com

Lay Renewal Ministries
3101 Bartold Ave.
St. Louis, MO 63143
1–800–747–0815
www.layrenewal.com

LifeWay Church Resources
One Lifeway Plaza
Nashville, TN 37234
1–800–458–2772
www.lifeway.com

Majesty Music
P. O. Box 6524
Greenville, SC 29606
1–800–334–1071
www.majestymusic.com

Marketplace 29 A.D.
P. O. Box 29
Stevensville, MI 49127
1–800–345–12AD
www.marketplace29ad.com
Email: bjgoetz@marketplace29ad.com

Radiant Light/Gospel Publishing House
1445 N. Boonville Ave.
Springfield, MO 65802
1–800–641–4310
www.GospelPublishing.com

Randall House Publications
   P. O. Box 17306
   Nashville, TN 37217
   1–800–877–7030
   www.randallhouse.com

Regular Baptist Press
   1300 N. Meacham Rd.
   Schaumburg, IL 60173
   1–800–727–4400

Standard Publishing
   8121 Hamilton Ave.
   Cincinnati, OH 45231
   1–800–543–1353
   www.standardpub.com
   Email: customerservice@standardpub.com

The Train Depot
   3244 Commerce Center Pl.
   Louisville, KY 40211
   1–800–229–KIDS
   www.TrainDepot.org

WordAction Publishing Company
   2923 Troost Ave.
   Kansas City, MO 64109
   1–800–877–0700
   www.wordaction.com

Employment Resources/Services
Group Publishing's Available Church Positions Postings
   P. O. Box 485
   Loveland, CO 80539–0485
   1–800–635–0404 ext.4479
   www.cmmag.com
   Email: swinter@grouppublishing.com

International Network of Children's Ministry
    P. O. Box 190
    Castle Rock, CO 80104
    1–800–324–4543
    www.incm.org

Event Planning Resources

Jtech Communications, Inc.
    6413 Congress Ave., Ate. 150
    Boca Raton, FL 33487
    1–800–321–6221
    www.jtech.com

Events for Children

Champions of Light
    Steve Geer
    www.championsoflight.org

Family Ministries Resources

Group Publishing Company
    P. O. Box 485
    Loveland, CO 80539
    1–800–747–6060
    www.grouppublishing.com

Flannelgraph

Betty Lukens, Inc.
    711 Portal Street
    Cotati, CA 94931
    1–800–541–9279
    www.bettylukens.com

Something Special for Kids
    Sam and Sandy Sprott
    1–800–Us 4 Kids

Gospel Magic and Performers

Dave and Jody
    Music that Matters
    708–479–8445

Dock Haley Gospel Magic
    P. O. Box 915
    Hermitage, TN 37076
    615–885–4800
    www.Gospelmagic.com
    Email: dockhaley@gospelmagic.com

Ned and Joan Way
    P. O. Box 19229
    Louisville, Ky 40259
    www.NoWay.org

One Way Street, Inc.
    P. O. Box 5077
    Engelewood, CO 80155–5077
    303–799–1188
    www.onewaystreet.com

Jeff Smith
    Salt and Light Ministries
    5105 Timbercreek Court
    Richmond, VA 23237
    804–743–8700

Steve Taylor
    Laughterthatuplifts.com
    1–888–473–7869

Mark Thompson
    P. O. Box 2321
    Redmond, WA 98073
    800–867–6579
    www.markthompson.org

Internet Resources

Children's Bible Activities Online
  Communication Resources
  4150 Belden Village St.
  Fourth Floor
  Canton, OH 44718
  1–800–992–2144

Childrensministry.com
  www.childrensministry.com

Children's Ministry Today
  8469 Seton Ct.
  Jacksonville, FL 32244
  909–777–3339
  www.childrensministry.org
  Email: info@childrensministry.org

Christianbook.com
  P. O. Box 8000
  140 Summit St.
  Peabody, MA 01961–8000
  978–977–5060
  www.christianbook.com

For Kids Only, Inc.
  P. O. Box 10237
  Newport Beach, CA 92658
  1–888–646–9584
  www.fko.org

Group Publishing Company
  P. O. Box 485
  Loveland, CO 80539
  1–800–747–6060
  www.grouppublishing.com

Leadership Training

Kidology.org
   Karl Bastian
   www.kidology.org

Children's Ministry Magazine
   6840 Meadowridge Ct.
   Alpharetta, GA 30005
   1–800–704–6562
   www.cmmag.com/cmml2003

For Kids Only, Inc.
   P. O. Box 10237
   Newport Beach, CA 92658
   1–888–646–9584
   www.fko.org

International Network of Children's Ministry
   Children's Pastors' Conference
   P. O. Box 190
   Castle Rock, CO 80104
   1–800–324–4543
   www.incm.org

Kids in Focus
   P. O. Box 1225
   Jamul, CA 91935
   Fax: 619–342–4474
   www.kidsinfocus.org

Magazines and Periodicals

Children's Ministry Magazine
   P. O. Box 481
   Loveland, CO 80539–0481
   760–738–0086
   www.cmmag.com

Group Publishing Company
    P. O. Box 481
    Loveland, CO 80539–0481
    760–738–0086
    www.grouppublishing.com
    www.groupmag.com

LifeWay Church Resources
    One Lifeway Plaza
    Nashville, TN 37234
    1–800–458–2772
    www.lifeway.com

The Children's Pastor
    P. O. Box 190
    Castle Rock, CO 80104
    1–800–324–4543
    www.incm.com

Ministry Consultants

Kids in Focus
    P. O. Box 1225
    Jamul, CA 91935
    Fax: 619–342–4474
    www.kidsinfocus.org

LifeWay Church Resources
    One Lifeway Plaza
    Nashville, TN 37234
    1–800–458–2772
    www.lifeway.com

Ministry to Today's Child
    Pat Verbal
    8415 Pioneer Dr.
    Frisco, TX 75034
    1–800–406–1011
    www.ministrytotodayschild.com
    Email: MTTC@aol.com

Preschool Resources

Churchnursery.com
    24 H.E. Wilson Ln.
    Seabrooke, SC 29940
    843–846–6339
    www.churchnursery.com

LifeWay Church Resources
    One Lifeway Plaza
    Nashville, TN 37234
    1–800–458–2772
    www.lifeway.com

Eerdmans Books for Young Readers
    255 Jefferson Ave., S.E.
    Grand Rapids, MI 49503
    1–800–253–7521

Group Publishing Company
    P. O. Box 481
    Loveland, CO 80539–0481
    760–738–0086
    www.grouppublishing.com

Lillenas Publishing Company
    2923 Troost Ave.
    Kansas City, MO 64109
    1–800–877–0700
    www.lillenaskids.com
    Email: music@lillenas.com &
    drama@lillenas.com

Randall House Publications
    P. O. Box 17306
    Nashville, TN 37217
    1–800–877–7030

WordAction Publishing Company
    2923 Troost Ave.
    Kansas City, MO 64109
    1–800–877–0700
    www.wordaction.com

Puppet Resources

Amaze Healing Wings
    Puppets with a Heart
    Darcy Maze
    Hesperia, CA
    www.amazehealingwings.com

Axtell Expressions, Inc.
    Dept. CM, 230 Glencrest Cir.
    Ventura, CA 93003
    805–642–7282
    www.axtell.com

Children's Ministry Today
    8469 Seton Ct.
    Jacksonville, FL 32244
    904–777–3339
    www.childrensministry.com

Maher Ventriloquist Studios
    P. O. Box 420
    Littleton, CO 80160
    303–346–6819
    www.maherstudios.com

One Way Street, Inc.
    P. O. Box 5077
    Englewood, CO 80155–5077
    303–799–1188
    www.onewaystreet.com

Plushpups—MT&B Corporation
    249 Homestead Rd.
    Hillsborough, NJ 08844
    1–800–682–1665
    www.plushpups.com

The Puppet Factory, Inc.
    P. O. Box 314
    Goodland, KS 67735
    785–899–7143
    www.thepuppetfactory.com

Puppet Partners, Inc.
    1343 W. Flint Meadow Dr., #2
    Kaysville, UT 84037
    1–877–262–4117

Swanson, Inc.
    1200 Park Ave.
    Murfreesboro, TN 37129
    1–800–251–1402

The Train Depot
    3244 Commerce Center Pl.
    Louisville, KY 40211
    1–800–229–KIDS
    www.TrainDepot.org

Vacation Bible School Publishers

Augsburg Fortress Publishers
    100 S. Fifth St., Suite 700
    Minneapolis, MN 55402
    1–800–328–4648
    www.augsburgfortress.org

Big Idea Productions
    206 Yorktown Center
    Lombard, IL 60148
    630–652–6000
    www.bigidea.com

Cokesbury
    201 Eighth Ave. S.
    Nashville, TN 37203
    1–800–672–1789
    www.cokesbury.com

Cook Communications Ministries
    4050 Lee Vance View
    Colorado Springs, CO 80918
    1–800–323–7543
    www.cookministries.com

Great Communications Publications
    3640 Windsor Park Dr.
    Suwanee, GA 30024–3897
    1–800–695–3387
    www.gcp.org

Bring Them In
    11323 Hughes Rd.
    Houston, TX 77089
    281–481–8770
    www.bringthemin.com

Caring Hands Ministries
    309 Hollyhill Ln.
    Denton, TX 76205
    940–367–4755
    www.chministries.com

CharismaLife
    600 Rinehart Rd.
    Lake Mary, FL 32746
    1–800–451–4598
    www.charismalife.com

Christian Ed Publishers
    9230 Trade Pl.
    San Diego, CA 92126
    1–800–854–1531
    www.ChristianEdWarehouse.com

Cokesbury
    201 Eighth Ave. S.
    Nashville, TN 37203
    1–800–672–1789
    www.cokesbury.com

Cook Communications Ministries
    4050 Lee Vance View
    Colorado Springs, CO 80918
    1–800–323–7543
    www.cookministries.com

Gospel Light
    2300 Knoll Dr.
    Ventura, CA 93003
    805–644–9721
    www.gospellight.com

Great Commission Publications
    3640 Windsor Park Dr.
    Suwanee, GA 30024
    1–800–695–3387
    www.gcp.org

Group Publishing Company
    P. O. Box 485
    Loveland, CO 80539
    1–800–747–6060
    www.grouppublishing.com

LifeWay Church Resources
    One Lifeway Plaza
    Nashville, TN 37234
    1–800–458–2772
    www.lifeway.com

Regular Baptist Press
    1300 N. Meacham Rd.
    Schaumburg, IL 60173
    1–800–727–4400

Standard Publishing
    8121 Hamilton Ave.
    Cincinnati, OH 45231
    1–800–543–1353
    www.standardpub.com
    Email: customerservice@standardpub.com

Subject Index

Scripture Index